Ruling But Not Governing

Ruling But Not Governing

The Military and Political Development in Egypt, Algeria, and Turkey

STEVEN A. COOK

The Johns Hopkins University Press
Baltimore

© 2007 The Johns Hopkins University Press
All rights reserved. Published 2007
Printed in the United States of America on acid-free paper

2 4 6 8 9 7 5 3 2

The Johns Hopkins University Press
2715 North Charles Street
Baltimore, Maryland 21218-4363
www.press.jhu.edu

Library of Congress Cataloging-in-Publication Data
Cook, Steven A.
Ruling but not governing : the military and political development in Egypt, Algeria,
and Turkey / Steven A. Cook.
p. cm.
Includes bibliographical references and index.
ISBN-13: 978-0-8018-8590-7 (hardcover : alk. paper)
ISBN-13: 978-0-8018-8591-4 (pbk. : alk. paper)
ISBN-10: 0-8018-8590-6 (hardcover : alk. paper)
ISBN-10: 0-8018-8591-4 (pbk. : alk. paper)
1. Civil-military relations. 2. Armed Forces—Political activity. 3. Authoritarianism.
4. Democracy. 5. Democratization. 6. Egypt—Politics and government. 7. Algeria—
Politics and government. 8. Turkey—Politics and government. I. Title.
JF195.C5C66 2007
322′.50961—dc22   2006026075

A catalog record for this book is available from the British Library.

Founded in 1921, the Council on Foreign Relations is an independent, national membership organization and a nonpartisan center for scholars dedicated to producing and disseminating ideas so that individual and corporate members, as well as policymakers, journalists, students, and interested citizens in the United States and other countries, can better understand the world and the foreign policy choices facing the United States and other governments. The Council does this by convening meetings; conducting a wide-ranging Studies Program; publishing *Foreign Affairs,* the preeminent journal covering international affairs and U.S. foreign policy; maintaining a diverse membership; sponsoring Independent Task Forces; and providing up-to-date information about the world and U.S. foreign policy on the Council's website, CFR.org.

For Lauren and Madelyn Sophia

CONTENTS

The idea for *Ruling But Not Governing* crystallized when I began asking questions about the intersection of religion and mass politics, the resilience of certain types of regimes confronting what seem to be serious challenges, and the inadequacy of prevailing scholarly work to explain authoritarian stability. This book brings the issues of Islamism, the military and politics, and the evolution of institutions together in an effort to explain, first, why some states have proved resistant to democratic change and, second, how external actors can play a role in breaking the authoritarian logjam.

Despite increasingly vocal questions about the sources of political power, legitimacy, and authenticity, regimes in the Middle East have remained remarkably stable. In the first half of the 1990s, scholars devoted considerable energy to what many believed to be an imminent wave of democratic transition in the region. In the latter part of that decade, when expectations of a more open and democratic Middle East were not realized, analysts turned their attention to understanding the staying power of authoritarian regimes. Although this work contributed important insights into authoritarian stability, it tended to overlook the effect of militaries and the legacies of military rule in a variety of Middle Eastern countries on this phenomenon.

The militaries of the Middle East relinquished their direct control of the ministries and agencies of government long ago, but countries like Egypt, Algeria, and Turkey have remained military-dominated. The soldiers and materiel of Middle Eastern militaries are the obvious outer perimeter of regime protection, but it is actually the less apparent, multilayered institutional legacies of military domination that play the decisive role in regime maintenance. The character of the military's interest in both a facade of democracy and in direct control of key aspects of political control is complex and nuanced. The officers seek to rule but not to govern.

Ruling but not governing has insulated Egyptian, Algerian, and Turkish officers from the vicissitudes of day-to-day governance; however, this strategy does pose risks to the military establishment. A democratic facade of elections, parliaments, opposition press, and the ostensible guarantee of basic freedoms and rights in these countries' constitutions have provided dedicated counter-elites (in the present cases Islamists) the opportunity to advance their agendas. The officers and their civilian collaborators not only tolerate but also in some cases benefit from including these groups. Yet this participation in the formal political arena has proven tenuous. As Islamist groups have accumulated political power, the regimes' defenders have seen to it that the Islamists were ultimately repressed. This pathological pattern in which Egyptian, Algerian, and Turkish Islamist groups have historically been included in and excluded from politics reflects the stability of these regimes.

Turkey has recently broken out of this pattern, offering insight into how military-dominated regimes can move away from authoritarian politics. Although a transition to democracy—a process that is far from complete in Turkey—is the result of internal problems and contradictions, it is clear that the European Union has had a dynamic effect on the Turkish political system. Indeed, the prospect of EU membership has altered the interests of Turkey's Islamists and constrained its officers, creating an environment in which wide-ranging and thoroughgoing institutional reform could take place. The relationship between Europe and Turkey is quite different from the United States and Egypt or France and Algeria, but the EU-Turkey story highlights how external actors can encourage political change through incentives.

In the end, my primary goal in this book is to provide scholars and policymakers alike with good assumptions about the political patterns and processes that are at the foundation of authoritarian stability and, in turn, how those patterns and processes can be weakened. This is vitally important at the present moment, as the United States is engaged simultaneously in a war in Iraq, a global war on terror, and an effort to promote democratic change in the Middle East.

When I think back on how this book came into being, from conception of the idea to the research to the writing, I am grateful to the people who gave their time, advice, and energy to assist me. Before naming names, however, I must acknowledge those individuals whose identities I promised not to share given the sensitive issues this research project addresses. So to begin, I offer generic and blanket words of gratitude to the officers (both retired and currently serving) of the Egyptian and Turkish Armed Forces who took the time to meet with me and offer their views on a range of issues. In addition, there were quite a few nonmilitary government employees in both Egypt and Turkey who also offered their time and assistance and prefer to remain anonymous. My deepest appreciation to them all.

In Egypt, I want to thank a group of friends, professors, and informal advisers including Mohamed Kamal, Mustafa Kemal al-Sayyid, Saad Eddin Ibrahim, the late Tahseen Bashir, Abdel Monem al-Said Aly, Hala Mustafa, Mohamed abd al-Salaam, the late Ahmed Abdalla, Gamil Mattar, Hazem Salem, Gehad Audah, Hassan el-Sawaf, Qadry Said, Mahmoud Khalaf, Abdel Raouf El Reedy, Ahmed Abdel Halim, Mustafa Alwy, the late Ismail Sabri Abdallah, Abdel Monem al-Mashat, and Randa al-Zoghbi.

In Turkey, special thanks to Ozlem and Hasan Yalcin, friends of friends whom my wife and I had never met, who picked us up along with our six absolutely mammoth-sized duffle bags on a freezing morning in early March 2000 at Ankara's Esenboğa Airport and welcomed us into their home. I am indebted to Metin Heper, Alev Çinar, Hootan Shambayati, E. Fuat Keyman, and Ergun Özbudun of Bilkent University in Ankara for all of their help and advice. In addition, I would like to thank Soli Ozel, Ziya Oniş, Ersin Kalaycioğlu, Mehmet Ali Birand, Kemal Yurteri, Cüneyt Ülsever, Steven Kimmel, and Andrew Finkel. The late Toni Cross and her staff at the American Research Institute in Turkey were exemplars of patience and assistance with my questions.

I want to single out my Turkish research assistant, Gulru Çakmak. Gulru, the great-grand-niece of Marshal Fevzi Çakmak—one of Mustafa Kemal's most important colleagues in founding the Turkish Republic—volunteered her services to me shortly after my arrival in Turkey. Her enthusiasm never failed and I am indebted to Gulru for all of her hard work.

The staff at various libraries I visited during the research for this book including those at the American University in Cairo, Dar al-Kutub, American Research Center in Egypt, Centre d'Etudes et de Documentation Economiques, Juridiques et Sociales—Cairo, Bilkent University, American Research Institute in Turkey—Istanbul, Milli Kütüphne—Ankara, State Institute of Statistics—Ankara, Dépôt des Archives d'Outre-mer—Aix-en-Provence, Institut de Recherches et d'Etudes sur le Monde Arabe et Musulman—Aix-en-Provence, Institut du Monde Arabe—Paris, Institut d'Etude Politique, Sciences-Po—Paris, and the Centre Culturel Algérien—Paris proved to be invaluable to me. The able librarians at the Africa and Middle East reading room at the Library of Congress were exemplars of professionalism. They found documents and articles in a few short hours that would have taken weeks to track down in Cairo and Ankara. I am particularly grateful to Dr. George Sfeir, the former Senior Legal Specialist in the Near Eastern and African Law Division of the Library of Congress, who took an interest in my work and opened his treasure trove of Arab legal documents and laws for me.

I must also acknowledge a series of language instructors whose patience and dedication were essential to the project even years before the study was conceived. *Alf shukr* to the late Sourraya Haddad, Gerry Lampe, Ibrahim Abdallah, Amin Bonnah, Mohamed Bakry, and Hatem Ahmed al-Said. Without the dedication of my Turkish teacher, M. Akif Kirecci, I could never have negotiated Turkey and in particular Ankara, a city where very little English is spoken.

I want to thank all of my friends for their patience and understanding. In particular, I am indebted to Rich Vuernick who never fails to take the time to offer wise counsel. Amy Hawthorne read various iterations of different chapters and always offered excellent advice. Hilary Driscoll and Kate Weaver, who served with me as research fellows at the Brookings Institution during 2001–2002, provided endless advice and encouragement. Michele Commerico and Joe Glicksberg were constant sources of support, intellectual insight, and friendship. Nancy and Danny Kaplan were wonderful sources of companionship, laughter, and good food in Aix-en-Provence.

I have always responded best to the toughest teachers. It is thus not surprising that I chose to attend the University of Pennsylvania for my doctoral studies with the hope that Ian Lustick would be my adviser. Ian proved to be everything that I had hoped: a peerless teacher, tough critic, patient soul, and unstinting advocate. I also owe tremendous thanks to a wider group of professors, advisers, and friends who took the time to read and comment on various parts of my work including Jose A. Cheibub, William B. Quandt, Robert Vitalis, Rudra Sil, Tom Callaghy, Lisa Anderson, Eva Bellin, Julie Taylor, John Entelis, Dani Miodownik, Jon Alterman, Peter W. Singer, Soner Cağaptay, Alan Makovsky, Craig Charney, Imran Riffat, Mahmoud Abdallah, Bart Friedman, and Rita Hauser.

Since January 2004, I have been a fellow at the Council on Foreign Relations, where I am blessed with an extraordinary group of colleagues. Rachel Bronson, Ray Takeyh, Adam Segal, Elizabeth Economy, Isobel Coleman, Elizabeth Sherwood-Randall, Jim Goldgeier, Walter Russell Mead, Michael Levi, Julia Sweig, Laurie Garrett, Lee Feinstein, Vali Nasr, Steve Simon, and Max Boot have been constant sources of insight, advice, and humor. I owe my deepest gratitude to Richard N. Haass, the president of the Council, who has provided me with a wonderful environment in which I can pursue my intellectual interests. Richard's expertise and advice, derived from his experiences in a variety of senior U.S. government positions, were invaluable in sharpening my thinking about the policy implications offered in the final chapter.

I am sure James M. Lindsay, the former vice president and director of studies at the Council, would not want me to offer any more to him than "thanks." Without the combination of his gentle encouragement, always-sensible advice, and commitment to intellectual rigor this book would never have been completed. Jim is all at once an unrivalled mentor, a master teacher, and a true friend. I will always be grateful for Jim's guidance and commitment to my professional development.

At the Council, I have had the pleasure of working with a number of extremely bright and talented research associates and interns. My deepest appreciation goes to Riad Houry and his predecessor Kareem Idriss, both of whom are treasure troves of knowledge about the Middle East, wise beyond their years, and true professionals. Danna Weiss proved to be a fearless researcher, plunging into vast amounts of material to answer my often obscure questions. Special thanks to Lindsay Iversen, who in a testament to her patience, fortitude, and good humor, read the manuscript twice and offered unparalleled advice regarding content and prose that vastly improved the book.

I would also like to thank Henry Tom and everyone at the Johns Hopkins University Press who made this book possible and, as a result of their hard work, better.

Finally, I must acknowledge the role of my family: my in-laws, Nancy and Richard Rossman, have been patient supporters and cheerleaders. I am grateful for their generosity and support.

My sister, Julie Schuster, has always been my best friend, confidante, and advocate. Julie's husband Glen, a scientist by training and businessman by vocation, demonstrated an interest in my work, which was always appreciated as my own interest waned from time to time. Moreover, Julie and Glen are the parents of my nephews, Seth and Justin, who have proved to be hours of entertainment and distraction for me.

My parents, Iris and Michael Cook, have instilled in me the value of learning and knowledge. They have endowed me with a great love of books and politics. In addition, they have made tremendous sacrifices to give me the best they could possibly provide. The rest of the world should have parents like my own because it would undoubtedly be a much better place.

I wake up every morning counting myself lucky that Lauren Rossman came into my life on September 18, 1995. She is my inspiration. My achievements are every bit her achievements. Lauren has read this book an untold number of times with patience and grace—each occasion with a level of concentration that I could not achieve. My only hope is that in the future I can somehow demonstrate my gratitude to her. Our daughter, Madelyn, who was born just as I was completing this book, is an amazing source of wonder and love for me. She is the center of my universe.

Ruling But Not Governing

CHAPTER ONE

A Logic of Regime Stability

In the days and weeks following September 11, 2001, as Americans were groping for ways to understand, and cope with, the attacks on the World Trade Center and the Pentagon, the news media supplied a welter of information concerning the Middle East. According to much of this reporting and analysis, instability was a principal characteristic of Arab states. The news media were not alone in portraying the Arab world in this manner, however. In private meetings and briefings, representatives of the Bush administration spoke of "non-evolutionary change"—that is, instability—in the Middle East as a singular challenge to the United States. Perhaps not surprisingly, the popular conception of the Middle East is of a region that is unstable as well as itself a source of global instability.

Phenomena such as extremism and violence may be indicative of a variety of interconnected problems, but they do not necessarily suggest instability. Given the time horizons and pressures with which the media and government must contend, it is understandable that they might promote a simplified notion that states of the Middle East are unstable and vulnerable to political challenges. Such a view, however, is too narrow and underestimates the proven capacity of Middle Eastern leaders "to muddle through" a variety of seemingly catastrophic crises. Consider, for example, Egypt's shattering defeat in June 1967; the civil war that erupted in Jordan in September 1970; the factional violence that shook Turkey for almost a decade between 1970 and 1980; the massacres at Hama, Syria, in 1982; the October 1988 riots that rocked Algeria's major cities; or Saddam Hussein's defeat in the first Gulf War. Each of these episodes challenged the stability of the regimes involved, yet none of them faltered.

Although Middle Eastern leaders have changed either through dynastic succession, palace intrigue, or even elections, authoritarian or semiauthoritarian political orders in that part of the world have remained remarkably stable.[1] This seeming anomaly raises two theoretically interesting questions about the durability of authoritarian political orders in the Middle East: First, what factors render these regimes so resilient? Second, given this stability, under what conditions might analysts expect authoritarian systems to collapse? The role of the military in politics is an old theme in political science and political sociology, but to explain the resilience of authoritarian regimes it needs a new twist. Analysts such as Lucien Pye, Manfred Halpern, and Edward Shils saw the military as the ideal instrument to direct the industrialization, institutionalization, and reform necessary for a modern society, but the military is actually a key variable in the stability of authoritarianism.[2]

The soldiers and materiel of Middle Eastern militaries are the obvious outer perimeter of regime protection. Yet it is actually the less apparent, multilayered institutional settings of states in the Middle East, themselves the legacy of military domination, that play the decisive role in regime stability. Some of these institutions resemble those found in democracies, while others reflect and channel the influence of the military. Because these systems are entrenched in the political landscape of their respective countries, officers in states like Egypt, Algeria, and Turkey have been able to rule without having to govern. The democratic facades and authoritarian institutions of Egyptian, Algerian, and Turkish political systems serve to defuse and deflect challenges to the status quo by sheltering those truly wielding power—the military. This state of affairs is reflected in the pathological pattern in which opposition groups in these countries have been included and excluded in politics. Under such circumstances it is unlikely that the combination of either political activism or domestic crises could set in motion a transition to democracy.

The implications of this argument suggest the critical importance of external actors in catalyzing democratic change in the Middle East. Warfare is, of course, one method an outside power can use to achieve regime change, but as the U.S. invasion of Iraq has shown, the costs of such a policy are high and the payoffs uncertain at best. Nevertheless, external actors can play a crucial role creating a political environment in authoritarian systems that is conducive to change. Through approaches based on incentives rather than sanctions and other punitive measures, outside actors can highlight regime vulnerabilities and contradictions, paving the way for transitions to democracy.

Islamists, Officers, and Institutions in the Middle East

Throughout the 1990s, political conflict between forces claiming to represent religion and those defending the state buffeted the Middle East. In 1992, after a decade of tacit cooperation, the Egyptian government sought to undermine the Muslim Brotherhood, which had garnered significant political power both within Egypt's lower house of parliament, the Majlis ash-Shaab, and the country's prestigious professional syndicates. What followed was five years of low-level warfare between the Egyptian state and Islamist extremists. The same year, the Algerian senior command nullified the results of Algeria's first competitive national legislative elections when it became clear that the Front Islamique du Salut (FIS), an organization composed of various Islamist factions, had garnered an outright parliamentary majority. The ensuing conflict was ferocious, leaving an estimated 100,000 Algerians dead. In Turkey, an Islamist party called Refah (Welfare) won a plurality of votes in the December 1995 national elections. Six months later, Refah became the senior party in a governing coalition. Yet within a year, that government stumbled under the intense pressure of Turkey's Kemalist elite, notably the military's senior commanders. There was no bloodletting in Anatolia, however. Although Refah and its leader were officially banned from politics, Turkey's Islamists quickly regrouped and reentered the political arena with new leaders and a new organization.

Indeed, the consistent and thoroughgoing exclusion of Islamist political activists is a common misperception of Middle Eastern politics. Reality is, in fact, far more nuanced. While formal bans on Islamist-oriented political parties are common throughout the Middle East, in practice, Islamist movements that have signaled their willingness to play by the existing rules of the political game are active participants in a variety of countries. These groups have, in turn, used the pseudodemocratic or semidemocratic institutions of these states to advance their respective agendas. For example, in the 1980s and early 1990s, Egypt's Muslim Brotherhood successfully harnessed these types of institutions such as elections to gain control of Egypt's professional associations, providing the Brothers with a platform to advance the organization's political program. And in Egypt's 2005 legislative elections, the Brotherhood secured an unprecedented 88 seats (out of 454) in the lower house of the Egyptian parliament.

Yet Islamist participation tends to be conditional and tenuous. Although they are not iron-clad rules, general parameters for political inclusion do exist: Islamist movements are likely to be accepted within the bounds of the political arena as long as they do not arrive in numbers significant enough to alter the prevailing institutional setting or as long as they suppress aspects of their political agenda in order to maintain their legal status. The result of these pressures tends to close off areas of debate—particularly in relation to questions concerning the sources of political power, legitimacy, and authenticity—and produces a measure of conformity that ensures the stability of the regime.

The inclusion of antistate political activists stems from two factors. First, the military elite and its civilian allies derive significant benefit from Islamist participation. Both legitimacy of the regime and the ability of authoritarian leaders to neutralize opposition are greatly enhanced. Second, the officers, like all individuals, do not possess a perfect theory of politics and tend to believe that they can manage the risks associated with Islamist political participation. When this proves to be a miscalculation, the senior command moves decisively to exclude Islamists from politics. Concomitant with this exclusion, military-political elites engage in a process of institutional revision and reengineering intended to tighten or close off channels through which opposition activists can pursue their agenda. For example, after the Turkish military's 1971 "coup by memorandum," the officers oversaw amendments to the 1961 constitution that reined in a variety of political rights and established barriers to political participation for certain groups.

Although in the short run this institutional reengineering and revision seems to be effective in curtailing political activity, these efforts actually trigger a new but familiar pattern of political inclusion and exclusion. In response to the revised institutional setting, political entrepreneurs seek new strategies to improve their own position and that of their constituencies. Again this activity is tolerated as long as it remains within certain limits, but when this (ill-defined) boundary is crossed, military-political elites engage in predatory policies to ensure the prevailing political order's survival. This pathological pattern of politics is common to Egypt, Algeria, and, until the early 2000s, Turkey. Critical to the latter's promising transition is the role the European Union has played in altering the interests and constraints of Turkey's primary political actors: Islamists and military officers.

The Theoretical Terrain

Throughout the 1990s, scholarly work on the Middle East typically viewed greater political openness in response to Islamist mobilization as an indicator that a transition to democracy was under way. Although the emergence of freedom of expression, the development of an independent press, and the concomitant deterioration in the coercive power of the state did augur the collapse of authoritarian politics in Eastern Europe and Latin America in the late 1980s and early 1990s, this was not the case in the Middle East. Leaders in this region introduced political changes—including the relaxation of police power—yet these developments represented revisions to authoritarian orders rather than political liberalization. Indeed, the Middle East seems to defy scholarly expectations of political development.[3] Microtheories of institutional change and macrotheories of transitions to democracy, civil society, and civil-military relations are particularly relevant to the present work but do not offer much theoretical traction on either the stability of military-dominated regimes or how these political systems can become more democratic.

Analysts have often written of the Middle East's weak institutionalization, but many countries in the region are, in fact, robustly institutionalized. It is the nature of institutions, not the number of them, that is the problem. In his 1968 work, *Political Order in Changing Societies,* Samuel Huntington argued that violence and instability in a given society was the result of "rapid social change and rapid mobilization of new groups in politics coupled with the slow development of political institutions."[4] The answer to these particular problems was clear: greater institutionalization.

The logic and simplicity of this hypothesis was seductive and had an effect on scholars and policymakers alike. In the almost four decades since the book was first published, analysts have tended, implicitly or otherwise, to see the strengthening of institutions as a critical factor in political development. It is important to recognize, however, that Huntington was merely interested in order. For him, the nature or kind of institutionalization did not matter as long as institutions were effective in establishing authority.

Huntington had no particular commitment to the institutions of liberal democracy at first. He averred that "liberty" could develop but only after the establishment of order. Huntington seemed to overlook a critically important implication of his hypothesis, the possibility of "perverse institutionalization."[5] He misjudged how authoritarian orders could be maintained or reproduced through effective institutions. As other analysts have demonstrated, institutional development takes place in the context of existing institutions and previous institutional innovations.[6] These types of path dependencies in authoritarian political systems are central to understanding Middle Eastern dictatorships.

In the hotly debated topics of the origins of institutions and how they change, there is a convincing body of theoretical work positing that institutions are the result of conscious design.[7] The modern states that we now think of as Egypt, Algeria, and Turkey emerged from circumstances characterized by dramatic discontinuities— defeat in war and nationalist revolution—that ultimately produced change. The new leaders of these states, Gamal Abdel Nasser, Houari Boumédienne, and Mustafa Kemal, along with their fellow officers designed a set of political institutions and structures that solved the problems they confronted in response to the exigencies of internal and external threats.

Despite the insights that theories of "intentional design" offer, there are limitations to this approach. As Kiren Aziz Chaudhry notes in her examination of the development and transformation of economic institutions in Saudi Arabia and Yemen, institutions do not "flow effortlessly from the design table of omniscient rulers."[8] The same is true, of course, in Egypt, Algeria, and Turkey. Although the institutional settings of the three states are firmly rooted in the conscious design of individuals, the process was not effortless, nor did it achieve the efficiency that some scholars have emphasized.[9] To treat institutions as merely instruments of resolving collective action problems forecloses important avenues of analysis that provide scholars with insight into conflict between the defenders of the state and opposition activists. Institutions are not necessarily designed for efficiency, but rather to preserve the power, prestige, privileges, and importantly, distributional advantage of the dominant elite and its allies at the expense of society.[10] This is precisely the situation in Egypt, Algeria, and, until its wide-ranging reform program began in 2002, Turkey.[11]

Although powerful in explaining the development of democracy in Latin America and Southern Europe, macrotheories of transitions to democracy are not generalizable to the Middle East. After exploring political change in countries such as Brazil, Argentina, Spain, Portugal, and Greece, analysts have concluded that there are two critical factors associated with transitions: (1) cracks within the regime, which represent a signal to society to organize, and (2) pacts that ensure the interests of former authoritarian leaders—what Adam Przeworski calls "democracy with guarantees."

Cracks have developed within a variety of Middle Eastern regimes—most notably in Egypt and Algeria. The resulting political crises did not lead to greater political openness, however. Instead, state elites acted to protect a system from which they, more than any other members of society, benefited. For example, in the early 1990s when both Egyptian and Algerian leaders confronted challenges to their regimes, they employed violence and other forms of coercion that ultimately ensured their power rather than pursuing political and economic reform or entering into a pact. The Algerian leadership specifically rejected a pact—the St. Egidio Agreement of 1995—in favor of continuing to fight Islamist insurgents. Moreover, while pacts—albeit implicit ones—are actually common in the Middle East, they tend to support the perverse institutionalization that prevails in many Middle Eastern countries.

Like the transitions literature, the scholarly work theorizing a link between civil society and political liberalization falls short in describing the Middle East. Although analysts have not agreed on a single definition of the concept, the term *civil society* is generally used to capture "that arena of the polity where self-organising groups, movements and individuals, relatively autonomous from the state, attempt to articulate values, create associations and solidarities, and advance their interests."[12] A prominent theme in much of this work casts civil society as a force for democratization in a pitched battle with the authoritarian state. For example, Baghat Korany has asked, "What general conclusions can we draw from the Egyptian case, with its tug-of-war between a dominant executive and an increasingly affirmative civil society?" In a response that is common in much of the civil society literature, Korany answers: "Egypt needs more civil society."

Many Middle Eastern countries are awash in civil society organizations—human rights, women's rights, labor, and social services organizations. Egypt boasts 19,000 of them; Algeria has experienced a flowering of these types of organizations since 1989, although there is no hard data on numbers; and as of the mid-1990s there were 65,000 registered "civic organizations" in Turkey.[13] Still, in Egypt and Algeria authoritarian political systems prevail, and the transition Turkey began in 2002 has had very little to do with civil society. In contrast, Argentina, which underwent a democratic transition in the 1980s, boasts approximately 1,000 civil society organizations.[14]

It seems then that Antonio Gramsci's conception of the linkage between civil society and the state is more accurate than contemporary images of this relationship. In his critique of liberalism, Gramsci argued that it would be naïve to assume that civil society could somehow disarm the "gendarme state." He based this claim on the contention that civil society may actually contribute to a more subtle and sophisticated form of state power. Indeed, contemporary Middle East politics vindicate Gramsci's insights. In recent decades civil society groups cooperated with the state as it pursued predatory policies. In Algeria, the Berber community, women's associations, labor unions, and a variety of groupings of intellectuals all supported the actions of the military command to interrupt and then cancel the 1991/1992 elections. Egyptian human rights activists serve on the government-created National Council for Human Rights, which has no power to compel the government to change its policies and serves only as window dressing. Likewise, in Syria, Tunisia, and other Arab countries, labor unions and business organizations enjoy government patronage in return for collaboration with the state. Those elements of civil society that do not cooperate with state authorities have little power to resist the authoritarian order given the circumstances of "extreme compulsion" under which they live.[15]

When Egyptian president Hosni Mubarak first learned about the ostensible connection between political liberalization and civil society, he reportedly asked his interlocutor, "What about 'military society'? Where do the military men fit in?" In many ways civil-military relations theorists have been asking similar, albeit more sophisticated, questions about the relationship between military officers and political development including: Why do militaries engage in coups? What types of military establishments are more likely to produce coups? How do military dictatorships fare? Under what conditions will militaries return to the barracks? What is the proper role for the military in newly democratic countries? The last two questions are of particular interest as a result of the attention militaries have received from scholars working specifically on democratic transitions in Latin America and southern Europe. A primary theme in much of this work is the relationship between a military's return to the barracks and political liberalization.[16] As civil-military relations theorists recognize, a return to the barracks does not necessarily imply that the central problem of who controls the military has been resolved. For example, despite democratic change in a variety of Latin American countries, the military tends to retain a measure of autonomy.[17] As Peter D. Feaver has noted, "A military can never [engage in a] coup and yet still systematically undermine civilian control."[18]

Feaver's assertion is relevant because the Egyptian, Algerian, and Turkish militaries withdrew to the barracks, yet have, in general, remained beyond civilian control. Although there does seem to be a connection between a military's departure from governance and politics and the processes of liberalization and democratization, establishing effective civilian control is much more than a "return to the barracks" per se. The three countries' militaries have been content to return to the barracks because they have overseen the development of an institutional setting—a system—that ensures the predominance of the officers. Institutional alterations have taken place, but both the broad contours of the military-founded regime and the institutions that enable the military's influence remain. The cases of Egypt, Algeria, and Turkey illustrate the "balance" between officers and civilians, demonstrating how officers in the Middle East can rule but not govern without ever having to step beyond the boundaries of their barracks.

Ottoman Legacies and Turkish Models

Egypt, Algeria, and Turkey have an interesting mix of similarities that would lead analysts to expect relatively common political outcomes. These military-founded and dominated political systems featured strikingly common patterns of political inclusion and exclusion that reflected the stability of these regimes. The similarities help analysts understand how and why Turkey has been able to undertake an extraordinary and wide-ranging program to dismantle its authoritarian institutions, whereas Egypt and Algeria have continued to experience the same political pathologies.

Although Turkey may only now be developing as a successful example of democracy in a Muslim society, policymakers and some scholars have long invoked the "Turkish model" as a path for political development in the Arab and wider Islamic world. According to these observers, the institutions of Turkey's political system have nurtured a relatively successful accommodation between religion and politics. They point not only to the regularly scheduled, multiparty elections that have been held since the mid-1940s but also to the fact that Turkey's political order has remained officially secular in a country that is almost entirely Muslim. These claims betray a superficial reading of Turkish history and politics. Conservative Muslims, Islamists, leftists, and Kurds do not view the Turkish experience as progressive or inclusive, despite the country's history of quasidemocratic practices. Nevertheless, in one sense Turkey has indeed been a model for a variety of countries, particularly those in the Arab world. After Mustafa Kemal and his coterie of army officers founded the Turkish Republic, a template of sorts was established for other nationalist officers in the Middle East. Yet, the lessons that the Turkish political system taught new leaders such as Egypt's Free Officers and Algeria's Colonel Houari Boumédienne had little to do with democracy and much to do with political control in military-dominated societies.

Like Mustafa Kemal in Turkey, Egypt's Free Officers and Algeria's new national army developed a set of political and social institutions that were critical to the consolidation and maintenance of their power. These included formal institutions such as single catch-all parties to better patrol the perimeters of the political system or laws, regulations, and decrees that formally limited political participation. Informal institutions also lie beneath officially espoused rules. Rooted in past practices and patterns of behavior, these informal institutions constitute the set of unspoken beliefs and uncodified norms that govern the expectations and behavior of political actors.

The web of formal and informal institutions that provides the framework for the authoritarian political system in Egypt, Algeria, and formerly Turkey is obscured behind an entirely different set of institutions and structures that conjure democratic polities. For example, various iterations of the Egyptian, Algerian, and Turkish constitutions provide for freedom of the press, freedom of associations, and legislative oversight. Scholars have generally dismissed the importance of the pseudodemocratic institutions of these states, but the officers have two interrelated interests in maintaining a democratic facade: First, pseudodemocratic institutions provide the capacity to satisfy certain demands emerging from society without fundamentally altering the character of the political order. Second, institutions resembling those of a democratic polity insulate the military establishment from the vicissitudes of everyday politics. As long as the public face of the government was not specifically the military, opposition would be directed at other political actors. Still, pseudodemocratic institutions contained significant risk for the military as these pretenses of democracy actually became powerful instruments through which dedicated Islamist groups could engage in wide-ranging political attacks on the prevailing regime.

In addition to these similarities, there are differences between the Turkish experience and those of Egypt and Algeria. Particular historical, social, and political contexts have shaped the way in which political actors in Egypt, Algeria, and Turkey view the world, calculate their interests and expectations, and understand their own constraints. Although the political patterns in the three countries have been remarkably similar, it would be remiss not to account for how context has contributed to important differences between them.

Consider, for example, the issue of Western colonialism and Western penetration. The nationalist Turks under the leadership of Mustafa Kemal successfully resisted British, French, Italian, and Greek efforts to dismember the Anatolian rectangle in the aftermath of World War I and forced the European powers to recognize the Republic of Turkey in the Treaty of Lausanne (1923). In contrast, both Egypt and Algeria have long histories of European domination. The British considered Egypt to be an important linchpin to their empire, particularly as a gateway to South Asia. By most measures, Algeria was the most thoroughly colonized country on earth between 1830 and 1962. During this time, the French engaged in a policy known as *Algérie française,* which claimed Algeria as a natural part of France. The differing historical legacies of colonialism and European penetration contributed to distinct institutional settings at independence and resulted in varying degrees of what Clement Henry Moore calls "moments of national consciousness."[19]

According to Moore, states undergoing independence struggles experience liberal assimilationist, traditional anticolonialist, and radical nationalist moments sequentially, culminating in the "consolidation of the nation-state" under a leadership that derives its legitimacy from the successful national struggle. Turkey, with the shortest history of European penetration, comes closest to this ideal type, passing through all three moments of consciousness in the process of establishing a coherent national state. As a result, despite ideological battles between different groups of elites, first order questions about the nature of the republic and the Turkish nation are largely settled. In contrast, although Egypt and Algeria reached the stage of radical nationalism and the military dominates both political systems, fierce competition among the forces representing each moment of national consciousness continues. As a result, there is little agreement in Egypt and Algeria over the appropriate trajectory for political development.

Historical, political, and social context is also important in understanding the nature of Islamist groups in Egypt, Algeria, and Turkey and how these groups have played a part shaping national politics. Egypt's Muslim Brotherhood is the oldest and perhaps most prestigious Islamist organization in the world. Founded in 1928 in response to what its first leader, Hasan al-Banna, believed was Egypt's moral degradation, the Brotherhood's goal has been to forge a just and pious society based on the principles of Islam.[20] Consequently, throughout its almost 80-year history, the primary component of the organization's political, social, and economic discourse has called for the application of *shari'a.* In this way, the Brotherhood is much more than a political organization; it is a social movement that seeks the Islamization of Egyptian society from below. The logic of this approach is clear: the transformation of society through a long-term strategy that emphasized Islamic values and the provision of services as mechanisms of mobilization. Those groups that oppose this vision would ultimately be swept away under the weight of the vast reservoir of Egyptians demanding to live in accordance with the Brotherhood's interpretation of Islam. The organization did drop its opposition to participation in Egyptian politics in the 1970s, but this did not fundamentally alter the Brotherhood's character as a social movement.

Founded in February 1989, Algeria's Front Islamique du Salut was less a social movement than a political organization, although its vision of Algerian society was similar in many ways to that of the Muslim Brotherhood in Egypt. Yet rather than a wide-ranging social or cultural project to forge an Islamic society, the FIS sought to realize its vision through the direct accumulation of power in Algeria's political arena. As a result, the FIS leadership of Abassi Madani and Ali Belhadj sought to take advantage of the relatively greater room for political activism that Algeria's 1989 constitution afforded them.

Turkey's Islamist party shares characteristics with both the Muslim Brotherhood and the FIS. Throughout the 1980s and 1990s, Turkey's Islamists maintained a rather extensive social services network that supported Turks in need and sought to advance the Islamist agenda through party politics. The origins of Turkey's Islamist parties can be traced to 1969 when Necmettin Erbakan, a German-trained civil engineer with an affinity for Turkey's Ottoman past and Islamist ideology, secured a seat in the Turkish Grand National Assembly (TGNA) as an independent. Shortly after taking office, Erbakan founded Milli Nizam Partisi (National Order Party), which was shut down as a result of the 1971 coup d'état. Two years later the party was resurrected under the name Milli Selamet Partisi (National Salvation Party) and served as a junior partner in both left-of-center and right-of-center governing coalitions during the mid- and late 1970s. Like its predecessor, the National Salvation Party was banned after the coup of September 1980. Three years later, when civilian government returned to Turkey, the Islamists re-created the National Salvation Party in the form of Refah (Welfare). Since that party's closure in 1998 it has spawned three additional political formations, Fazilet (Virtue), which was banned in 2001 and subsequently split into two parties, Saadet (Happiness) and Adalet ve Kalkinma (Justice and Development).

Turkish Islamists have been able to participate in politics, but, more importantly, they have been allowed to do so even over the objections of the defenders of the Turkish state. That is to say that Turkey's quasidemocratic institutions had content and meaning even before Ankara's transition to democracy began in earnest in 2002. That electoral laws, the judiciary, and to some extent the Grand National Assembly permitted civilians to exercise a certain amount of power created expectations among the Turkish public about the proper role of state organizations. Although the military is consistently the most popular and well-respected of these organizations, Turks have shown a limit to what they would permit from it. For example, the Turkish public repudiated the officers' efforts to engineer the outcome of elections after the return to civilian rule in 1961 and 1983. In contrast, the historical, political, and social environments in Egypt and Algeria offered little opportunity for the development of institutions that would provide their citizens the means to oppose effectively the military-dominated state.

The most notable contextual variation between the three countries is, however, the relationship between religion and state. Gamal Abdel Nasser and Houari Boumédienne did not disestablish religion as Mustafa Kemal did. Islam remains the religion of state in both Egypt and Algeria. Moreover, whereas Kemal regarded Islam as a source of Ottoman backwardness and corruption, the Egyptian and Algerian officers sought to demonstrate that their political agendas conformed to Islamic principles. In a telling symbolic gesture, the first place that Nasser and his fellow Free Officers visited after forcing King Farouk to flee to Italy was al-Azhar, the oldest and most venerated center of Islamic thought and learning in the Muslim world. The officers of Algeria's Armée Nationale Populaire sacralized the role of fighters against the French colonial presence by calling them *moujahideen,* a term that has religious connotations and is derived from the same root as *jihad.* More than that, the official statements of independent Algeria's leaders and the country's array of constitutions and national charters place Islam in a central role in the Algerian revolutionary project.

Yet within these differences concerning the relationship between religion and state there is an important similarity. In the battle against the remnants of the Ottoman Empire and the British, French, Italian, and Greek militaries for control of Turkish territory, Mustafa Kemal often used Islam as a critical component of his nationalist message in an effort to garner the support of sheikhs and hodjas in the Anatolian interior. Kemal's descendants at the senior level of the Turkish officer corps have periodically sought to harness Islam in pursuit of some national goal. For example, despite the oft-repeated appellation of the "staunchly secular" character of the Turkish officer corps, the military promoted mosque building and the establishment of *imam-hatip* (preacher) schools throughout the 1980s in the belief that more religion would depoliticize society after left-right violence wracked Turkey in the 1970s. The unintended consequence of this emphasis on Islam has been the accumulation of Islamist political power in Turkey's officially secular political system.

While Turks often chafe at the suggestion, the processes and patterns that characterized the Turkish political system until the early 2000s resembled those in Egypt and Algeria. Turks often point to their different historical, political, and social experiences as proof positive that Turkey cannot possibly be compared with Egypt and Algeria. Although context is important to the details of each case, the broad narratives of

Egyptian, Algerian, and Turkish politics are strikingly similar. This is not at all surprising given the role of military officers in the founding of the three states, the formal and informal institutional legacies of military domination, and the continuing importance of the military establishment in the countries' political orders. What is surprising, however, is Turkey's ability to break from the logjam of authoritarian stability and begin the process of consolidating a more liberal democracy. Paradoxically, it is the Turkish military establishment, which is widely regarded as the most interventionist and politically influential of the three, that has experienced a diminution of its once vaunted autonomy in a significantly changed political environment.

This book examines the claims about the crucial connection between military establishments and regime stability. Chapter 2 provides insight into the autonomy and critical interests of the Egyptian, Algerian, and Turkish military establishments. Chapter 3 uses Egypt's political experience since the Free Officers' coup in July 1952 to explore the institutionalization of military dominance. It also analyzes the political dynamics that led to the exclusion of Islamist groups from the political arena and sheds light on the process of institutional revision designed to ensure the armed forces-founded order. Chapter 4 examines the contest between Algeria's military and Islamist movement to leverage the pseudodemocratic institutions of the state to their own respective advantages. Chapter 5 outlines Turkey's pathological patterns of regime stability and explains the political dynamics that triggered the Turkish transition to more democratic politics since 2002–03. Chapter 6 highlights the theoretical concepts related to military-dominated systems and regime stability, helping policymakers understand both what is necessary to effect change in military-dominated political systems and how external actors can most effectively pursue such a strategy.

CHAPTER TWO

The Egyptian, Algerian, and Turkish Military Enclaves

The Contours of the Officers' Autonomy

The modernization paradigm dominated the social sciences between the 1950s and 1970s. During that era, scholars of the Middle East hypothesized that relatively autonomous militaries were progressive forces of modernization and democratization. The basic tenets of modernization theories are fairly straightforward: (1) the combined effects of the French Revolution and Great Britain's industrial revolution undermined the old social, political, and economic order in favor of societies that were increasingly complex, differentiated, and free; (2) social change is the product of internal political dynamics; and (3) industrialization produces modernity, which leads to "convergence" among industrialized societies.[1] For Manfred Halpern, Lucien Pye, Edward Shils, and others interested in questions relating to the military and political development the last of these principles was most important.[2] These analysts saw the military—fused as it was with organizational capacity, sense of mission, and nationalist sentiment—as the ideal instrument to direct the processes of industrialization, institutionalization, and reform necessary for the development of a modern society.[3] Once national goals were met, the scholars assumed, the "new authoritarians" would relinquish their prestigious positions. The empirical evidence suggests that military officers in developing countries were, indeed, successful in generating significant economic performance and carried out successful programs of national infrastructure development. In time, however, state-directed economies stagnated, and the officers became conservative elements clinging tenaciously to regimes in which they were (and remain) the primary beneficiaries.

These officers, mostly of senior rank, make up the *military enclave*.[4] They represent an elite preserve that is in many ways separated from society in military-only facilities such as schools, hospitals, clubs, and residential areas. Yet, more profound, and politically more salient, than the actual physical separation between the military and most civilians is the distinctive worldview to which senior military personnel tend to subscribe. Within the Egyptian, Algerian, and Turkish military enclaves, commanders maintain specific ideas about the military's organizational and technological capacities as well as a particular nationalist narrative that places the officers in a superior position to civilians.

The military officers who founded contemporary Egypt, Algeria, and Turkey were all "high modernists" par excellence. High modernism's worldview, which places a premium on the scientific knowledge necessary for modernization, is "inherently authoritarian."[5] According to high modernists, only those with these types of specialized skills, that is to say themselves, have a mandate to exercise political power. The successors to the Free Officers, Houari Boumédienne, and Mustafa Kemal have, in general, maintained this worldview, considering themselves to be great modernizing forces—vanguards of society—imbued with organizational capacity and the technology of the West. These assertions are based on the officers' (generally correct) assessment of the incompetence of their nations' civilian politicians. Moreover, the military in all three countries can quite rightly claim to be the only state organization with the capacity to undertake infrastructure development and other public works projects. Notwithstanding the trend in which senior commanders have become adept in the discourse of democratization and liberalization, military officers in Egypt, Algeria, and Turkey have over time demonstrated less interest in progressive political programs than in protecting the prevailing political order from which the commanders derive significant benefit.

Yet Egypt, Algeria, and Turkey are not to be confused with military dictatorships. They are better characterized as military-dominated states. The officers of the military enclave, along with their civilian allies, strategically created political systems that have benefited themselves at the expense of the rest of society. By overseeing the development of political institutions that allow for the *appearance* of pluralism but also incorporate key mechanisms for oversight and political control, the officers sought to guarantee the maintenance of their political order. Over time, the officers sought to conceal themselves behind the veneer of democratic institutions, representative structures, and legitimizing institutions that came to characterize their respective political systems. During periods of crisis, however, the military elite tend to strip away this facade, revealing themselves as the locus of power and reinforcing the authoritarian core of the political order.

Given historical precedent this political dynamic seems fairly straightforward, but the behavior of the officers and what members of the military enclave perceive as a crisis is complex. Scholars often cite *interests* as the factor determining whether the military will remain docile or will intervene in politics. For example, John Waterbury has written of Hosni Mubarak's succession in Egypt: "It was no surprise that Sadat chose someone from the military. For his own survival, Sadat had to reassure the senior officers that he would not ignore their interests in an era that was already being dubbed as one of peace."[6] Ümit Cizre Sakallioğlu has described the Turkish military's autonomy in relation to an array of interests linked to the Turkish presidency, promotions within the armed forces, and the defense budget.[7] And William Quandt has identified interests as an explanatory variable in the Algerian military's decision to force President Chadli Benjedid from office in early 1992.[8] These examples are merely illustrative but nevertheless represent the tone of much of the scholarly work examining politics in these countries. However, it is often unclear how scholars derive the interests they impute to political actors.

The Egyptian, Turkish, and Algerian military enclaves maintain a hierarchy of interests, which can tell analysts much about the behavior of the officers. These levels include lesser-order interests; core parochial and institutional interests; and existential interests, which represent the regime. Political activity that encroaches on or assails these interests tends to result in different responses from members of the military enclave. For example, attacks on lesser-order interests are not likely to provoke the military establishment into repressive or exclusionary policies; encroachment on core parochial and institutional interests will more likely, though not always, engender a response of this nature; and perceived threats to the political order will almost certainly trigger a military crackdown. This should be taken not as a rule, but rather as a guideline intended to capture the tendencies of the officer corps. Military officers, like all individuals, do not have the capacity to perfectly assess a given political situation and as a result may deviate from these behaviors.

But how cohesive are the interests within the Egyptian, Algerian, and Turkish militaries?[9] Militaries, like all large organizations, can hardly be thought of as unitary actors. Within the U.S. military, for example, there is intense interservice rivalry over budgets and missions. The officers of the Egyptian, Turkish, and Algerian militaries are no different. The air force is Egypt's favored service in terms of equipment and resources, largely because President Mubarak is an accomplished air force officer. In both Algeria and Turkey, land forces are almost always the privileged branch of service.

Moreover, military officers represent cross-sections of society, with a variety of political positions and orientations. Rival *shillas* (connections based on school and family ties) remain important means of advancement for Egyptian officers. The Algerian officer corps is composed of a variety of clans, which are key sources of patronage. These differing groups are based on where the officers come from, where they serve, and their functions. It is clear that even at the most senior officer levels, the Turkish General Staff can be roughly divided into hardliners and liberals. When, for example, General Hilmi Özkök was slated to become the chief of the General Staff in 2002, some officers quietly undertook a campaign to extend the term of the outgoing chief, Hussein Kıvrıkoğlu, due to Özkök's reputation as a liberal.

Despite these differences the senior commanders of the Egyptian, Algerian, and Turkish militaries have, at key moments, tended to act coherently and decisively. In Egypt, the officers who run the presidency and the defense ministry are generally united under the leadership of the president—a fellow officer—and have demonstrated that they will march in lockstep to counter perceived challenges (as they have done, for example, against Islamists movements). In early January 1992, Algeria's 60 top military officers met in a "conclave" and agreed that President Chadli Benjedid—whom they had selected as president at a similar meeting 14 years prior—must be forced from office and the elections cancelled. It was only when Algeria was plunged into virtual civil war later that year that differences emerged between *éradicateurs* and *conciliateurs*. Yet even these differences hardly crippled the Algerian military's war effort, as the high command successfully pursued a military solution to the problems of the Armée Islamique du Salut and the Groupement Islamique Armé, though the fight against the Groupe Salafiste pour la Prédication et le Combat continues. Since the 1960 coup, which a group of junior officers undertook, all levels of Turkish military education have emphasized a Prussian-like devotion to the hierarchy of command in an effort to prevent another episode of junior-level insubordination. The Turkish General Staff's subsequent interventions—the 1971 coup by memorandum, the 1980 coup, and the 28th of February Process, which brought down Turkey's first Islamist-led government—demonstrate the significant capacity of Turkey's senior command to act coherently and decisively when necessary.

Two Ends of the Spectrum: Lesser Order and Existential Interests

Lesser-order interests cover issues that have been, and remain, important to the officers but are not so crucial that they will engage in aggressive or predatory activities to protect them. As one knowledgeable Ankara insider explained of the Turkish military's willingness to countenance a certain amount of political change: "If you hold ten cards, and six are more important to you than the other four, it is probably not worth it to fight to protect those that are less important to you."[10]

The relevance of lesser-order interests to the military enclaves can be gauged by two factors: First, the officers have demonstrated that lesser-order interests—for example, certain institutions and structures that contribute to political control—may be beneficial to either their political project or their capacity to influence politics but do not seem necessary to ensure either of these. Second, in the aftermath of political crises when state elites engage in institutional revision and reengineering, aspects of the political apparatus that represent lesser-order interests may or may not be revived. Consider, for example, the single, dominant, state-affiliated parties that had at one time been a hallmark of the Egyptian, Algerian, and Turkish political systems. These parties represented important means of political control when the nations were founded yet in time slipped into oblivion with virtually no resistance from officers. Moreover, once the barrier to multiparty politics was breached, the commanders never sought to reestablish single-party systems even after crises or in response to political pressure. In Egypt when the *manabir* (platforms) within the Arab Socialist Union were established in the mid-1970s, they were intended to become loyal opposition groups of the left and right. Instead, they became political parties that were sharp critics of President Anwar Sadat. Rather than cracking down on these newly formed parties, the president and his allies—both military and civilian —merely ignored developments in Egypt's legislature, the People's Assembly. Other examples of lesser order interests include laws governing the press, aspects of penal codes, and regulations concerning the activities of nongovernmental organizations.

It is rational that members of the military enclaves would intervene to preclude or undermine threats to their respective regimes. The officers *may*, of course, intervene for another reason—for example, to ensure core parochial or institutional interests— but analysts can be reasonably certain that when the officers perceive a threat to the political order, the military will respond. The regime is an existential issue for the officers. Not only have the commanders been either founders of these regimes or the direct descendants of these founding officers, but the very nature of the political order provides significant benefits to the members of the military enclave and their allies. Like an individual who senses that his or her life is in jeopardy and will take extraordinary action to survive, so too will Egyptian, Algerian, and Turkish officers endeavor to ensure that their regimes remain intact.

Core Interests

The Egyptian, Turkish, and Algerian officer corps share a roughly similar constellation of core interests relating to the economy, foreign and security policy, the political and state apparatus, and nationalism. Given the generally closed nature of the military barracks, knowing precisely what constitutes the officers' interests can be difficult, yet officers have, over time—through their actions and discourse—privileged four issue areas over others.

Economic Interests

Military leaders have stressed economic independence as the best means to economic development in their respective states. In the years after the founding of contemporary Egypt, Algeria, and Turkey this translated into statist economic policies. Yet, as state-led development faltered between the 1970s and late 1980s, the officers tended to shift their rhetorical emphasis in favor of neoliberal economic policies such as structural adjustment and privatization.[11] Regardless of the economic model, however, the officers in all three countries have consistently demonstrated that personal financial gain or advantage to the military establishment is more important than economic development.

In Egypt, although state-led development became a cornerstone of economic policy after the Free Officers consolidated their power in 1954, the officers concomitantly developed significant economic interests independent of their lofty rhetorical goals. Despite the existence of the Committee to Eradicate Feudalism, which fell under the leadership of the armed forces, Field Marshal Abdel Hakim 'Amr and his fellow officers parlayed their predominant positions within the Egyptian state to enhance their personal wealth. Once Anwar Sadat came to power in 1970, a nexus between private economic interests and the military developed. The new president's policy of *infitah* (opening) allowed the members of the military enclave and the economic elite to benefit mutually from the "commissions game," which enriched the officers and ensured that, in return, contracts from the military continued to flow.

In the early 1980s, the military establishment, under the command of Defense Minister Mohamed Abdel Halim Abu-Ghazala, carved out its own significant and lucrative portion of Egypt's commercial and industrial sectors through a combination of the National Service Projects Organization (NSPO), the Arab (later "Egyptian") Organization for Industrial Development, and a variety of cooperative ventures with both domestic and foreign manufacturers. This diverse portfolio, which includes the manufacture of weapons, electronics, and consumer goods; infrastructure development; various agribusinesses; as well as services in the aviation, tourism, and security sectors has rendered the military perhaps Egypt's single most important economic entity. The official rationale for this economic activity has been budget relief, based on the argument that the military's economic self-sufficiency permits Egypt to maintain large military structures without placing pressure on state finances.[12] Yet, many of the inputs critical to the military enclave's economic activities are subsidized, which not only places the officers and their civilian allies at a considerable advantage but also negatively affects state finances—precisely the outcome the military's economic activities are supposed to avoid.[13] Further, although during the mid-1990s the Egyptian government embarked on a program of privatization and structural adjustment, the military enclave declared its economic assets off-limits. A new Egyptian government established in 2004 under Prime Minister Ahmad Nazif placed a new emphasis on economic reform. While Egypt's senior command has signaled its qualified support for economic change, there is no indication that the military is willing to allow its own considerable economic interests to be privatized.[14]

Like the senior military command in Egypt, Algeria's officer corps has particular economic interests that it has protected at the expense of Algerian society. Despite the relative success of centralization and planning during the first two decades of independence, the logic of the rentier state has had powerful, and distorting, effects on the Algerian economy. Within a few years of Colonel Chadli Benjedid's ascension to the presidency in 1978, his partial liberalization of the economy in the 1980s provided an opportunity for members of the military establishment and their allies to benefit from new sources of rent. The reinvigorated private sector supplemented the considerable economic advantage officers already enjoyed given their proximity to the state. Like the apparatchiks who became capitalists as the Soviet Union collapsed, Chadli's version of *infitah* permitted the privatization of previously public assets whose new owners were often military officers or their civilian allies. This business activity provided little measurable relief to average Algerians confronting economic dislocation resulting from the collapse of oil prices in the mid-1980s.

In the early 1990s, Algeria's senior commanders fought International Monetary Fund (IMF) recommendations to establish greater economic transparency while they simultaneously sought to leverage economic reforms for their own benefit. For example, a Central Bank regulation allowing for intermediaries to manage foreign exchange transactions permitted members of Algeria's military enclave to "become pseudo-private actors, importing through their own companies, taking commissions on imports, or facilitating access by private companies to import contracts."[15] Overall, the officers' efforts to maintain their economic advantage produced a bleak economic picture for Algeria. While rents circulated through the military, the public sector, and a commercial private sector, the general population was forced to contend with limited economic opportunities and its attendant social dislocations.[16] By mid-decade, the economic situation forced the officers to accept a series of IMF economic reforms to address the problems of inflation, massive unemployment, and external debt. The program of stringent macroeconomic adjustment, which included rescheduling Algeria's high-interest debts to the Paris Club helped refloat the economy. The restructuring of the country's debt had the immediate benefit of freeing up additional resources for the military to effectively prosecute the war against Islamist insurgents. This was not the only benefit, however. Inflation dropped from 30 percent in the mid-1990s to 2 percent in 2003. Employment levels also improved, and as the price of oil and gas spiked in 2003–2006, Algerians began to experience expanded economic opportunities.[17]

The officers of Turkey's military enclave also maintain significant economic interests, but these interests remain somewhat different in both degree and kind from those of their Egyptian and Algerian counterparts.[18] For example, the instances in which Turkish officers have engaged in corruption or used their status to extract rents from state-owned or private enterprises are relatively few. Still, the Turkish General Staff historically has had a compelling interest in the health of certain companies and sectors of the economy. Under Law 205/1961 the military established OYAK (Army Mutual Aid Association), which was designed as an insurance system and means of obtaining subsidized mortgages and other loans for the officer corps and civilian employees of the Ministry of National Defense. OYAK invests a mandatory 10 percent salary contribution from its members in a variety of industrial and financial ventures, giving the military establishment a significant stake in the large holding companies that dominate the Turkish economy. In addition to the military's OYAK-related activities, the Turkish General Staff's historical autonomy in the realm of weapons procurement has allowed the senior command to direct contracts toward a number of favored domestic and foreign firms, further reinforcing the military's abiding interests in particular sectors and firms operating in the Turkish economy.[19]

Turkey's most recent economic crisis, which began in November 2000, underscored the economic interests of its military enclave in two ways. First, the military demonstrated that its economic interests and those of the firms that did business with the armed forces trumped prudent economic management. For a time the General Staff blocked efforts to privatize Turk Telekom—a commitment that the government of Bülent Ecevit made in order to secure $10 billion in emergency financing from the IMF. Second, although some high-profile defense contracts with foreign firms for a new generation of battle tanks and attack helicopters have been cancelled as a result of Turkey's continuing economic weakness, the projects themselves continue. For example, a local Turkish consortium will build the new tanks, and a variety of new weapons systems remain in the pipeline. While the Turkish General Staff has made much of the reduction in the country's defense budget, down to 3.3 percent of gross national product in 2004, defense expenditures increased to 7 percent of the government's total budget in 2005.[20]

Security and Foreign Policy

The military enclaves also maintain a common core interest in the realm of security policy—both domestic and foreign. With regard to the former, perhaps it is enough to point out that Egypt, Algeria, and Turkey all maintain special units and forces whose respective missions are related to public order and/or surveillance of society.[21] Moreover, in all three countries military and/or mixed military-civilian courts have been used extensively to repress opposition groups.

In 2003 and 2004 both Turkey and Egypt abolished their state security courts. On close examination, however, these changes are not as dramatic as they first might seem, especially in Egypt. The reforms that Egypt's legislature undertook merely transferred the specialized jurisdiction of the state security courts to the "ordinary courts" that were established through the 1950 Law on Criminal Procedure. The changes in Turkey are overall more substantial, but even some of these reforms are not as thorough as press reports and official statements might suggest. The legislation abolishing the state security courts established new courts with similar jurisdiction. In addition, in May 2003, the General Staff and the government disagreed over a proposed amendment to Article 8 of the Anti-Terrorism Act that would eliminate "propaganda crimes from terror crimes." The amendment was passed, yet offenders of "propaganda crimes" remain subject to prosecution under other articles of the Turkish penal code.[22]

On the international front, all three military enclaves have historically demonstrated that the formulation and execution of security policy remains the sole province of the officer corps. In Egypt, the Palestine War of 1948 helped crystallize the opposition of the Free Officers to the *ancien régime*. The officers believed that while they were fulfilling their solemn duty to protect Arab land from Zionism, corrupt commanders and politicians had betrayed the army with poor planning, cronyism, and faulty equipment. Once in power, the officers retained autonomy in this area—a situation that has continued over the last five decades. For example, while the Free Officers' alliance with the Muslim Brothers was important in the prelude and immediate aftermath of the July 1952 coup, the benefits of the relationship were not as relevant as establishing and retaining exclusive control over Egypt's foreign and security policy. As a result, the Brothers were repressed soon after their political value waned, not least for the Islamists' opposition to the 1954 Anglo-Egyptian Agreement, which afforded Great Britain access to bases in the Canal Zone in the event of a crisis.

Beginning in the mid-1970s, Egypt's leadership has been able to establish and maintain relations with Israel, including a formal treaty of peace, despite significant domestic opposition. In 1982, notwithstanding commitments to political liberalization after Anwar Sadat's assassination, Hosni Mubarak and his advisers refused to break Egypt's relations with Israel over that country's invasion of Lebanon. The issue that was of paramount interest to the military establishment in both cases was not peace with Israel per se but the attendant benefits that came with this conciliation, primarily strategic ties with the United States. Egypt's military-political elite value these ties to the extent that the public discussion of relations between Washington and Cairo were placed off-limits. In the mid-1980s, the opposition press broke this informal taboo and sought clarification of U.S.-Egypt relations expressing concern over the integrity of Egyptian sovereignty. Spokesmen for the armed forces responded tersely that while "democracy and opposition" were respected in Egypt, such inquiries only compromised national security.[23] For the same reason, the military has shielded the defense budget and its procurement policies from public view. More dramatically, the military establishment's autonomy in security policy was further highlighted when, against the backdrop of domestic opposition, Egypt sent 35,000 troops to Saudi Arabia during the 1991 Gulf crisis.

Algeria's commanders also retain a core interest in the development and implementation of security and foreign policy. At the time of Algeria's independence Ahmed Ben Bella assumed the presidency with broad support, including that of the military, but he was unable to wield power in security and foreign affairs. The officers of the Armée de Libération Nationale (ALN), which was transformed into the Armée Nationale Populaire, reserved for themselves such critical positions as the ministers of war, foreign affairs, and interior. As Ben Bella established a popular mandate, however, he sought to undermine the position of each of these officials and announced his intention to establish "popular militias." The combination of these policies placed the ability of the officers to control foreign and security policy in jeopardy and was, in part, a reason for Ben Bella's ouster in June 1965. While the officers of the ALN had been willing to allow the president and his loyalists to control certain areas of policy and decision making, their command of security policy was clearly of paramount importance. The military enclave's control over foreign and security policy remained unproblematic during both the Boumédienne period and the presidency of Colonel Chadli Benjedid, as civilian ministers served as little more than legal cover for the military in the realm of foreign and security policy.[24]

During the 1980s, however, President Chadli sought to venture beyond what Algeria's military establishment believed was acceptable on the foreign policy front. The senior officers were willing to allow Chadli to engage in diplomatic efforts to improve relations among the countries of the Maghreb, including those with Morocco, Algeria's subregional competitor, but they would only permit the president to operate within certain parameters. In 1988, for example, when Chadli's efforts seemed to actually hold out the possibility of improved relations between Algiers and Rabat, the senior commanders thwarted his efforts and the longstanding border dispute between the two countries remained unresolved.[25] Similarly, in the mid-1990s, the commanders prevented President Liamine Zeroual, a retired officer, from establishing a security policy independent of the military. In 1995, despite Zeroual's desire to begin the process of national reconciliation, under pressure from the military he rebuffed the Platform for a Political and Peaceful Solution of the Algerian Crisis—the St. Egidio Agreement—which most of Algeria's political factions, including the Islamists, had signed.

When he became president of Algeria in 1999, Abdelaziz Bouteflika, widely regarded to be the military's candidate, sought to step beyond the bounds of the military on foreign policy and security issues with decidedly mixed results. Although like his predecessor Zeroual, Bouteflika intended to improve ties with Morocco, he has met resistance from the military. Rather than warming relations, Bouteflika has instead routinely accused the Moroccan government of harboring drug dealers and terrorists. Bouteflika has had more success in pursuing national reconciliation. Just three months after his election, the National People's Assembly adopted the Civil Harmony Law, which was overwhelmingly ratified in a national referendum three months later. Although an important step forward in rebuilding Algeria, the law was not as far reaching as initially understood.[26] The initiative was undertaken only after the Islamists were thoroughly beaten on the battlefield. The Armée Islamique du Salut (AIS), the largest armed militant organization and a component of the FIS, had, in fact, been adhering to a truce with the military since 1997. Besides prompting anywhere from 5,000–15,000 militants to return to their homes and jobs without fear of prosecution, the amnesty effectively split the FIS from its military wing.[27] Ali Jeddi, the most senior FIS official not in jail or exiled as of 2000, accused the AIS commanders who accepted the amnesty of betrayal. In this way, Algeria's national reconciliation served to reinforce the officers' military and political victory, as well as its continued primacy in security policy. While the 2006 Charter for Peace and National Reconciliation is more far-reaching than the Civil Harmony Law, it nevertheless specifically outlaws the FIS, bars the exploitation of religion for political gain, and shields the officer corps from prosecution for excesses during Algeria's decade of civil insurrection.

The Turkish military establishment also has an influential role and a key interest in the development of foreign and security policy. In 1950, when the 27-year reign of Mustafa Kemal Atatürk's Republican People's Party came to an end, outgoing president Ismet Inönü—an accomplished officer and Atatürk's second-in-command—met with the Demokrat Partisi's leadership and warned them that two issues were off-limits to their incoming government: secularism and foreign policy. Four decades later, when the Islamist-oriented Refah Partisi was slated to become the senior member of a coalition government, the military indicated that it would accept such a government (with reservations) as long as Refah politicians did not hold the interior, foreign, and defense ministry portfolios. This was extraordinary because as the senior member of the government, it would have been Refah's prerogative—in consultation with the president of the republic—to determine the allocation of cabinet portfolios.

In the 36 years between the Demokrat and Refah periods, the officers worked to institutionalize their exclusive control over foreign and security policy. Turkey's 1961 constitution formally established the Milli Güvenlik Kurullu (National Security Council, or MGK)—a mixed civilian-military body weighted in favor of the officers—which was charged with conveying to the Council of Ministers the military's view on a range of issues related to a broad conception of security. After the 1980 coup, the powers of the MGK were enhanced such that Turkey's civilian leaders were directed to give "priority consideration" to its recommendations. According to a former senior Turkish official who attended MGK meetings in the 1990s, the officers there were open to the discussion of all issues of national import with the notable exception of security policy.[28] The military establishment underscored this autonomy as it prosecuted the war against the Kurdistan Worker's Party (PKK) with little regard for Turkey's civilian leadership, and in mid-1997 invaded northern Iraq in pursuit of Kurdish insurgents without informing the government.[29]

There have been significant changes to the size and structure of the MGK since the mid-1990s. First, it was expanded from five officers and five civilians (not including the president) to include additional civilian ministers. This was an important change in terms of creating the impression that the military was willing to accept greater civilian participation but did little toward establishing civilian superiority over the MGK. The most dramatic change occurred in late 2003 when in an effort to conform to European norms, the Turkish Grand National Assembly adopted changes to the MGK that reduced the number of officers to one (the chief of staff), emphasized the body's advisory role, and established that a civilian must hold the office of MGK secretary-general—a post previously reserved exclusively for a military officer who answered to the chief of staff.

Despite these changes, the military enclave continued to wield significant influence in the development of Turkish security and foreign policy, especially in northern Iraq. The General Staff is unwaveringly opposed to the emergence of an independent Kurdish state there. Although few within Turkey advocate publicly for the establishment of an independent Kurdistan, there is a range of opinions on this issue within the ruling AK party. Yet the official position of the Turkish government is distinct for its lack of nuance, adhering closely to the thinking of the senior command.[30]

State and Political Apparatus

In all three countries officers and their civilian allies forged political systems with well-developed democratic facades, permitting the commanders to rule but leaving it to others to govern. Given the benefits of this situation, the officers have an interest in ensuring that these facades remain precisely little more than the pretenses of democracy they represent. In order to achieve this goal, the military enclaves have embedded within these political systems various means of control and have demonstrated that protecting the integrity of these tools is of primary importance.

During the almost two decades after the Free Officers assumed power in Egypt, the commanders constructed a democratic facade that only became more sophisticated and institutionalized with President Anwar Sadat's "political liberalization." By the 1980s, Egypt featured a parliament that included a variety of parties, a relatively freer press, and parliamentary influence in certain policy areas. Moreover, the Egyptian political-military elite permitted non-state-based groups to operate in cultural and social spheres relatively unencumbered. On the surface it seemed as if the Egyptian political system was becoming more open, but the military-political elite actually retained and refined the means of political control. Restrictive electoral laws, poll rigging, continued limits on the press, and the considerable power of the president, including his ability to appoint a full third of the upper house of Egypt's legislature, ensured that political activity remained circumscribed. According to one former high-ranking officer, "In Egypt, the machinery of the state is used to maintain the status quo."[31]

In an indication that the military regards political control of primary importance, the officers have demonstrated a willingness to expose themselves to the risks associated with direct involvement in politics and governance. In addition to the president —an officer and the leading member of Egypt's military enclave—and the officers who staff the presidency, a majority of Egypt's 26 governors are senior-ranking military and police officers, who, although removing their uniforms for their posts, remain integrated within the military establishment. The role of these officer-governors is relatively straightforward: they ensure that at the local and regional level opposition activists do not engage in activities that would undermine political control, potentially raze Egypt's democratic facade, or (worst of all) actually empower political institutions. In addition, Egypt's Emergency Law and its related regulations essentially place the country under military rule, if not martial law, and have been used as a pretext for the creation of a parallel judicial system and the widespread use of military tribunals. These courts have been used against not only those who have perpetrated violence against the state but also those who have advocated for the reform of elements of the state apparatus that contribute directly to the military enclave's ability to maintain control.[32]

The Algerian military enclave—"the real power in Algeria"—played a central role in state building.[33] Yet officers can exercise power and influence from the relative safety of the barracks through an elaborate facade of democracy that nevertheless contains various means of political control. In the first 25 years after Algeria's independence, the state's democratic veneer consisted of formal arrangements providing for the separation of powers, a functioning legislature with considerable powers of oversight, and an independent judiciary. Power, however, was weighted heavily in favor of the executive at the expense of the legislature, the party of the FLN remained the sole legal political formation in the country, and the judiciary proved far from independent. In October 1988, Algerians demanded an end to this *hogra* or arbitrary government. In response, Algeria's officers, who had popularized and retained a certain mystique stemming from their role in the revolution, placed both this legitimacy and their desire to forge a modern and professional military at risk with the brutal suppression of the disturbances.

In the immediate aftermath of the rioting, the military oversaw what was billed as a significant political liberalization. Yet this reform was an effort to restore and update Algeria's democratic facade that would permit the officers to maintain their predominant position in the political arena. The military withdrew from FLN structures, and Algerians were permitted to form "organizations of a political character." But these changes were accompanied by restrictive electoral, political parties, and press laws, designed to ensure that the country's politics remained circumscribed and controlled. The officers routinely expressed their support for the inclusion of political opposition in Algeria's National Assembly, but military spokesmen also made it clear that they preferred these parties have little power to influence policy.[34] Clearly, the officers were willing to countenance unprecedented political participation, but they retained their abiding interest in aspects of the state apparatus that provided them a veto in the political arena.[35]

In Turkey, members of the military enclave have long engaged in a discourse about democracy and the officers' unfailing support for a democratic republic. To some extent, the officers have been true to their word, accepting the outcomes of elections and referenda that directly contradicted their very public wishes.[36] Yet the military enclave's willingness to risk exposure to politics in order to establish or safeguard key aspects of political control is abundantly apparent from the officers' periodic coups d'état and interventions in politics. Turkish officers and their allies suggest that at each of these moments intervention was warranted to preserve democracy and that no further proof, other than the fact that the officers returned power to civilians, is necessary to support this claim.[37]

As these episodes came to a close, the officers, while reinforcing their commitment to democracy and upholding their commitment to multiparty politics, simultaneously established ever-more restrictive political constraints. In 1961, the officers established the MGK, which was not only a key component in the preservation of the officers' core interest in foreign and security policy but also provided the opportunity for the officers to monitor political developments. In 1971, the military forced the government to tighten various aspects of the 1961 constitution that the officers deemed too liberal. The 1982 constitution upheld the value of democracy and personal freedoms but simultaneously sought to ensure that political activity remained within certain parameters.

Nationalist Narratives

In Egypt, Algeria, and Turkey, the military has derived a significant measure of legitimacy from nationalist narratives that place the officers at the center of struggles against colonialism, external aggression, and the realization of the "national will." The three military establishments have demonstrated again and again the importance of these particular accounts through not only their discourse but also their willingness to take risks to suppress alternative narratives. The nationalist account of the Egyptian armed forces, for example, revolves around the following stylized version of contemporary Egyptian history: "In 1952, the military toppled an alien and corrupt dynasty. Four years later the armed forces heroically defended Egypt's independence when it repelled the Israeli, British, and French invasion of 1956. The loss of Sinai in 1967 was the result of Israeli aggression and came at a time when one-third of the armed forces was fulfilling its Pan-Arab duty in Yemen. The heroism of the officers and soldiers of Egypt's military made the Crossing of the Suez Canal possible in October 1973 successfully restoring Egypt's collective national honor and ultimately its land. The Egyptian military is the guarantor of domestic stability and a source of regional stability." It should be of little surprise that over the course of the last five decades, Egypt's military-political elite would seek to burnish and reinforce this particular narrative and take significant risks to defend it. After all, this narrative serves as a wellspring of the armed forces' legitimacy.[38]

More so than their Algerian or Turkish counterparts, the Egyptian military enclave's core interest in preserving its nationalist narrative is closely associated with the military's autonomy in security and foreign policy. Consider, once again, the 1954

Anglo-Egyptian Treaty. Although the Free Officers and the Muslim Brotherhood benefited mutually from their cooperation against the *ancien régime,* they were in many ways nationalist competitors. Both organizations played important roles in, and derived significant prestige from, the nationalist agitation against the British and the war of 1948. When the Brothers assailed Colonel Nasser and his fellow officers over the provisions of the 1954 agreement, it represented a challenge not only to the officers in the realm of foreign/security policy but also to the military's commitment to Egyptian nationalism—the very issue on which the officers' legitimacy rested. As a result, risking both popular support and domestic order. After all, the Brothers maintained a paramilitary organization called the "Secret Apparatus." Hence the Free Officers repressed their erstwhile, yet important, allies. Once the Brotherhood was rehabilitated in the 1970s and again in the 1980s, the organization was given significant autonomy in the areas of culture and social services but was officially prohibited from engaging in political activity that would likely include a critique of the military enclave's nationalist narrative.

In the peace treaty with Israel the Egyptian military enclave upheld the critical importance of its nationalist narrative. A key component of the agreement is a provision that limits the Egyptian military from moving more than 50 kilometers east of the Suez Canal. This was perhaps the only way the Egyptians could close off the possibility of any Israeli territorial claim to Sinai and thereby ensure that all land occupied as a result of the June 1967 war was returned to Egypt. Regaining sovereignty over the entire Sinai was of critical importance to the officers' legitimacy; their willingness to demilitarize a section of Egypt's territory in order to regain the peninsula illustrates their commitment to the perpetuation of their nationalist narrative.

The Algerian military establishment also maintains a core interest in a nationalist narrative in which the officers retain an unrivaled position. An examination of the military's flagship publication, *el-Djeich,* from the period immediately following the founding of independent Algeria through the mid-1980s, indicates that the officer corps has sought to foster and preserve an organic connection between the military and Algerian nationalism.[39] Initially there was some urgency to this message as Boumédienne and his fellow officers of the ALN worked diligently to synthesize their role in Algeria's war of independence with the internal commanders. It was not the officers of the ALN—the army of the frontiers—who bore the brunt of the war of liberation, but the *moujahideen* who fought the French military from within Algeria. Yet it was critical to the political project of Boumédienne and his cadre of commanders to establish that the ALN had played the crucial role in Algeria's independence struggle, rather than distinguishing itself for its general ineffectiveness along the Moroccan and Tunisian borders.

The officers considered this nationalist narrative so critical that they were willing to place national unity in jeopardy as Boumédienne and his fellow commanders sought to liquidate all competing claimants to Algeria's nationalist mantle who refused to be co-opted.[40] Further, the officers' 1965 coup, which deposed their hand-picked president, Ahmed Ben Bella, was based on their perception that as Ben Bella sought to consolidate his power he was compromising both the military's authority and the officers' nationalist credentials. Ben Bella promoted Tahar Zbiri, an ex-leader of the internal *maquisards,* to lead the État Major of the Armée Nationale Populaire. Ben Bella also planned to establish popular militias. These groups would not only serve as a potential counterweight to the military but also held out the potential to supplant the military as the ultimate expression of Algerian nationalism.

After the coup, Boumédienne reminded the public that the army was Algeria's leading nationalist body, proclaiming: "We are . . . nationalists worthy of the name . . . [We] are the people, [wc] are the Revolution."[41] With the coup of June 1965, all potential challengers to the military's hegemony had been undermined and the officers' central place in Algeria's nationalist credentials was seemingly secure. The officers did face challenges to their nationalist narrative over the next 20 years—notably, what has become known as the Berber Spring of 1980 and the Islamist agitation that began in 1982 under the leadership of Moustapha Bouyali. In both instances, Algeria's military elite responded ferociously with harsh crackdowns intended to ensure that Algeria's prevailing nationalist narrative remained unchallenged.

The Turkish military's nationalist account is bound up with the principles of Kemalism—secularism, democracy, modernization, unity, and cultural affiliation with the West. It was, after all Mustafa Kemal, who, according to Şerif Mardin, "took up a non-existent, hypothetical entity, the Turkish nation, and breathed life into it."[42] And it was Kemal, a military officer, who placed the Turkish Armed Forces at the very center of this nationalist project. On the fifth anniversary of the republic, he proclaimed: "When speaking of the army, I am speaking of the intelligentsia of the Turkish nation . . . The Turkish nation . . . considers its army the guardian of its ideals."[43] Turkey's military enclave has carried this torch ever since, invoking its connection to Kemal, his reforms, and Turkish nationalism to justify its role and ensure its legitimacy. Consider, for example, the words of General Kenan Evren, who led the 1980 coup d'état: "I am . . . fully confident that the Turkish Armed Forces, the indivisible and essential element of the nation, will continue to fulfill the honourable tasks befalling them tomorrow, just as they are doing today, under Atatürk's inspiration."[44] Evren's statement and similar declarations of his successors suggest that Turkey's military enclave would brook no deviation from a nationalist narrative based on Kemalist principles.

In fact, the military establishment has consistently demonstrated this rigidity in relation to Kurdish ethnic consciousness. In response to defeat, occupation, potential partition, ethnic cleavages, and massive underdevelopment after World War I, Kemal conjured a Turkish nation coterminous with the boundaries of the Anatolian rectangle. He was convinced that political, economic, and cultural development could not take place unless the Turkish nation was free of ethnic and religious differences within clearly defined territorial boundaries. Over the course of the republic's subsequent history, the military elite has welcomed ethnic Kurds to participate in the political and economic life of the country, though only if they refrain from using any public or official ethnic affiliation other than "Turk."

Beginning in the mid-1980s and throughout the 1990s, however, coinciding with the terrorism of the Kurdistan Workers' Party (PKK), the military—with the assistance of allies within the media—intensified its nationalist message. Not only did the officers see to it that Kurdish dialects continued to be banned and Kurdish-related cultural activities outlawed, but they also routinely jailed nonviolent activists advocating for greater Kurdish cultural autonomy. These actions risked both alienating the larger Kurdish community, particularly those in the southeast, and the possible expansion of the Kurdish insurrection beyond the PKK, all in order to protect the officers' Kemalist nationalist narrative. Potential resolutions to the problem of Kurdish ethnic consciousness, notably "neo-Ottomanism," which would shift identity away from ethnicity to one based on common religion, were dismissed out-of-hand as a violation of Kemalist and nationalist principles.[45] The reforms Turkey has undertaken to meet European Union requirements allow for Kurdish cultural and linguistic expression. Yet while Kurdish-language broadcasts can now be heard on the state-affiliated Turkish Radio and Television, the opportunity to learn or study in Kurdish dialects remains limited.

Egyptian, Algerian, and Turkish military enclaves maintain a hierarchy of interests and share a common constellation of core interests. Knowledge of the commanders' worldview and an appreciation of the derivation of the officers' interests provide analysts with insight into the behavior of the officers. It remains difficult, however, to determine clear red-lines that would allow analysts to predict precisely how officers behave. Military officers are unable to assess perfectly any given political situation, and as a result their behavior may deviate from what observers expect. Understanding the outlook and interests of the military enclaves provides a credible guideline that captures the tendencies of the commanders. It also underscores the challenges to the stability of the military-dominated systems in Egypt, Algeria, and Turkey.

CHAPTER THREE

The Pouvoir Militaire *and the*
Failure to Achieve a *"Just Mean"*

With its slide into civil insurrection in the 1990s, Algeria became the prism through which observers viewed the struggle between Islam and the state in the Middle East. Arab leaders used Algeria's descent into violence, which by decade's end had cost an estimated 100,000 lives, as a reason why they could not undertake political reforms for fear that Islamists would overwhelm their political systems. For their part, U.S. policymakers were concerned that the establishment of an Islamic state in Algeria would profoundly influence the political trajectory of other states in the region, notably Egypt.

The damage to Algerian society that the brutality of both Islamist extremists and the armed forces wrought tends to overshadow the political contest that preceded the country's decade of bloodshed. Between 1988 and 1992, Islamists and officers were initially engaged in a peaceful political battle. Whereas the Islamists of the Front Islamique du Salut (FIS, also referred to as the Front) sought to advance their agenda through the state's pseudodemocratic institutions, Algeria's military enclave sought to ensure the authoritarian status quo. The officers believed that this could be achieved through the establishment of what was referred to as a "just mean," which would effectively split the political arena between several competing groups, neutralizing opposition and ensuring the continuance of the military-founded political system.

A close examination of this period undermines two prevailing myths about Algeria: (1) that the FIS was by its very nature prone to violence and (2) that the political liberalization of the late 1980s and early 1990s was a "real democratic opening." First, the FIS was, true to its name, a political front composed of a variety of different Islamist organizations, none of which had a history of violence. It was actually the army's cancellation of the 1991–1992 elections that radicalized Algerian politics and contributed decisively to the subsequent fighting. Second, the military oversaw the "political liberalization" to serve the interests of the officers in their efforts to preserve Algeria's prevailing authoritarian political order, not to promote any real openness.[1]

Evolution and Character of the Regime

The evolution of the Algerian regime is intimately associated with the Armée de Libération Nationale (ALN) and its successor, the Armée Nationale Populaire (ANP). On paper, the military was subordinate to Algeria's civilian leadership: the agreements initialed at the Soumman Conference (1956), as well as the Tripoli Program (1962), the constitution (1963), and the Charter of Algiers (1964) all confirmed the principle of civilian superiority. The reality was, however, quite different. Algeria's first president, Ahmed Ben Bella, owed his position exclusively to the military. In 1963, a year after independence, Colonel Houari Boumédienne told *Le Monde:* "The choice of the armed forces to present Ben Bella the presidency of the Republic is not a sentimental choice. We want brother Ben Bella to occupy this post because he is a man capable of assuming it."[2] The installation of Ben Bella, a breach of the Soumman agreements and Tripoli Program, indicated that the military establishment, its political instincts already well developed at the time of independence, was intent on being a central actor in Algeria's political development. Even though the general staff played an indirect role in the actual drafting of the country's first constitution, that the officers chose the president suggests that the military reserved for itself a key position in the founding of the Algerian regime.[3]

In 1965, less than two years after the ratification of the constitution, the Algerian officer corps deposed Ben Bella and dissolved parliament. The military establishment had been content to obscure its role behind the presidency and the constitution, but after the coup the officers set about refashioning the institutions of the state.[4] The 26 members of the Council of the Revolution, all officers, charged themselves—in the absence of the National People's Assembly—with overseeing the development of state structures capable of realizing the goals of the revolution.

Over the following 11 years, the Council of the Revolution further entrenched the military establishment as the founders and backbone of the Algerian regime.[5] This was reinforced with the promulgation of the 1976 National Charter and subsequent constitution. Reflecting on this formative period in the development and consolidation of the Algerian regime, Abderrezak Bouhara, a former officer in the ALN and the ANP, argues that the military sought to establish a "state [that] outlives men and events."[6] Indeed, the choice of Chadli Benjedid, the former commander of the Oran military district, to become president after Boumédienne's death indicates that although the officer corps had increasingly sought to insulate themselves from everyday involvement in the politics of governing, they were unwilling to risk their regime by ceding political control to any other group. In sum, the military establishment, not revolutionary bodies such as the Gouvernement Provisoire de la République Algérienne (GPRA) or the Conseil National de la Révolution Algérienne (CNRA), was the founding body of the Algerian regime.

Yet what can be said about the character of this political order? The regime that Algeria's officers founded looked strikingly similar to a democratic polity. In addition to an array of seemingly democratic institutions, the Algerian political setting featured representative structures and a series of normative principles intended to elicit the loyalty of the populace. Although these types of institutions, structures, and principles were not unique to Algeria, they became crucial instruments in the confrontation between the Algerian state and its opponents in the late 1980s and 1990s.

Democratic Institutions, Representative Structures, and Legitimating Principles

In September 1963, after political scores within and among various factions of the GPRA were settled, Ahmed Ben Bella, who had become Algeria's first president with the support of the ALN, promulgated Algeria's first constitution. Its preamble issues a clarion call for Algerians "to continue their march toward democratic and popular revolution."[7] Within the *tiers mondiste* language typical of Algeria's postindependence discourse, Algerians were endowed with fundamental rights as the ultimate sovereigns of the state. For example, the Front de Libération Nationale (FLN)—the *parti unique* that was to be the principal agent of Algeria's national development—"derives its force from the people in order to break the economic structures of the past and substitute an economic power exercised democratically for the *fellahin* and the laboring masses."[8] As Articles 1 and 3 of the constitution declare, "Algeria is a democratic popular republic" whose motto is "Revolution of the people, for the people."

The legitimating principles enshrined in the constitution not only conjure images of a democracy but also emphasize culture and cultural authenticity. This should come as little surprise as Islam and Arabic were the primary factors that bound Algerians in their struggle for independence.[9] The constitution reminds Algerians that "Islam and the Arabic language were effective forces of resistance against the attempt to undermine the identity of Algerians carried out by the colonial regime" and declares Islam the state religion and Arabic the official language.[10]

The constitution provided for a National People's Assembly whose representatives were to be elected by secret and universal suffrage for terms of five years. Although the constitution established a strong presidency, the National People's Assembly was empowered "to exercise supervision over the actions of the government through hearings, written questions, and oral questions with or without debate." Moreover, the Algerian judiciary was declared independent with the power to engage in judicial review.[11] Finally, the presidency, in conjunction with the National People's Assembly, could initiate constitutional revisions, but such action required an absolute majority of members of parliament and was subject to approval through popular referendum.[12]

Even though there was an 11-year interregnum between the coup d'état of June 1965 and the return of constitutional politics, the Council of the Revolution during this time initiated two formal mechanisms for popular participation, the Assemblées Populaires Communales (APCs) and the Assemblées Populaires de Wilaya (APWs), established in 1967 and 1969 respectively. The APCs were founded to serve as representative and administrative bodies at the local level, and the APWs were set up to perform similar functions for Algeria's then 33 *wilayat* (or provinces). By 1971, opposition movements emerged from a number of important areas of Algerian society, notably elements of the middle class and a nascent Islamist movement. The Islamists insisted on greater adherence to Islamic strictures and, along with their middle-class allies, demanded *shura* (consultation). Boumédienne's effort to co-opt these groups resulted in the criminalization of gambling, the establishment of Friday as the weekly holiday, and the elaboration of a National Charter in April 1976 and the subsequent return to constitutionalism in November of that same year. The purpose of the charter was to offer Algerians a retrospective assessment of their revolution after almost 20 years and to present a roadmap for future progress.[13] Before its ratification through a referendum, the content of the charter was subject to open and public debate.[14]

The 1976 constitution, based on the National Charter, maintained both the legitimating principles and a formal institutional framework resembling a democratic system like its 1963 predecessor. Given Boumédienne's leftward ideological shift, the normative appeals of the new constitution placed greater emphasis on socialism but nevertheless still firmly situated the legitimacy of the Algerian state in the "popular and democratic" struggle for independence. The opening paragraph of the constitution stated: "The Algerian people acquired their independence at the price of a hundred years battle and a war of liberation, under the guidance of the National Liberation Front and the Army of National Liberation, which stands in history as one of the great episodes in the resurrection of the peoples of the Third World. In the period after independence, [the Algerian people] resolutely devoted itself to the construction of the State and the building of a new society founded on the elimination of the exploitation of man by man and in the final analysis, in the framework of the option of socialism, the full development of man and the promotion of the popular masses."[15] Once more, the constitution encouraged Algerians to "continue ... the untiring enterprise of the decade since the historic rectification of 19 June 1965, in order to endow the nation-state with a modern and democratic base."[16]

The egalitarian ethos of the preamble, which exhorted Algerians to battle the "exploitation of man by man," was further developed in Article 37, which warned them: "The functions in the service of the state are not a privilege. They constitute a responsibility. The agents of the state must act exclusively in consideration of the interests of the people and the greater public. The exercise of public responsibilities is neither a means to enrichment nor a means to serve private interests." As a corollary to this principle, all Algerians were deemed "equal in rights and responsibilities" before the law (Articles 39–40). Significantly, citizens were endowed with the freedom of expression, though with the admonition that this right should not be exercised to undermine the state. On the cultural level, Islam and Arabic retained their primary places as key cultural touchstones employed to evoke the legitimacy of Algeria's political order.

The return of constitutionalism in 1976 also meant the restoration of Algeria's National Popular Assembly (APN). Elected by universal, secret balloting every five years, the parliament was deemed the "institutional base" of the Algerian state and provided "decentralization for the participation of the popular masses and the management of public affairs at all levels."[17] The third chapter of the constitution—"The Legislative Functions"—endowed the National Popular Assembly with legislative, consent, and oversight functions. Members of the assembly were also permitted to establish a commission of inquiry "into all affairs of general interest," in addition to their established rights to question the government, which was enjoined to respond to any query within 15 days.[18] One significant institutional innovation was the establishment of a Court of Accounting, "charged with auditing all the public spending of the State, the Party, the local and regional collectivities, and the socialist enterprises of the state."[19] Given that Ben Bella's drive for power and self-aggrandizement was the justification for the coup of June 1965, the array of legislative and particularly oversight functions built into the 1976 constitution were ostensibly to ensure that no individual or group could use the Algerian state for personal gain.

A decade later, Boumédienne's successor, Colonel Chadli Benjedid, offered the Algerian public the "Enhanced" (or "Enriched") National Charter. Keeping with Boumédienne's precedent, this latest statement on the Algerian revolution was the subject of open and public debate before being put up for a referendum. Although relying less on revolutionary discourse, the Enhanced Charter differed little from the two constitutions and National Charter that preceded it, with one significant exception: to counter the Algerian state's flagging legitimacy, the Enhanced Charter placed significantly greater emphasis on Islam. The opening section of the document reviewed Algerian history, giving Islam pride of place for "providing protection from the Crusades and colonial control." It also pointed out that the Algerian people "derived strength from this spiritual power making possible the hope of victory."[20] Building on the historical role of Islam in Algeria's struggle, the charter indicated that "there is a fusing of Islam and Algerian society which provides the power to hold together a united land."[21] The emphasis on Islam was to be operationalized in the educational policies of the Algerian government. Accordingly, the charter recognized "the promotion of spirituality of young people, the necessity of supporting religion as an academic subject, and improving the means of studying religion as a basic subject."[22]

While the Enhanced Charter represented the ideological rationale for Chadli's new policy initiatives rather than a blueprint for a new constitution, the impetus for such a change developed in the wake of the October 1988 riots that swept Algeria's cities. The government, which had already undertaken a series of economic initiatives to confront a marked deterioration in the country's economic performance, was badly shaken by the events of *cinq octobre* and embarked on what seemed to be wide-ranging political reforms. This process culminated in the 1989 constitution.

Like its predecessors, the preamble of the constitution underscored the historic legitimacy of the Algerian state through the struggle for independence. Yet the document also betrayed an implicit understanding that evoking that struggle was no longer sufficient to elicit the loyalty of the Algerian public. A string of events including student riots in Constantine during 1986, persistent wildcat strikes in the industrial sector throughout the 1980s, the perceptible growth of Islamist-related social activity, and, of course, the October 1988 riots demonstrated that Algeria's revolutionary mystique could no longer ensure social cohesion. In addition to conjuring images of the struggle against French colonialism, therefore, the 1989 version of the constitution emphasized both cultural authenticity and a new concept to enter the Algerian political lexicon, the "state of law." Consider, for example, the following excerpts from the opening section of the new constitution:

> The 1st of November 1954 was the zenith of our destiny, resulting in a long resistance to the aggressions against our culture, our values and our personality, the 1st of November is anchored solidly in the present battles and the past glory of the Nation [*sic*].

> The Constitution is above all the fundamental law that guarantees the individual and collective rights and liberties, protecting the rule of freedom of choice of the people and conferring legitimacy to the exercise of these powers. It assures the juridical protection and the control of public powers in a society where legality and the development of man in all his dimensions prevail.

> Strong of spiritual values, profoundly rooted, and of the traditions of solidarity and justice, the people are confident in the capacities to work fully toward cultural, social, and economic progress of the world today and tomorrow.

Algeria is an Islamic land, an integral part of the Greater Maghreb, an Arab, Mediterranean, and African country . . .[23]

These passages underscore the effort to fuse the revolution, cultural issues, and the rule of law to bolster the Algerian state's flagging legitimacy.

Formally, the 1989 constitution maintained many of the same attributes as its forerunners—an elected National People's Assembly with legislative and oversight power, an independent judiciary and judicial review, and an elected president, to name just a few. There were, however, two important changes: First, clauses from the 1976 constitution endowing the military with a role in "the development of the country" were excised. Second, the monopoly of the FLN, which previous constitutions charged with realizing the democratic aspirations of the Algerian public, was terminated and Algerians were granted "the right to create associations of a political character."[24]

The Authoritarian Reality

Despite the inventory of formally democratic institutions, structures, and legitimating principles, Algeria was never a democracy. Even the rapid development of multiparty politics, the emergence of an independent press, and the freedom of expression following the ratification of the 1989 constitution did not indicate a transition to democracy. Within the array of seemingly democratic institutions, structures, and normative principles is, in reality, an authoritarian regime in which the military establishment predominates. Rather than a democracy, Algeria features a facade of democracy, which shields the real locus of power—the officer corps.[25] The regime is designed to maintain the prevailing balance of power in the political system.[26] Formal and informal structures and institutions ensure the power, prestige, privileges, and distributional advantages of the military and its allies among the civilian elite.

From the outset, the Algerian political system featured a number of constitutionally mandated structures such as the High Council of Defense (later to be named the High Security Council), the Constitutional Council, and the High Council of the Magistrature. Although officially advisory bodies to the government, these could be instrumentalized to serve the interests of those at the summit of the Algerian state. The High Security and Constitutional Councils played pivotal roles in the army's 1992 intervention. In addition, the single-party system and the presidency served as institutional outposts from which the military officers could patrol the perimeters of the Algerian regime.

Without diminishing the officer corps' initial commitment to the idea of a vanguard party entrusted with mobilizing the Algerian masses to reclaim their patrimony while constructing a new state, a system based on a *parti unique* precluded the emergence of autonomous centers of power, thus ensuring control of the regime and its attendant benefits to the military enclave. In addition to the party of the FLN, the presidency, which is endowed with a formal set of powers that far outstrips those of any other political actor, has continuously rested in the hands of the officer corps. As noted, Ben Bella was the military's "choice," and his two immediate successors were officers of considerable stature—Boumédienne was the historic leader of the ALN, while Chadli had long held the prestigious position of commanding the Oran military district.[27] Even the ostensibly liberal reforms of the 1989 constitution maintained a presidency boasting robust authority and influence.

At the time the 1989 version of the constitution was promulgated, analysts hailed its relative liberalism and pointed to it as the prime example of Algeria's anticipated transition from an authoritarian to a democratic regime. Behind the document's apparent political innovations, however, the prevailing authoritarian system remained in place. Rather than democracy, the goal of the constitution was to infuse the regime with greater legitimacy through liberalization in several key areas. Consider, for example, the hallmark of Algeria's so-called transition to democracy, Article 40 of the constitution: "The right to create associations of a political character is recognized. This right is not, however, to be invoked to violate fundamental freedoms, national unity, territorial integrity, the independence of the country and the sovereignty of the people." Although the categories outlined in the second sentence were open to rather expansive and imprecise definitions, the law implementing Article 40 was demonstratively restrictive.[28] For example, under law 89-11 (July 1989), in order to operate legally, political parties were required to: obtain an *agrément préalable* (prior licensing) from the Ministry of the Interior, use standard Arabic in all official business, and collectively behave in accordance with "Islamic morals and the spirit of the November 1 revolution." Moreover, donations were limited to 200,000 Algerian dinars (about $2,800), and fundraising from abroad was forbidden. This restriction severely hampered Berber parties, which had significant émigré followings in France and other European countries. The law did provide for state financial assistance for parties, but the level of that support was dependent on the number of seats held in the parliament. This provision favored the FLN. Indeed, the status of the FLN under the implementing law was decidedly ambiguous. Since the party was not subject to the prior licensing requirement of law 89-11, the question remained whether it was subject to the other provisions of the law.[29]

Informal institutions also exist beneath officially espoused rules and regulations. Rooted in past practices and patterns of behavior, these informal institutions constitute the set of unspoken beliefs and uncodified norms that continue to govern the expectations and behavior of political and social actors. The origins of these institutions lie in the military establishment's successful efforts to undermine Algeria's founding documents, while publicly expressing fealty to them. The result has been the open secret of Algerian politics since independence: the yawning gap between the subordinate military of the formal texts and the actual autonomy of the commanders.

The dichotomy of formal and informal power in Algeria extends to a variety of issue and policy areas, including presidential succession.[30] The informal institutions that govern the selection of the president and his relationship with the military enclave underscore the officer corps' autonomy. Consider, for example, Chadli's ascension to the presidency in early 1979. While the process appeared to conform to the regulations concerning presidential succession elaborated in the 1976 constitution, closer examination reveals the military's capacity to determine the president without consent of those outside the rarefied preserve of the senior officer corps.[31] In short, Chadli was *not* selected at the Congress of the Party of the FLN called upon the death of Boumédienne but rather at a simultaneous conclave of senior commanders held under the auspices of Commander Larbi Belkheir. Once the commanders agreed on Chadli to succeed Boumédienne, the new president was presented to the gathered FLN delegates, who could do little to oppose the military's fait accompli.[32]

Once selected, the Algerian president has had to abide by a specific set of unwritten rules and norms that condition his relations with the officers: a president may govern how he wishes, yet he must not pursue policies anathema to the military establishment. Even Boumédienne, who by the time he brought forth the 1976 National Charter had accumulated significant personal power, was to some extent beholden to the officers because they alone could remove him from power—just as Boumédienne had done to Ben Bella a decade earlier.[33] This relationship was even more pronounced during Chadli's presidency. With far less personal prestige and power than his predecessor, President Chadli was forced to strike a delicate bargain with his fellow officers, providing them with guarantees in return for their support.[34] As a result, the senior command retained wide latitude to pursue its own military, political, and economic prerogatives with little interference.

When President Chadli was ultimately forced from office in 1992, the military selected General Liamine Zeroual—a former minister of defense—to lead the country. Although Zeroual was a member of the military establishment, he was, like Chadli, beholden to the officers for his position and limited in his ability to pursue independent policy initiatives, especially on foreign and domestic security issues. After Zeroual's resignation in 1998, Abdelaziz Bouteflika was elected president in polling that the Algerian opposition accused of being fraudulent. Six other presidential contenders asserted that Bouteflika, a former foreign minister who had been close to Boumédienne, benefited from military-sponsored vote rigging and ballot stuffing. Still, Bouteflika learned quickly that being the military's candidate did not afford much room for maneuvering. In fact, during the early weeks and months of his presidency, the Algerian government was paralyzed because the military objected to Bouteflika's selection of ministers in the government.

Notwithstanding the existence of institutions that resemble those of liberal democracies, Algeria's political order is clearly rigged to benefit the military elite and its allies. As a result, the *pouvoir militaire,* as the military establishment is known, will likely endeavor to prevent any alteration to the prevailing institutional setting. Given this imbalance in benefits, however, political entrepreneurs are—at opportune moments and in the face of extreme compulsion—likely to seek strategies to improve their condition and that of their constituencies.

The Benefits and Risks of the Democratic Facade

The web of formal and informal institutions that provided the framework for Algeria's authoritarian regime was obscured behind an entirely different set of institutions, structures, and normative principles critical to a political facade that conjured a democratic polity. Yet what benefits did Algeria's dominant military—the unrivaled master of its political domain—derive from the elaborate facade of democratic institutions, representative structures, and normative principles?

Benefits to the Military Enclave

There are three interrelated reasons why the Algerian military enclave either established or countenanced the trappings of a democratic polity. First, the very existence of institutions and representative structures that matched both the regime's founding texts and its ostensibly democratic principles could only serve to enhance the legitimacy of the political order.[35] It was not, however, just their existence, but the functionality of these institutions and structures that was a critical component of regime legitimacy. Though the rules, regulations, norms, and structural attributes of a democratic polity were superimposed on Algeria's authoritarian regime, they could be, and were at times, invested with power. The Assemblée Nationale Populaire was not merely a shell devoid of content; it passed legislation and sought to hold the government accountable in some areas. In 1979, for example, the parliament managed to approve a constitutional amendment mandating that the post of prime minister be filled.[36] Still, the political arena remained circumscribed. The appointment of a prime minister, after all, made little difference in the overall character of the authoritarian regime. Nevertheless, Algeria's elite could claim, without being totally disingenuous, that the founding texts and legitimating principles roughly corresponded to practice.

The second reason the Algerian military enclave either encouraged or tolerated institutions that resembled a democracy was that this facade served as a convenient means of co-optation. Authoritarian political systems, as opposed to their totalitarian counterparts, have neither the ideological nor organizational capacity to destroy potential counter-elites and thus must buy off these would-be challengers. The democratic facade instilled a measure of flexibility into Algeria's authoritarian regime, providing it with the capacity to satisfy certain demands emerging from society without fundamentally altering the underlying character of the political order. Boumédienne and his allies restored the National People's Assembly and other key elements of Algeria's democratic facade in response to demands for *shura* (consultation). The reforms of late 1988 and early 1989 resulted from a similar dynamic. Though the demonstrators taking part in the October 1988 riots did not make any explicit demands for political liberalization and democracy, their calls for an end to *hogra* (arbitrary government) produced modifications to Algeria's political facade in an effort to mitigate the political pressure on Chadli's government.[37] The strategy—which the military supported and some even suggest demanded—was to allow limited pluralism within the context of Algeria's authoritarian regime.[38] This remains the current state of Algerian politics, where "pseudo-opposition" groups are permitted to attack the policies of the government but are barred, by sets of formal and informal institutions, from asking questions about the sources of power and legitimacy of the political order.

Finally, the officers of the military enclave sought to avoid—with the exception of their representative at the presidency—the day-to-day governance of the country. This was not merely a matter of preference, as the officer corps devoted its energies to developing a modern, professional fighting force, but a matter of survival. Exposure to the vicissitudes of politics, the Algerian commanders believed, would unnecessarily jeopardize their coherence—a crucial component of their power.[39] As long as the public face of the government was not specifically that of the military, opposition would be directed toward other political actors, notably the FLN.[40] The benefit of Algeria's political facade is thus obvious: the officers need not govern, though they retain their position as society's undisputed power brokers.[41]

Risks to the Military Enclave

Algeria's political facade has been a benefit to the officer corps, but it also contains a certain amount of risk. Historically, politics within Algeria's authoritarian regime have revolved around access to rents from the well-developed system of patronage networks. Whatever ideological predilections Algerian civilian politicians maintained —there were, to be sure, a variety of tendencies within the FLN—these principles were seemingly not as important as the advantages associated with state largesse. In such an environment, it was relatively easy for the leadership to purchase political docility. Yet, Algeria's political facade always held out the possibility that a determined counter-elite, resistant to co-optation, could exploit the formally democratic institutions, representative structures, and legitimating principles that overlay Algeria's authoritarian core to engage in a bid for political power. This is precisely what occurred between 1989 and 1992.

In the relatively more liberalized political environment of the period after the 1988 riots, the pretenses of democracy became powerful instruments through which a dedicated opposition could engage in a wide-ranging attack on the Algerian government and the prevailing elite. Although the risks to the military establishment were clear, they were not as immediate as some analysts might suspect. The scholarly literature has emphasized the interests of the officer corps, but members of Algeria's military enclave withstood the Islamists' withering assaults on these interests yet allowed their foes to continue to operate legally in the political system. The judgment to not suppress the Islamists resulted from the combination of the military establishment's inability to forecast the consequences of FIS activities and the officers' own rhetoric about democracy, however disingenuous. The minister of defense General Khaled Nezzar indicated that he welcomed the political participation of the Islamists so long as a "just mean" was established in the National People's Assembly, preventing any party from dominating that body.

Less than two weeks after the ratification of the 1989 constitution a faction of Algeria's Islamist movement founded the Front Islamique du Salut. Under the leadership of Abassi Madani, a professor at the University of Algiers; Ali Belhadj, a preacher at the al-Sunna mosque in the Bab el-Oued neighborhood of Algiers; and Shaikh Ahmed Sanouni, the imam of al-Sunna, the new party used its network of mosques and social service centers to mobilize and recruit political activists to man the developing party bureaucracy, establish publications, and ultimately run in local, provincial, and national elections. Moreover, within a month of its founding, the party promulgated its official statement on the condition of Algeria's economy, society, and polity. Analysts of Algerian politics have often pointed out that the Front's program, manifested in both its official *Projet du Front Islamique du Salut* and the myriad policy statements of its leadership, were incoherent, vague, hopelessly naïve, and downright unworkable.[42] Although this assessment may, in fact, be correct, it does not diminish the important *effect* the Front's emotionally and materially satisfying counter-narrative had on the Algerian population.

Economic Interests

Given Algeria's deteriorating economic performance throughout the mid-1980s, and particularly following the collapse of the world oil market in 1986, the economy was a primary component of the Front's political strategy. Its platform sought to empower the private sector while also advocating a strong role for the state in the economy in order to protect Algeria's independence.[43] As a result, the party positioned itself in opposition to the worst distortions associated with both the state sector and President Chadli Benjedid's economic reform program initiated in the early 1980s.[44] In doing so, the Front used themes and language eerily similar to that of Algeria's founding texts:

> Our country has suffered colonial pillage for more than a century, its economy was derived under the reign of previous regimes that are responsible for an economic crisis characterized by a rupture of equilibrium between consumption, production, and the scarcity of basic necessities, like medicine and housing . . .

> The FIS maintains an Islamic project devoted to the salvation of man and civilization, recognizing how the economic dimension can serve man. Whether it is proceeding in production or consumption, proceeding with investment in order to alleviate poverty or in order to build projects of a civilizational character, the final objective is the promotion of man. This is our point of departure . . .[45]

In placing itself between the depredations of state-led planning and the deleterious effects of Chadli's policies, which encouraged consumption at the expense of investment and exacerbated already widespread corruption, the FIS was able to hold itself out as the true custodian of Algeria's economic well-being.[46] Moreover, as was typical of Islamist movements throughout the Middle East and North Africa, FIS's founding document also called for the establishment of Islamic banking in an effort to stamp out usurious practices.[47] In all, the Front's critique was potentially potent, insinuating that both the Boumédienne and Chadli governments had betrayed their solemn commitment enshrined in the 1976 constitution to eradicate the "exploitation of man by man."

The issue of corruption also figured prominently in the Front's economic analysis, given the legitimating principles of Algeria's founding texts, which expressly prohibited state agents from using their positions as a means for personal profit.[48] For example, the relative freedom resulting from Algeria's democratic facade permitted Abassi to excoriate the government on the issue of outstanding foreign debt in the daily *Horizons:* "First of all, the politics of intrigue pursued by the *pouvoir* has revealed its result: Bankruptcy. Can you imagine anything other resulting from these policies?"[49] In April of the same year, the Front once again took advantage of the democratic political facade to stage a march through central Algiers and present a series of demands to Chadli at, literally, the doors of the presidency. Among its 15 demands, the Front called for the "rehabilitation of the Court of Accounting with the establishment of immunity for its members."[50] Both the 1976 and 1989 constitutions had established such a court, which had the authority to audit the finances of the state and all public enterprises. The FIS, like other opposition parties that had come into being as a result of the 1989 constitutional revisions, had a ready-made issue on the question of corruption, seeking to leverage the elite's misuse of Algeria's economic institutions to improve its political prospects.[51]

The Islamists' vision of Algeria's economy potentially undermined the officers' well-developed economic interests. The Front positioned itself so that it could snipe at both the persistent and robust state sector and assail Chadli's economic liberalization. These criticisms attacked the military enclave's economic interests. Since the beginning of Chadli's reforms in the early 1980s, it was precisely at the muddled intersection of Algerian *étatisme* and circumscribed *infitah* (economic opening) where the commanders had a distinct advantage over other economic actors. Not only were the rent streams guaranteed from clients within the state sector, but greater emphasis on private enterprise also opened an entirely new area of revenue for the senior commanders. The private economic interests that were encouraged during the Chadli period tended to be concentrated in the commercial sector and were linked to the army and the state.[52] Retired or currently serving officers became *parrains* (godfathers) to these businesses, ensuring they obtained the appropriate licensing and had access to goods and materials often still under the control of the state sector in exchange for a percentage of the profits.[53] The distorting effects of this liberalization "based on the circulation of rent among the military, a deficient public sector, and a largely commercial private sector," actually benefited the military enclave and its allies.[54] Yet, FIS rhetoric concerning the gross inefficiencies and corruption of Algeria's prevailing economic arrangements, to which the military enclave was intimately linked, failed to elicit a response from the officer corps.[55]

Foreign and Security Policy

The FIS also developed what it considered an alternative vision of security and foreign policy. On the domestic side, the *Projet* sought "to ban abuse and oppression" within a security system that guaranteed the interests of the *umma* (community of Muslims) and the freedoms enshrined in the *shari'a*.[56] While the April 1990 demands reiterated these broad themes, Abassi and Belhadj also called on Chadli to release and rehabilitate all political prisoners who had been convicted in state security courts.[57] The Front's demand for the release of prisoners who had been convicted in the state security courts threw open the question of the military establishment's stated commitment to legalism. The FIS was, after all, implying something that was an open secret of Algerian politics, yet one that was never discussed. The *cours de sûreté* represented an efficient means through which the military establishment undermined and ultimately destroyed opponents of the officer corps' regime. In addition, the FIS call for a security policy free of abuse and oppression was a direct challenge to the officers' prerogatives relating to domestic order. Among other things, the Front's attack was a response to the brutal conduct of the military, particularly the *sécurité militaire*, in its efforts to quell the rioting of October 1988.[58]

Externally, the FIS envisioned an Islamist-oriented foreign policy that would involve Algerian diplomats in efforts to protect their co-religionists in regions where Muslims were under threat, notably China, India, the Soviet Union, Bulgaria, Palestine, and Afghanistan. Closer to home, Abassi told *Jeune Afrique* that the Front sought "equal relations based on the respect for the mutual sovereignty of each" with the European powers of the Mediterranean basin, including France. He also underscored the party's deference to the "political choices . . . and way of life" of its immediate neighbors: Tunisia, Libya, and in particular, Morocco.[59]

Iraq's invasion of Kuwait in August 1990 provided an opportunity for the FIS to further exploit Algeria's facade of democratic institutions, representative structures, and legitimating principles in its campaign to achieve political power. While FIS support for Saddam Hussein—a "Godless Ba'athist"—required some ideological contortion, the Front's leadership recognized the political profit of riding the Arab nationalist ferment gripping much of Algeria's population as the United States deployed military forces to the Persian Gulf. Thus, the FIS framed the crisis in the Gulf as both a religious and colonial conflict, as Abassi told the government-aligned *Algérie-Actualité*:

> . . . It is inadmissible that Iraq annexes Kuwait by military force, but the arguments used by the United States do not justify its presence [in Saudi Arabia]. Iraq never constituted a danger to Saudi Arabia. The violation of the Arab and Islamic lands is not a disgrace to Saudi Arabia only. It is a disgrace to the entire Arab-Muslim world . . . The FIS considers the frontiers that were traced by colonialism perpetuate the [colonial] presence in a direct or indirect manner all with the support of the regimes it bought. The presence of Western forces in the Gulf is a new crusade. The military forces are there in order to occupy Arab land and take their riches. The FIS believes that the Crusades have not ended and the battle against colonialism continues.[60]

The Front tried to show ostensible vigilance in the face of the colonial threat, in contrast to Algeria's official neutrality. From the perspective of the FIS, the government's impartiality highlighted the negligence in the continuing Arab struggle against foreign influence and intervention. Exercising Algerians' rights of freedom of expression and assembly, the FIS staged demonstrations in front of the Ministry of National Defense pledging assistance to Baghdad.[61] These protests featured Ali Belhadj dressed in battle fatigues organizing volunteers for the defense of Iraq.

The FIS position on both internal security and foreign policy matters represented an incursion into areas reserved solely for the military establishment.[62] Despite the Front's insinuation that the achievements of the revolution had been betrayed through close relations between Paris and Algeria's "*hizb Fransa*" (French party), a direct reference to leading members of Algeria's high command, the officer corps remained restrained. In response, the military establishment preferred to portray the Front as a foreign-inspired implant that sought to compromise Algeria's independence. On the question of the Front's overtures to Morocco, Algeria's rival for sub-regional hegemony, the officers did not move against the FIS, but rather chose to signal the Moroccan leadership that Rabat would pay a heavy price for interfering in Algeria's domestic political realm.[63]

Perhaps most irritating to the officer corps was what had become the contentious issue of Iraq. Commenting on the activities of Ali Belhadj and other FIS activists, the military's flagship publication *el-Djeich* argued: "The Algerian state is exposed to public condemnation, in fact, for its constant positions of principle; extreme measures of retaliation that the state should have adopted, against all logic, are identified; the absence of direct military engagement is deplored; and in these cases the opening of training camps and the formation of true militias are demanded . . ."[64] In the same editorial, the military implied that the militias Belhadj had demanded were not truly for the defense of Iraq, but were to be "recentered" for other activities, presumably to take up arms against the Algerian government. Still, the military enclave remained content to do little more than warn the Front. Major General Khaled Nezzar, minister of national defense, underscored the military's resolve to "respond to any organized excesses that might jeopardize the national unity of the country . . . [and] would not hesitate to intervene to re-establish order and unity so that force remains in the hands of the law."[65] While the military establishment was putting the FIS on notice regarding what the officers perceived as a potential threat to domestic order, the military did not hinder the Front's ability to stage subsequent political rallies until the FIS-sponsored general strike of May–June 1991.

State and Political Apparatus

The FIS also made an assault on the constituent parts of Algeria's political machinery: the National People's Assembly, presidency, judiciary, and the electoral process. By holding the government to its professed democratic ideals, the Front sought to highlight that the Islamist narrative was most appropriate for the development of Algerian society. The idea of a consensus, with its religious as well as political connotations, was a central feature of the FIS discourse on Algerian politics. Indeed, an overall theme of the *Projet* suggested that the historic nexus of religion and politics, which was so important to Algeria's independence struggle, had been broken to Algeria's detriment.

Though defiance to French colonial rule took a variety of forms, Algerian nationalism began to cohere around religion in the early part of the twentieth century. The Association of Algerian Ulema (founded in 1931 under Abdelhamid Ben Badis, who had been influenced by the Islamic reformism of Mohamed Abduh) focused its attention on what the organization's members believed were the two crucial components of Algerian identity: Islam and Arabic. With independence, Islam's place was upheld in the founding documents as Algeria's new leaders clearly recognized the nexus between Islam, nationalism, and the imperatives facing newly independent Algeria.[66]

Recognizing this linkage—not only in the minds of the FIS leadership and its activists but also in the official narrative of the Algerian revolution—Abassi Madani, Ali Belhadj, and other FIS activists used it in their bid for political power. The FIS program consequently sought to highlight that any divergence from Islam had a deleterious effect on the efficacy of government. Politics explicitly based on Islam could not, by its very nature, permit anything other than government by consent: "Politics according to the FIS is *sharique* [sic] politics that combines practical wisdom, harmony in action . . . and flexibility in dialogue. All in the pursuit of what is just and true, equitable and moderate. These politics are a synonym for sincerity: it is founded on the effort of persuasion and not destruction . . . This is the politics of *shura* and not of despotism . . . In order to end despotism, the Front adopts *shura* and in order to put an end to monolithic politics, and monopoly of the economy and society, it calls for equality in political, economic, and social opportunity . . ."[67] By valorizing the role Islam played in the revolution, the FIS sought to undermine Algeria's political elite, who had incorporated religion as an important theme of the national narrative. The Front claimed that the authoritarian practices of the state betrayed the revolution by ignoring its essentially Islamic and thus consensual character.

The FIS strategy of fusing political reform with religious principle became clear in the run-up to, and aftermath of, the June 1990 local elections and then again in the prelude to the 1991–1992 legislative elections. In addition to the overarching political vision expressed in the *Projet,* the April 1990 march through central Algiers culminated in a series of specific political demands on Chadli and the Algerian government. First, the FIS asked the government to identify areas for reform and to set out a program determining how and when these reforms would take place. Second, the Front sought the dissolution of the National People's Assembly and new elections within three months. Third, the party called for the establishment of a political authority independent of any political party to audit the electoral process, and it called on the Constitutional Council to guarantee the integrity of municipal, provincial, and national legislative elections.[68] As part of the Front's campaign in the months prior to the communal and provincial elections, the petition underscored the Front's counter-narrative of a society based on the religiously tinged concept of consensus. The Front's message resonated deeply with a large portion of the Algerian public, producing landslide victories in June 1990 for the party on both the commune and *wilaya* levels.

While FIS activists, flush with their victory at the local and provincial levels, took up their positions of responsibility in the 853 (of 1,539) communes and 31 (of 48) *wilayat,* the leadership continued to exploit Algeria's democratic facade in its bid for political power at the national level. Six weeks after the local and provincial victories, Abassi, who had become ubiquitous with the development of independent newspapers, magazines, and journals, reiterated the themes he had taken up at the FIS demonstration outside the presidency the previous April. In an interview with the French publication *Jeune Afrique,* the FIS spokesman took Prime Minister Mouloud Hamrouche to task over the continuing existence of the FLN-dominated Assemblée Nationale Populaire, presumably a relic of the single-party system. Abassi stated that Hamrouche "has no sense of politics. Moreover, there are contradictions [in his position]. In one instance, Hamrouche recognizes the outcome of the elections; in the other, he refuses to do so." And, on the same issue, Abassi subtly, yet with unmistakable condescension, challenged Chadli to live up to the democratic principles of the new constitution: "[W]e hope that President Chadli will be logical with himself. He has chosen the best way, this is democracy. He promises free elections and with courage accepts the results . . . A man who attains such a level of political maturity is not able, to our minds, to hesitate in the dissolution of parliament."[69]

Chadli and Hamrouche did eventually agree to clean and fair legislative elections, which were scheduled for July 1991. In preparation for this contest, the outgoing FLN-dominated parliament promulgated a new electoral law. Law 91-06 (March 1991) was, quite simply, designed to keep the Front from gaining a parliamentary majority through gerrymandering that favored less populated areas in which the FLN was likely to win at the expense of coastal and urban regions, which had proven to be FIS strongholds.[70] The FIS leadership, along with most other political parties, with the notable exception of Said Saadi's Rassemblement pour la Culture et la Démocratie, called for the new code to be repealed or amended. When Chadli and Hamrouche resisted, the Front—once again taking advantage of Algeria's political facade—called for a general strike to express displeasure with the government's determined effort not to live up to the democratic/legitimating ideals of the 1989 constitution. Launched at the end of May, the strike initially met with only limited success, as the other parties refused to take part. Although municipal services in Algiers were interrupted, businesses and industry in the city were unaffected.[71] Controversial within the Front's *Majlis ash-Shura* to begin with, the lackluster response to Abassi's appeal for a work stoppage had serious implications for both FIS's political prospects and his continued leadership of the party.

Determined not to relinquish his control of the party, Abassi calculated that whipping up the emotions of FIS activists on the street would produce at least the impression of an effective strike.[72] The result was violence pitting FIS members against the police and ultimately a declaration of a state of siege leading the way for the army's deployment throughout the streets of the capital. Making good on Nezzar's warning of the previous September concerning domestic unrest, the military arrested hundreds of FIS militants, including Abassi and Belhadj, and for a time occupied the Front's headquarters. The general strike, which violated the military's core interest regarding internal security, resulted in a crackdown that brought the officers to the forefront of Algerian politics. After reestablishing order in the streets of Algiers, the military establishment left the FIS intact. Abassi and Belhadj were to remain in prison, as were many other FIS activists, but the party was not dismantled. By August, the FIS had regrouped under the provisional leadership of Abdelkader Hachani. While proclaiming his fealty to the Front's jailed leaders, Hachani went about the process of developing a strategy for its continuing bid for political power.

In general, FIS's consistent message that Algeria's political apparatus was in need of reform encroached on the military establishment's interest in maintaining the political facade that had served them so well. The type of reform the Front was calling for would have either razed the facade, exposing the officer corps to the type of political risks it historically sought to avoid, or infused the institutions and structures that encompassed Algeria's pretense of democracy with power. Still, other than a response to the turmoil associated with the general strike, the military made no precipitous moves against the Front. This is not to suggest that the military remained docile. In fact, the officers sought to match the Front's rhetoric with their own, suggesting to the public that the party's calls for political reform were artificial. In April 1991, *el-Djeich* addressed the issue and sought to shed light on what it considered the true nature of the Front's political discourse: "The double language, their particular manner of not worrying about sincerity and scruples and adapting their rhetoric and public discourse to circumstances . . . have also revealed the ease with which, in the face of new problems and the unforeseeable evolution of situations, the religious explanation becomes adventurous when it is put to the service of obscure strategies."[73]

Aside from the crackdown during and after the general strike, the military establishment's response to the FIS was generally limited to this type of rhetoric. Moreover, the officers, in light of the Front's activities, sought to convince Algerians that the military, not the FIS, was the true guardian of democracy.[74] *El-Djeich* editorialized: "The present challenge is also the reinforcement of democracy, which requires each person's contributions, active engagement, and fight against extremism—against all extremisms which, for Algerian society, are recent evils, foreign to natural evolution, true abscesses of fixation, whose goal is to eclipse the constants and the references to the Algerian Nation, its thousand-year-old history, its ferocious resistances, its community solidarity, and to create division and hate." Major General Mustafa Chelloufi, secretary general of the Ministry of Defense, emphasized that the army favored liberalization and also indicated that the military was "the defender of the constitution."[75]

Nationalism

Finally, an integral part of the FIS campaign for political power was to highlight its nationalist bona fides. It did so using the legitimating nationalist principles located in Algeria's founding texts and espoused by the country's leadership. Analysts have often cited the selection of the name "Front" (*jabha* in Arabic) and the fact that the acronym FIS is pronounced the same way as the French *fils* (son) as clear evidence of the party's effort to hijack the nationalist mystique of the Front de Libération Nationale (FLN) and the ALN/ANP. Moreover, the FIS tended to highlight the personal biography of Abassi Madani—who, according to the Islamists, had been a member of the Mouvement pour le Triomphe des Libertés Démocratiques and later an FLN militant who was jailed for seven years after attempting to blow up Radio Alger on the first night of Algeria's liberation struggle. Yet, it was much more than one man's story or FIS's ostensible connection to the revolution as the true heir to the FLN. As Dirk Vanderwalle has indicated, FIS rhetoric turned the key phrases of the liberation and early independence period against the Algerian elite.[76] In language strikingly similar to that of Algeria's various political texts, the Front's *Projet* declared:

Conforming to the aspirations of the Algerian Muslim people desiring to move ahead and to definitively break the yoke of colonialism and break the multidimensional burden of underdevelopment and the diverse forms of neocolonialism, the axes we propose will put the popular will into action: It inspires the genius of our people . . .

In order to break the perverse dialectic of nepotism . . . the Front works to codify responsibilities, to offer guarantees in order to accomplish the duties due to the people, to encourage the spirit of collective work in an environment opposed to egoism, corruption, and individualism . . .

After the colonial invasion our army was subjugated, but the people's army never capitulated and the popular resistance and organization testifies to the tenacity and courage of our faithful people. The battle was to be crowned by the victory of colonialism and our lions recovered our independence and our sovereignty with the grace and assistance of God. The successive revolutions in our land and particularly liberation have demonstrated that the army is the people and the people are the army.[77]

Clearly calculated, the Front's rhetorical flourishes and its ideological pretensions tracked quite closely with those of Algeria's founding texts. In using this type of language, the FIS sought to demonstrate that Algeria's prevailing elite had failed to live up to their own professed ideals and commitments.

Nationalism had become an issue on which the FLN, and even the army, had grown significantly vulnerable; therefore, it was an issue the FIS sought to exploit. The Front's criticisms sought to draw a clear distinction between the prestate FLN and the postindependence FLN. From the perspective of the FIS, the FLN's incompetence and corruption subjected Algeria to a new form of colonialism: the FLN and the government's failure to achieve industrialization had compromised the *pouvoir's* claim to nationalist legitimacy.[78] In the words of Abassi Madani, the former *parti unique* was no longer among the "respectable militants."[79]

When the FIS directly criticized the military it was often related to the issue of nationalism. By opposing the military establishment's position on the Gulf War, the FIS had tried to demonstrate its commitment to the nationalist cause. Even before the crisis in the Gulf, however, the military establishment had suffered scrutiny over its nationalist claims.[80] Though nothing in the *Projet*, for example, represented an overt challenge to the military, the document did call for the reform of the military establishment so that the armed forces would become an "instrument of protection of the country and the people from all dangers to sovereignty, freedoms, rights, duties and the interests of the entire *umma.*" The implication, of course, was that the officer corps, despite its nationalist image, did not always act in the best interests of the

Algerian people. Abassi expanded on this theme when, in an interview with *Algérie-Actualité,* he suggested that the 1965 coup was an error that had disrupted Algeria's proper political development.[81]

Not all of the Front's critique was, however, as disciplined or subtle as the *Projet* or Abassi's oblique references. In the run-up to the June 1990 commune and *wilayat* elections, the Front was apparently concerned about a military intervention. Speaking to a large gathering, Abassi warned the army: "If you are manipulated by the hands of foreigners, know that the Algerian people are ready for every eventuality." By insinuating that the National People's Army was susceptible to foreign (French) influence, Abassi again highlighted the unfailing nationalism of the FIS. At the same time, Ali Belhadj reminded his audience that "the blood of 5 October is still not dry." Given the military's conduct during the riots, this was clearly a statement calculated to cast aspersions on the nationalism of the officer corps.[82]

The officers' commitment to, and image as vanguards of, Algerian nationalism are key elements in the political, social, and economic prominence of the country's military establishment.[83] The ALN/ANP has consistently underscored the organic connection between the military and the Algerian people, identifying itself as "an avant-garde force . . . the result of the legitimate will of the popular masses to realize their national aspirations."[84] It has a vested interest in maintaining an official narrative that places the officers at the center of the country's nationalist pantheon. The war of liberation, fought between 1954 and 1962, is, of course, the fundamental and essential source of Algerian nationalist legitimacy, and the officer corps maintains almost exclusive control over the struggle's official narrative.[85] One would expect a ferocious response from the military in response to the Front's attempts to undermine—in the eyes of ordinary Algerians—the military enclave's commitment to nationalism. Yet, again, the military seemed to remain committed to, and satisfied with, its strategy of rhetorical counter-fire.

The military's objective was to portray itself as the ultimate guarantor of democracy in contrast to the FIS, which, the officers claimed, harbored sinister ambitions. General Chelloufi warned in February 1990: "I will not be tolerant of those who use democracy in order to return dictatorship once they have achieved power." More directly related to the issue of nationalism, *el-Djeich* sought to portray the FIS, just as the Front had portrayed the military, as an unwitting instrument of Western imperialism: "[I]n its manifestation as a small group, a social movement, or political party, the religious extremist sphere of influence serves western strategy aimed at maintaining a balance between monarchies and nationalist regimes in order to prevent the birth of Arab unity."[86] The officers also emphasized the Front's ostensible connection to that other enemy of Arab nationalist aspirations: the House of Saud. Once again, according to *el-Djeich:* "So many Saudi flags brandished on certain marches on Algiers and elsewhere! In fact, the supposed demarcation between Algerian religious extremists and the Saudi regime . . . is only, in the final analysis artificial and purely due to circumstance. Through *ulema* intermediaries and other parallel channels, their ties are more steadfast than ever . . ."[87]

As part of this tactic, the military establishment drew a distinction between the religious-political current that the FIS represented, which necessarily divided the nation, and "authentic Islam," which, they claimed, played so integral a role in the national liberation movement and continued to be a source of unity. Yet beyond these and similar statements between February 1989 and December 1991, none of the military's actions indicated efforts to outlaw the Front.

Regime Maintenance and the Military Enclave's Perception of Threat

Given the FIS attacks on the military enclave and against its interests, analysts would expect the officers to have intervened before January 11, 1992.[88] Yet despite encroachments by the FIS and its activists on the military's core interests in economic matters; national security and foreign policy; the country's prevailing political arrangements; and the nationalist narrative, the military made little effort to exclude the Front.[89] The military did take action against the FIS as a result of the May 1991 general strike, but the organization was only banned from the political arena for a short period.

This lack of a reaction on the military's part does not prove that interests are unimportant; rather, it demonstrates that military officers are not perfect assessors of fluid and dynamic circumstances. It is plausible that the officers did not believe that the Islamists were in any position to follow through with their political program. After all, despite the Front's electoral success in the June 1990 elections, the March 1991 revisions to the electoral law were designed to prevent the Islamists from gaining a majority in the National People's Assembly. Needless to say, it was a surprise to members of Algeria's military enclave when the FIS seemed poised to achieve precisely this outcome after the first round of voting in December 1991. Still, it was not until the officers considered the implications of an apparent political deal between Chadli and the FIS against the backdrop of the Islamists' overwhelming victory that the military moved to exclude the FIS from the political arena. That the agreement held out the potential to alter Algeria's political order rendered the military's intervention virtually certain.

Coinciding with the first round of balloting at the end of December 1991, both the

Algerian president and the FIS leadership signaled to each other that they viewed the possibility of cohabitation favorably. Indeed, during the two years of the Front's legal existence, there is evidence that Chadli and Abassi, by virtue of their common confrontation with leading elements of the FLN, had made a political deal.[90] According to Hugh Roberts, Chadli offered support to the FIS at the expense of the FLN, with which he was engaged in a bruising political battle. The aim was to weaken the FLN just enough to discredit Chadli's critics and pave the way for the president to lead the party unencumbered. The FIS, Chadli calculated, would draw off support from the FLN but not enough to capture a majority in the National People's Assembly. In return for this support the FIS was expected to refrain from criticizing the virtues of the president himself.[91]

In general, during the electoral campaign in the spring of 1990 the FIS held to its commitments, reserving its toughest criticism for government policies and the FLN, which did not represent a direct censure of the president. Prime Minister Hamrouche was singled out for apparent incompetence, but not Chadli; the FLN was increasingly identified with France though Chadli was spared; and when former prime minister Abdelhamid Brahimi revealed that government officials had skimmed $26 billion from state coffers, the FIS seized on the issue without implicating the president.[92] In October 1988 the rioters had leveled accusations of corruption against Chadli and his family, but the FIS held back from this type of attack. Moreover, the tacit cooperation between the FIS and Chadli may have extended into the actual functioning of the electoral process. During the June polling, there was a conspicuous absence of official oversight at many polling stations. This neglect, apparently intentional, permitted the FIS to ensure its large-scale victories.[93] Immediately following the polls, Chadli and Abassi held a meeting during which the president committed to holding free and fair legislative elections and reportedly the question of cohabitation was raised. From the perspective of one of the military enclave's most outspoken and leading members, the "flagrant complicity" of Chadli and Hamrouche in the Front's significant showing in the elections was disturbing.[94]

The March 1991 electoral law and the Front's subsequent general strike later that spring seemed to signal a termination of the FIS-Chadli relationship. After all, from the Front's perspective the president had gone back on his word to hold clean and fair elections. With Abassi, Belhadj, and other leaders in prison, the Front refused to take part in the government-parties conference held in August under the auspices of new Prime Minister Sid Ahmed Ghozali and was similarly disinclined to take part in the legislative elections, scheduled for late December. Yet, ten days before the election the Front reversed its position, as its provisional leader Abdelkader Hachani declared, "To take a step towards the establishment of an Islamic state . . . the FIS will take part in the forthcoming legislative elections."[95] Though the electoral procedures still heavily favored the FLN, the December 26 balloting produced an overwhelming FIS victory. In the period in between electoral rounds, the FIS resumed a solicitous approach to Chadli. Hachani went so far as to indicate rather explicitly that the Front would not seek presidential elections and that the Islamists were prepared to work with the president.[96]

Even before the balloting took place, Chadli had indicated that although "he preferred an Islamist defeat, he was ready to come to terms [with the FIS] should the occasion arise."[97] While Chadli may have believed that cohabitation was the best way for him to survive as president, and perhaps even enhance his stature, the military enclave was clearly unnerved at the prospect of cooperation between the president and the FIS. Indeed, Major General Nezzar reports in his memoirs that within days of the first round of voting, the military resolved not to allow the FIS to attain a majority in the National People's Assembly.[98]

The deal between Chadli and the Front, had it been consummated, represented a precursor to an alteration of the Algerian regime. Many observers indicate that a FIS majority in the National People's Assembly represented a threat to Algeria's constitutional order and an important step toward the establishment of an Islamic state, but the agreement with Chadli was, in fact, far more relevant in this regard than the Front's parliamentary representation. Put simply, though the FIS may have been able to secure an outright majority in parliament, it would not have necessarily led to constitutional changes. Under the 1989 constitution, the power to initiate constitutional revisions was vested with the president. The officers could not trust Chadli—despite his efforts in early January to convince them to the contrary—to be the firewall between the Front's ambitions and the constitution, and ultimately the regime. After all, in return for not calling for early presidential elections, Chadli was to acquiesce to the Front's political program, which included, among a range of issues, dismissing several senior officers, investigating official corruption, arresting those officers involved in political repression, and diluting the powers of the presidency.[99]

The Chadli-FIS deal would have effectively separated the armed forces from the presidency, an office historically dependent on the military establishment. Chadli's political maneuvering would have exchanged the officer corps for FIS activists as the primary pillar of the Algerian executive. With the president no longer in need of the military's mandate, but dependent on the FIS, the field would have been wide open for the Front to assert control over the armed forces and ultimately restructure the country's political system. In the years since the intervention, leading military figures of the period have often made self-serving declarations indicating that their actions were in the best interests of democracy. Nezzar has written: "Certain leaders believed that halting the electoral process was a blow to the democratic process. In reality it was precisely to the contrary; stopping the elections assured the survival of the democratic process."[100] At the same time, however, the former minister of defense betrays his disdain for the democratic process. Reflecting on a meeting he held with Hocine Aït Ahmed, leader of the Kabyle-based Front des Forces Socialistes, between the two rounds of elections, Nezzar states: "I asked that he consider the eventual halt of the [electoral] process. He was opposed. His argument was that 'democracy was the best' and that 'in all respects, the president maintains the prerogative to dissolve the Assembly.' I realized that he did not grasp all the elements. I responded to him that [Chadli] does not have the presidency in the real sense of the term and was an appendage of the FIS.[101]

These statements concerning the need to "take extreme measures in order to preserve the republican State" betray the officers' grave concern not for democracy but for maintaining their regime. In the end, the second round of voting was canceled, the results of the first round annulled; Chadli was pushed from office, and within a few months the Front was declared illegal.[102] Yet these actions were only initial steps in the process of regime maintenance.

Whereas the military enclave had signaled its willingness to countenance an Islamist presence in Algerian politics and even had withstood an assault on the core interests of the officers, it was decidedly unwilling to allow the Front to use Algeria's political facade to upend the regime. Although the institutions and structures that lay just beneath Algeria's democratic facade failed to contain the threat to Algeria's political order, they could nevertheless prove useful to the military as the officers engaged in an effort to safeguard the political order. For example, the military enclave instrumentalized Article 24 of the constitution to provide legal justification for their intervention. On the heels of the constitutional revision of early 1989, analysts pointed to this provision, which states in part that the army "is charged with safeguarding national independence . . . and assuring the unity of the country," as unambiguous evidence that separation of Algeria's military establishment from politics had been achieved. Unlike the 1963 and 1976 documents, the ANP was no longer identified as "an instrument of the Revolution, [which] participates in the development of the country." Even well before the elections, however, the military establishment was indicating that it would not be held to a strict interpretation of the constitutional provisions regarding the armed forces. In February 1990 *el-Djeich* editorialized: "It is thus that the National Popular Army defines its permanent mission as 'safeguarding national independence and the defense of national sovereignty,' as stipulated in Article 24—an article that must be read in a deep and global way rather than interpreted in an exclusive, purely literal sense. Article 24 should be considered, understood, and interpreted as much by its spirit as by its text."[103]

The military also sought to instrumentalize other constitutionally mandated structures, including the Constitutional Council and the Haut Conseil de Sécurité (High Security Council, HCS). The Constitutional Council, though ostensibly independent, was actually weighted heavily in favor of the executive, as four of the seven members owed their positions either directly or indirectly to the president. It was precisely at this point that the informal institutions resulting from past patterns of civil-military relations became so crucial. With their patron forced from office and little political clout of their own, members were subject to pressure from the military high command and as a result forced to approve the actions of the military establishment.[104]

The HCS was the structure through which the officer corps affected its intervention. It was intended only as an advisory body to the Algerian presidency, but as with the Constitutional Council, the informal rules that conditioned Algerian politics held sway.[105] Although military officers were a minority on the HCS, with Chadli forced from office the civilians—the prime minister and the ministers of foreign affairs and justice—found themselves in the company of three of the most powerful commanders in Algeria: Major General Khaled Nezzar, Major General Larbi Belkheir, and Major General Abdelmalek Guenzaïa.[106] The civilians were in no position to challenge the military's actions, even if they wanted to do so. Employing the Haut Conseil de Sécurité clearly had no legal foundation; it is questionable whether the body could even convene without a request from the president. But the legacy of 37 years of military domination and the officers' control over the means of coercion rendered it a fait accompli.

On January 16, the HCS issued a proclamation that although acknowledging the constitutional vacuum resulting from the simultaneous dissolution of the National People's Assembly and vacancy of the presidency due to resignation, nevertheless invoked constitutional Articles 75, 79, 129, 130, and 153 to provide legal imprimatur to the establishment of the Haut Conseil d'État (High Council of State, HCE) and an unelected Conseil Consultatif National (National Consultative Council).[107] Though the military enclave endeavored through no small amount of tortured reasoning to legally justify its action, the effort was transparent. Unlike the HCS, the Constitutional Council, or various institutional/structural arrangements that had been embedded in the constitution to protect the regime, the Haut Conseil d'État, which was to function as a collective presidency, had no precedent. Again, informal institutions played a critical and determinative role. The obvious lack of legal foundation made little difference given the existing balance of power in Algerian society. Influential political parties such as the FFS could protest the military's action, but there was little else they could do. With no other relevant political actor possessing the power to challenge the military's prerogative, the HCE, whose members included Khaled Nezzar, served out the remainder of Chadli's term before handing power to former minister of defense Major General Liamine Zeroual.

The HCE and later Zeroual set about renovating Algeria's formal political institutions to ensure that potential political competitors could not threaten the integrity of the regime. The result was a new constitution, ratified in 1996, which retained many of the features of Algeria's facade of democratic institutions, representative structures, and legitimating principles. It reiterated the "people's sovereignty," equality before the law, and the importance of the National People's Assembly as a democratic and representative body. It upheld the right to form political parties, but in addition to the text lifted directly from the 1989 constitution, the 1996 version added prohibitions that had been included in implementing law 89-11.[108]

The new constitution also sought to insulate the political order from further risks. It imbued the presidency with even greater power; codified several emergency decrees and laws that restricted the rights of assembly, expression, and association; and established a second legislative body, one-third of whose members were presidential appointments.[109] This new upper chamber of the National People's Assembly, called the Conseil de la Nation (Council of the Nation) was a particularly important innovation. With legislation requiring the approval of three-quarters of the Council of the Nation, the president could easily hamper lawmaking through his directly appointed deputies.[110] The goal was (and continues to be) to check any future political competitors who might seek to alter the basic structures of the Algerian political order. In short, as was the case with the 1963, 1976, and 1989 constitutions, the 1996 version rigged Algerian politics in favor of the *pouvoir militaire* and their civilian allies.

Paradoxically, these efforts to protect the regime have resulted in seemingly greater political contestation. Analysts and spokesmen for the Algerian government point to the existence of 60 political parties (including Islamist organizations), 30 independent newspapers, and a series of parliamentary, as well as presidential, elections as indicators that Algeria has undergone a fundamental transformation.[111] These developments are positive but have all occurred within the parameters of Algeria's continuing authoritarian political order. Party leaders have questioned the wisdom of various government ministers; advocated greater Islamization; assailed President Abdelaziz Bouteflika for his handling of the "second Berber Spring" of April–June 2001; savaged Prime Minister Ali Benflis for his government's woeful response to the devastating floods in the autumn of 2002, which left more than 1,000 dead and untold numbers homeless; and criticized Bouteflika and his then-prime minister, Ahmed

Ouyahia, over the government's woeful response to the May 2003 earthquake. Yet, as Lahouri Addi asserts, political "opposition can oppose the government, but not the overall system."[112]

With the defeat of the FIS and its armed wing, the Islamic Salvation Army, in 1999, a modicum of peace has returned to Algeria. Although the terrorism of Islamist extremist groups like the GSPC continues, this violence no longer represents a significant threat to the country's political order. In September 2005, President Bouteflika felt confident enough in the continuing stability to put his Charter of Peace and National Reconciliation to a referendum. According to the Interior Ministry, 97.4 percent of the almost 80 percent of eligible voters approved the charter. A central feature of Bouteflika's broad vision for Algeria's future, the charter, which was formally enacted in February 2006, contains four primary components. First, members and supporters of the armed groups will be granted amnesty so long as they did not commit collective massacres, rape, or use explosives in public. This amnesty covers those individuals already convicted of these crimes who will be released from prison. Second, the approximately 6,000 Algerians missing as a result of the decade-long civil insurrection will be designated "victims of the national tragedy" and their families will be entitled to compensation once a court determines that a missing person is dead. Third, any party exploiting religion for political gain will be banned. Finally, the charter shields any "individual or a collective entity, belonging to any component of the defense and security forces of the Republic" from prosecution for their conduct during the years of civil conflict.[113]

The establishment of the Charter of Peace and National Reconciliation—now Algerian law—shows how the relationship among the military, Islamists, and the political system has changed. The defeat of the Front Islamique du Salut and its armed wing led the Algerian military establishment to conclude that an existential threat to the regime no longer exists. As a result, the officers have taken a step back from the political arena, though they have not abandoned their self-endowed mission to stand watch over and protect the republic. Flush with oil and gas revenues, as well as a more stable security environment, Algeria's commanders have demonstrated a willingness to countenance an Islamist presence in the National People's Assembly. In 2006, the Islamist representatives from the al-Islah, Mouvement de la Société pour la Paix, and an-Nahda parties held approximately 20 percent of the seats in the legislature.

While Bouteflika enjoys the tacit support of the senior command, he has used the size of his victory in the April 2004 presidential elections to establish some distance between the presidency and the military and to assert his own authority.[114] Beginning in the summer of 2004 with the retirement of the chief of staff, Bouteflika was able to manage a significant reshuffling of the military command. By 2006, several of Algeria's most powerful officers, including Generals Mohamed Lamari and Mohamed Touati, had retired or were reassigned and a new crop of officers were promoted to command positions. Another leading member of the officer corps, General Larbi Belkheir, who had been in charge of the president's office, was named Algeria's ambassador to Morocco. Bouteflika is clearly engaged in an effort to create a cadre of officers that is personally loyal to the president so that he can carry out a program of economic reform and national reconciliation unencumbered.

These developments, however, do not necessarily represent a transformation of the dominant feature of Algeria's political order: stability. The Islamist presence in the National Popular Assembly is enough to legitimate Algeria's ostensibly more democratic political system, but it is clearly not sufficient to mount a significant challenge to the prevailing political order. Moreover, the changes Bouteflika undertook regarding the military are unprecedented, but the reshuffling of commanders does not in and of itself indicate that the influence of the Algerian military is waning. First, Bouteflika obviously understood that his electoral mandate aside, the military continues to be the critical powerbroker in the political system. Otherwise he would not have believed it was necessary to cultivate a group of officers to assure his position. The Algerian presidency remains ultimately dependent on the officers.

Second, although some of the most important hardline commanders have retired or moved into new positions, former officers have retained significant influence through vast patronage networks. In addition, Bouteflika has not succeeded in thoroughly revamping the senior command. Generals Mohamed Mediène and Smain Lamari, both of whom are closely associated with the military's intervention in January 1992, continue to command the Securité Militaire. Finally, General Larbi Belkheir's move from the presidency to Algeria's embassy in Rabat may not be as dramatic as it appears. Generally when an officer is "rewarded" with an ambassadorship it is a clear indication that his influence has diminished, but Belkheir's reassignment can be seen differently. Belkheir is no longer at the center of decision-making, but given his prominent position within the armed forces, the sensitivity of the post due to the often tense relations between Algeria and Morocco over the southwestern Sahara, and the officers' past efforts to watch over the conduct of Algeria's relations with Morocco, his assignment betrays the continuing influence of the military.

Indeed, Algeria is likely to remain ultrastable due to the organic connection between the military enclave and the regime. Although opposition movements may divine strategies and use features of the democratic political facade to improve the position of their constituencies, the military enclave can be expected to thwart the political projects of these entrepreneurs. Of course, Algeria has undergone institutional innovations—though primarily intended to ensure the continuity of the regime—and political dissent is generally tolerated, but the officer corps has refused to tolerate what it perceives to be threats to the regime. Moreover, this dynamic is likely to repeat itself. As long as the officer corps maintains its unwavering interest in preserving the rigged quality of Algeria's political order, this situation will likely encourage opposition activism and potentially result in the continuation of the logic of regime response to Islamist political mobilization.

CHAPTER FOUR

Institutionalizing a
Military-Founded System

Israel's stunning defeat of Egypt's armed forces in June 1967—known commonly in Arabic as *al-naksa* (the setback)—is widely regarded as the event that began the demilitarization of Egyptian politics. The standard narrative of the period immediately following holds that the hegemony of Egypt's military establishment was compromised with the death of Field Marshal Abdel Hakim Amer, apparently by suicide, in 1967; the trials of the commanders deemed responsible for the setback; popular protests in 1968 directed against the armed forces; and President Gamal Abdel Nasser's March 1968 commitment to reconstruct the armed forces into an effective fighting force. By the time of the Corrective Revolution in May 1971, this account suggests, the demise of Egypt's officers as important political actors was complete. Undertaken at the behest of Nasser's successor, Anwar Sadat, the Corrective Revolution sought to resolve the perceived shortcomings of what Egypt's official history calls the "July 1952 Revolution." Sadat's program involved the elimination of a number of powerful and politicized senior military officers. Analysts have consistently pointed to the subsequent decline of officers with cabinet portfolios as a primary indicator that Egypt's commanders were returned to the barracks and have, in general, remained there.[1]

Events of the late 1960s and early 1970s did help define the trajectory of the Egyptian political system. Perhaps the most important consequence was the institutionalization of the presidency as the undisputed principal actor in Egyptian politics. Military officers, with a number of notable exceptions, have sought to maintain a low profile—certainly in comparison with their Algerian and Turkish counterparts. Yet Egypt's senior command retains a crucial and influential position in the political system.[2] Just as in Algeria and in Turkey until the early 2000s, the logic of the Egyptian political system's stability is tied directly to the multilayered institutional setting that is a legacy of military rule.

Evolution and Character of the Regime

On July 23, 1952, a group of predominantly midlevel Egyptian army officers undertook a coup d'état ending the Albanian-Ottoman dynasty that had ruled Egypt since
1805. United in their loathing of the continued British penetration of Egypt, palace
corruption and intrigue, as well as the incompetence and venality of Egyptian politicians, the Free Officers sought at first merely to reform Egyptian politics and return
power to civilian politicians. Yet, after only a short time, the Free Officers began to
view their intervention in a different light.[3] Rather than reform, the commanders
undertook a thorough reconstitution of the political system, which ultimately was to
have little similarity to the order that prevailed on July 22, 1952.[4] In February 1953,
Gamal Abdel Nasser, the dominant personality among the leading cadre of Free
Officers, declared that bringing in a new government "is a minor objective compared
to the wider aims of our revolution. The latter [objective] seeks to change the political
system."[5] Indeed, in their effort to alter Egypt's political system and to begin work
toward achieving the six goals of their revolution—the eradication of all aspects of
imperialism; the extinction of feudalism; the abolition of monopolies and capitalist
control over the system of government; the development of a strong national army;
the institutionalization of social justice; and the establishment of a sound democratic
society—the officers systematically stripped away remnants of the *ancien régime*. This
began as early as July 26, 1952, when King Farouk was forced to flee the country for
exile in Italy, and continued with the dissolution of Egypt's parliament and the
outlawing of political parties in 1953.[6]

During this period, political power was concentrated within a Revolutionary
Command Council (RCC) comprising the leading nine to twelve Free Officers;
though even before he assumed the Egyptian presidency, Nasser was the undisputed
leader of this body. It was through the RCC that the Free Officers—and the Egyptian
military establishment in general—constructed their new order. In addition to dis-
banding parliament and political parties and terminating the monarchy, the officers
undertook a series of economic measures, including agricultural reform and sequestration of private property, which forced changes to the social structures of
Egyptian society. Overall, it was from this program, which was intended to bring
"greater material well-being, justice, and freedom within a democratic polity" to the
Egyptian people, that the officers derived revolutionary legitimacy.[7] The officers'
challenge was institutionalizing these profound changes.

The establishment of the Liberation Rally in 1953, which was a mass-based organization intended to bond the Egyptian people to the new order, was the officers' first
effort to institutionalize their regime. It was not until three years later that they

promulgated a constitution, which formally delineated the country's new political order.[8] The 1956 constitution, and the series of texts that followed it, contained a variety of institutions, structures, and principles that resembled those of liberal political systems. The officers and their civilian allies recognized that situating Egypt's revolution within the formal institutions of a democratic polity was crucial to mobilizing the masses in support of the officers' revolutionary objectives.

A Formally Liberal Polity

In June 1956, Egyptians overwhelmingly approved the first constitution of the postmonarchy era. The document's preamble—a series of statements beginning with the phrase "We, the people of Egypt"—emphasized that as the people had "wrested [their] rights to a life of freedom," their liberty was based on a "sacred belief in equality, justice, and dignity." These principles, moreover, were derived from the "ideals proclaimed by the masses" for which martyrs had sacrificed their lives in the struggle for national dignity. The result promised a society that "assured . . . freedom of thought and worship in an atmosphere where there are no dictates save those of conscience and reason."[9] Within the context of these rights, Article 3 of the constitution also established Islam as the religion of the state.

The constitution defined Egypt as a "democratic republic" in which sovereignty laid in the *umma* (nation, though also translated officially as "people") and "liberty, security, safety, and equality of opportunity" were guaranteed. In a further elaboration of legitimating principles reflecting democratic norms, the 1956 constitution established the equality of all Egyptians before the law and endowed citizens with the rights of freedom of opinion and expression. These principles were subsequently bolstered with provisions guaranteeing freedoms of the press, assembly, association, and an independent judiciary. Concurrent with the promulgation of the constitution was Law 73/1956, "On the Exercising of Political Rights," which codified the right to vote.

The centerpiece of the constitution was the establishment of a National Assembly. Composed of 350 members elected by secret ballot, the National Assembly was empowered with the legislative functions of the state. It was also endowed with the power to override a presidential veto, and it maintained considerable formal powers of oversight concerning the functions and performance of the government and the state administration. For example, each member of the National Assembly had the right to direct questions and interpellations to government ministers and any group of ten legislators could initiate discussion on key issues of public policy and demand a full exchange of views with the government during a parliamentary session (Articles

90–91). This oversight also extended to the critical area of the state budget, which, the constitution required, was to be submitted to the National Assembly at least 90 days before the end of the fiscal year for parliamentary approval. Parliament was also vested with the power to withdraw its confidence in a government minister, thereby forcing the official to resign. Finally, the legislature was to nominate the president of the republic. That nomination—by a two-thirds majority—would then be referred to the Egyptian people in a plebiscite by secret ballot.

Six years later, President Nasser—who had by that time consolidated significant personal political power and prestige—presented a National Charter. The 1962 document offered both a retrospective look at the achievements of the first decade of the revolution and an outline of what Egyptians could expect in the coming years. While analysts have quite correctly held out the National Charter as evidence of Cairo's leftward shift in the early 1960s, the socialist cast of the charter's text did not in any way diminish the key components—nationalism, democracy, and social justice—of the legitimating principles that served as justification for the Free Officers' coup. In general, the charter integrates all of these factors in a narrative that indicates the ostensibly populist character of the events of July 1952.

> By the beginning of the year 1952, a crucial year in the history of Egypt, the masses both in town and in country had already given adequate expression to their real will.
>
> The greatest thing about the Revolution of July 23rd 1952 is that the armed forces who [*sic*] set to stage it were not the makers of the Revolution, but its popular tool . . .
>
> Furthermore, the genuineness and strength of this [revolutionary] consciousness made it impossible to accept the possibility of a military dictatorship, but placed the popular forces, with the forces of the peasants and the workers at the head, in the position of actual leadership.[10]

Devotion to those legitimating principles permitted the "vanguard of the revolution" (the military) to realize many achievements since its intervention, most notably the creation of a progressive and democratic order in place of the retrograde regime the "alien monarchy" had presided over. In addition to nationalism, democracy, and social justice, the charter included an "unshakeable faith in God" as a crucial element in the continuation of the revolution's progress.[11] This was a more conscious and demonstrative affirmation of the role of religion in society than in the 1956 constitution.

The 1964 constitution represented an effort to institutionalize the broad vision outlined in the National Charter two years prior. Despite the charter's emphasis on "true democracy," socialism, and social justice, the new constitution did little more than reaffirm the salience of the legitimating principles, representative structures, and

democratic institutions found in the 1956 constitution. There were additions addressing the role of the state in economic development and the relationship between the
public, cooperative, and private sectors. The most notable innovation of the 1964
constitution granted parliament the power to withdraw its confidence from the
government, obliging the president to appoint a new cabinet.[12]

Within three years of ratification of the 1964 constitution, the regime that had
been established at the behest of the military establishment and its civilian allies
confronted a substantial challenge. Israel's victory in June 1967 produced significant
pressure from across Egypt's political spectrum for thorough reform of both the state
administration and politics in general. In response to these demands, Nasser produced the "March 30 Program" (1968), which diagnosed the problems that contributed to the defeat, outlined Egypt's achievements over the critical months since the
setback, and developed a blueprint for the future. The statement identified "powerful
actors"—in particular, Field Marshal Abdel Hakim Amer and the cadre of senior
officers tied to him—as the primary cause for both the military's poor battlefield
performance and the apparent deficiencies of the Egyptian political system.[13] Holding senior officers accountable for Egypt's defeat was consistent, at least in spirit, with
Law 4/1968, "Regarding the Control of State Defense Matters and the Armed Forces."
Promulgated on January 25, 1968, the law was ostensibly a formal remedy to the
military establishment's autonomy. In practice, however, the Israeli presence on the
East Bank of the Suez Canal meant that the military remained the most privileged of
state organizations as Egyptians prepared for a decisive battle with Israel.

Yet, Nasser also asserted in the March 30 Program that the struggle to recover both
Egyptian land and honor lay not just with military preparations but with the mobilization of society to achieve democracy and social justice. Nasser thus outlined a ten-
point program for a new constitution that underscored the importance of such basic
individual rights as freedom of expression, thought, opinion, and the press. Once
again affirming the supremacy of the law, the March 30 Program went a step further
than previous founding texts in proposing a High Constitutional Court vested with
the power of judicial review.[14] On the whole, the document stressed the necessity of
deepening Egypt's democratic practices as a primary means of confronting the problems the country encountered and which the June 1967 war had laid bare.

Within a little more than three years of the plebiscite that ratified the March 30
Program as Egypt's roadmap for military and political redemption, a new "permanent Constitution" was promulgated. Anwar Sadat, Nasser's successor and a fellow
Free Officer who had assumed the presidency in September 1970, presided over its
final drafting and confirmation. The 1971 constitution invoked now-familiar legitimating principles. And just as in previous founding texts, it asserted the sovereignty

of the law as the "only guarantee for the freedom of the individual" and "the sole basis for the legality of authority."[15]

The new constitution acknowledged the importance of religion in Egyptian society, specifically invoking the name of God and in supplication for "His assistance" in achieving national objectives. This, in and of itself, did not represent a dramatic shift from the National Charter or the March 30 Program. Yet, Article 2 read, "Islam is the religion of the state; the principles of the Islamic *shari'a* are a principal source of legislation, and Arabic is the official language." Beyond the new emphasis on Islamic law and the formal establishment of due process—a hallmark of democratic polities—the 1971 version of the constitution differed little from either the 1956 or 1964 constitutions.[16]

In May 1980, the public ratified five amendments to the 1971 constitution, which have remained in force. Four of these changes came in the first section of the document, entitled "The State." According to official dispatches at the time, these were undertaken to reflect changes taking place in Egyptian society. The amended articles stressed familiar themes of democracy and social justice, including constitutional recognition of the multiparty system that Egypt had inaugurated in 1976. The second addressed the issue of religion, specifically the relationship of *shari'a* to Egypt's legislative process. The new text read, "Islam is the religion of the State and Arabic its official language. Islamic jurisprudence [*shari'a*] is *the* principal source of legislation."[17] The inclusion and identification of *shari'a* as the basis of law reflected the ideological dominance that Islam had achieved. In time, the Muslim Brotherhood would use this phrase to point out the significant gap between objective reality and the constitutional principles that the Egyptian government was duty-bound to uphold.

The amended constitution also established a new parliamentary chamber—the Majlis ash-Shura (Consultative Council). Defined as the upper house in Egypt's new parliamentary arrangement, the Consultative Council comprises 264 members, two-thirds of whom are elected by direct and secret elections, with the remaining third subject to presidential appointment. The purpose of the council is "to protect the alliance of the working forces . . . public rights, liberties, and duties, and to entrench the democratic socialist system and widen its fields."[18] The council's responsibilities include "consultation" on a variety of issues including proposals to amend the constitution, draft laws, the implementation of economic and social development programs, and general state policies.

In May 2005, the Egyptian constitution was once again amended. In what the Egyptian establishment press and the ruling National Democratic Party hailed as a historic step toward "deepening" democracy, the constitutional changes provided for multi-party presidential elections. Previously, the People's Assembly nominated a presidential candidate (by a two-thirds majority) who then stood in a public referendum in which Egyptians were asked either to vote "yes" or "no." Beginning with the 2005 elections, Egyptian presidents would face challengers for their office.

The Authoritarian Reality

Shortly after the founding of the Free Officers' regime, Nasser and his colleagues on the Revolutionary Command Council established such organizations as the Islamic Congress and the Liberation Rally (both in 1954). These organizations were supposed to foster the political participation of the Egyptian people but in reality served two primary purposes: First, they were channels through which Egypt's leadership bolstered the legitimacy of its political project. Second, given the nature of these groups, which encompassed all political tendencies, the state elite could more readily monitor the political arena and thus preclude the development of autonomous centers of political power.[19]

In the mid-1970s, Sadat effectively brought an end to the era of the single, mass-based vanguard party when he first called for the establishment of *manabir*, or platforms—representing the left, right, and center—within the Arab Socialist Union, a successor to the Liberation Rally. Dismantling the Union was a significant change but cannot be considered an unfettered commitment to democratic politics.[20] The president's rhetoric about democracy aside, Sadat sought to engineer a parliamentary configuration in which a ruling party would receive the support of "loyal opposition" parties on both the right and the left.[21]

Moreover, the legislation that enabled the establishment of political parties—Law 40/1977—was subject to the manipulation of Egypt's ruling party (in 1978 renamed the National Democratic Party, NDP) and the government. The law required that party programs and activities conform to a specific set of principles: national unity, the alliance of working people, social peace, democratic socialism, and protecting the basic gains of workers and *fellahin*. The NDP-dominated Committee for the Affairs of Political Parties (Political Parties Committee) tended to use—as circumstances required—either purposely expansive or narrow definitions of these parameters in order to disqualify political opponents from obtaining legal recognition. The law further demanded that proposed parties must not be similar to those already in existence in order to be granted a license. Yet with no clear metric by which to determine the differences and similarities among existing and proposed parties, the approval process was inevitably politicized, leaving it difficult to establish a new party.[22] Rather than a means of fostering greater political participation and representation, Law 40 became a mechanism of political control.[23]

The authoritarian nature of Egypt's regime was also reflected in the consistent and overwhelming parliamentary majority of the ruling party. The NDP's dominance was assured through state largesse that allowed its members to enjoy unrivalled financing and access to the state media, electoral laws that favored the ruling party, and considerable fraud.[24] The dominance of the NDP has had two primary and interrelated effects on Egyptian politics. First, it limited the influence of opposition parties within the legislature and hampered their ability to attract members, reinforcing the power of the regime loyalists (the bourgeoisie, some rural notables, and members of the public sector) who made up the NDP. Second, with the hegemony of the NDP assured, the People's Assembly became little more than an extension of the executive branch, ensuring both the implementation of government policy and the tenure of the president. The presidency remains the crucial institutional mechanism of the military establishment's political influence. As a result, engineering the dominance of the NDP was (and remains) a means through which the leadership of Egypt's military-dominated state sought to ensure both the regime and its attendant benefits.

Since 2003, the NDP has positioned itself as a reformist party. A string of proposals originating from its policy secretariat, which President Mubarak's son, Gamal, leads, have championed individual rights, political liberalization, and economic opportunity. Bold pronouncements and position papers aside, the NDP's proposals were intended to further institutionalize the power of the party rather than forge a genuine transition to a more democratic political system. The arrest and imprisonment of Ayman Nour, the leader of the liberal al-Ghad party, in 2005–06 on what were widely regarded as politically motivated charges belies the NDP's commitment to democratic reform.

The NDP leadership also has forced changes in Egypt's institutional setting to ensure the ruling party's supremacy. Consider, for example, amendments to the Political Parties Law, the origins of which are found in a September 2004 NDP position paper titled "Citizens' Rights and Democracy."[25] Although removing stipulations that Egyptian political parties adhere to principles of national unity and *shari'a* as well as uphold the gains of the 1952 revolution, the law placed new restrictions on groups seeking to become political parties. Whereas the previous version of Law 40 required that potential parties be distinct from existing parties, the amended version required that they represent a "new addition" to the political arena. In order to gain legal recognition, would-be parties must also now obtain 1,000 signatures of citizens from 10 of Egypt's 27 governorates. Previously, only 50 signatures were required and there were no geographic requirements. Parties seeking approval must also detail their sources of funding, none of which may come from foreign entities.

The People's Assembly also made a number of changes to the Political Parties

Committee. In 2005, the committee was expanded to nine (from seven) members to accommodate new seats for the ministers of interior and People's Assembly affairs, both of whom were leading members of the NDP. The chairmanship of the committee remained in the hands of the secretary-general of the ruling party. The other members include three retired judges and three independent political figures. Although the judiciary has, at times, demonstrated its independence, the former judges have generally been closely aligned with the NDP. The amendments do not only change the composition of the committee but also provide it with new powers. For example, if the Political Parties Committee determines that a political party or one of its leading members deviates from the party's platform, the party can be shut down. Party activities can also be suspended if the committee believes that it is in the national interest. Moreover, if a party is found to be violating the national interest, the committee has the power to refer the matter to the Socialist Public Prosecutor. Rather than taking steps to open the political system, the NDP has clearly sought to ensure the authoritarian status quo under the guise of reform.[26]

Other freedoms outlined in Egypt's founding texts are similarly restricted through strategic use of the phrase *fi hudud al-qaanun*—within the framework of the law. For example, while Article 48 of the constitution establishes freedom of the press, the Press Law (93/1995) actually institutes stiff penalties—including prison terms and heavy fines—for publishing false or defamatory information. Fines and prison sentences are increased for those whose actions are judged to have harmed the national economy, the national interest, or both. Law 93/1995 was repealed in June 1996 in favor of a new version, Law 96/1996. While the government touted Law 96 as testament to press freedom in Egypt, the provisions of the new law differed little from the previous version.[27]

The most significant of Egypt's dizzying array of regulations, statutes, and decrees intended to ensure the prevailing political order is the Emergency Law (162/1958).[28] This law, which has been amended several times since its promulgation and has been in force almost continuously since 1967, extends military rule throughout Egypt.[29] Under the Emergency Law, newspapers and periodicals have been subject to censorship and closure, workers have been barred from striking, and political organizations may meet only at the discretion of the Ministry of Interior. Without the proper permit, opposition groups are unable to hold public rallies or demonstrations, leaving private rooms or buildings as the only venues in which to gather and organize.

The Emergency Law also establishes a parallel judicial system—the Supreme State Security Court (not to be confused with the State Security Court, which was abolished in 2003). Responsible for adjudicating crimes related to public safety and national security, these courts, unmentioned in any of Egypt's founding documents, lack basic guarantees such as due process. International organizations such as Human Rights Watch and Amnesty International have determined that the Supreme State Security Court falls well short of internationally held judicial standards, primarily because of provisions in the enabling statute that limit a defendant's right to appeal.[30] This court has thus become a blunt instrument with which state elites have confronted their opponents. Armed with a purposefully expansive definition of security and order, Egypt's leadership has sought to undermine political activists and advocates dedicated to, among other causes, the expansion of human rights, political freedom, and good governance. Between 2000 and 2003, human rights and reform activist Saad Eddin Ibrahim and 27 of his colleagues from the Ibn Khaldun Center for Development Studies were tried in the Supreme State Security Court for conspiring to bribe public officials, receiving donations from abroad without prior permission from the government, deliberately disseminating false information harmful to Egypt's interests, and defrauding the European Union. Ibrahim and his codefendants were eventually acquitted and released in early 2003 after the Bush administration brought pressure to bear on the Egyptian government.

Beginning in 1992, the Emergency Law was also employed as a basis to justify the referral of civilians to Egypt's military system of justice. Originally intended to provide for swift sentencing in cases related to terrorism, military tribunals were increasingly used to try civilians who were not involved in violent antistate activity. Members of Egypt's Muslim Brotherhood, for example, have consistently been tried and convicted in the military court system even though the organization has not engaged in violence for over three decades.

In addition to Egypt's legal system, the office of the presidency is one of the primary institutional mechanisms designed to ensure the authoritarian status quo. As noted, one of the key consequences of the 1967 defeat was the institutionalization of the president as the most significant actor in Egyptian politics. Yet, even before 1967, the presidency had already become a focal point in the Free Officers' political order. Both the 1956 and 1964 constitutions endow the president with considerable powers. These powers ranged from the decidedly mundane to more robust prerogatives such as the capacity to dissolve the People's Assembly, promulgate decrees with the force of law, declare a state of emergency, and command the armed forces. Egypt's 1971 constitution restricted the president to two six-year terms in office, but the constitutional amendments of May 1980 rescinded this safeguard.

Although the president will encounter challengers as a result of amendments made to the constitution in May 2005, would-be candidates must surpass a number of significant legal hurdles to even enter the presidential campaign. Only parties that have been established for five years *and* obtain 5 percent of the seats in the People's

Assembly *and* hold 5 percent of the seats in the Shura Council may put forward a candidate. That candidate must also be a member of a higher committee of his/her political party. Independent candidates must obtain the signatures of 250 members of Egypt's representative structures—at least 65 endorsements from the People's Assembly, 25 signatures from the Shura Council, and ten local council endorsements from 14 of the 27 governorates.[31] The majority that the ruling party invariably enjoys in all of these bodies favors the incumbent president. Ultimately, the combination of the full weight of legal regulations and presidential powers interlocking with the ruling-NDP places the balance of power decidedly in favor of the president—who has always been a military officer. One strategic analyst, also a retired military officer, explained that at the highest level of the Egyptian state there is no appreciable difference between military and civilian.

Analysts have often described civil-military relations in Egypt as a bargain, but it is actually much more than a transactional relationship.[32] The military and the president share interests and worldviews linking their fortunes in a more significant way than a mere bargain. The military establishment trusts the president as the steward of the state and political development.[33] Socialized in the same manner as the officers through military education, training, and experiences, Egypt's head of state maintains a perspective that tracks closely with that of his uniformed colleagues.[34] Even during the early years of the Sadat period, when the prestige and influence of the military establishment was at its lowest ebb, the president found it necessary to cultivate officers in order to oust his rivals both within and outside the armed forces.

There have been moments of presidential-military discord. During the January 1977 "Bread Riots," for example, Egypt's commanders agreed to intervene and restore order throughout the country, thereby rescuing Sadat from a potentially fatal political crisis, only after the president agreed to rescind economic austerity measures. Throughout the 1980s, President Mubarak and Field Marshal Mohamed Abdel Halim Abu Ghazala had an uneasy relationship as they both competed for the loyalty of the officer corps—a contest Mubarak eventually won.

In general, however, it is the military's crucial and intimate association with the presidency that ensures the continuity of Egypt's political system. If the officer corps needs to, it can influence political events through the president. This mutually reinforcing relationship with the president has allowed the officers to remove themselves from day-to-day governance.

Critical though the formal institutions of political control may be, informal institutions are equally, if not more, important to the maintenance of Egypt's authoritarian regime. The origins of informal institutions lie in precedents from the time of the Free Officers' coup, which placed the military establishment in an exalted political and social position. Despite the attenuation of the military's prestige after June 1967 and the alteration of the overt role of the officer corps, the nexus between the presidency and Egypt's commanders indicates that informal institutions relating to the power of the military establishment endure.

Consider, for example, the much-discussed issue of presidential succession. Egypt's constitutions all specify in detail the procedures for the selection of a new president in the event of retirement, resignation, incapacity, or death of the incumbent.[35] In practice, Egypt's heads of state have been selected through the officer corps.[36] When Anwar Sadat chose Air Force general Mohamed Hosni Mubarak to be his vice president in 1976, the move was widely regarded as both Sadat's effort to further undermine his opponents from the cadre of officers who took part in the 1952 coup and an acknowledgment that the "October Generation" (commanders who took part in the 1973 war with Israel) would become politically influential. Although constitutionally the Speaker of the People's Assembly, rather than the vice president, is the next in line to the presidency, there was never any question that Mubarak would succeed Sadat after the president's assassination in October 1981.[37] A basis of support within the military high command has historically been an informal requirement for the position.[38] A potential unintended consequence of severing the link between the presidency and the armed forces could, in fact, be a more autonomous military establishment.[39] After all, without the benefit of a fellow officer serving as president, the military establishment would need to ensure its interests more actively.

The informal institutional power of Egypt's military establishment is reflected in the pattern of relations between the presidency, its military-affiliated personnel, and the parliament.[40] For example, although the executive's authority in areas related to armament allocation and procurement—particularly from foreign suppliers—is subject to parliamentary review, this has never occurred. Indeed, despite the wide-ranging oversight with which the People's Assembly is formally vested, no actual oversight ever takes place. Egypt's minister of defense makes an annual presentation to the assembly's standing Committee on Defense, National Security and Mobilization and is obliged to answer parliamentarians' questions, but such questions are rare.[41] As one military informant explained, "The minister of defense may brief the parliament, but there is no real dialogue, the members are not culturally inclined to question the military."[42] As this officer suggests, the historically high regard with which the military has been held in Egyptian society has placed it generally beyond reproach.

Egypt's prevailing political institutions, which were founded shortly after the Free Officers' coup, ensure both continuity and the highly influential, yet low-key, role of the officer corps. This institutional setting clearly privileges Egypt's military enclave. At the same time, however, this asymmetry in benefits creates incentives for the emergence of counter-elites who oppose the military-dominated political order.

The Benefits and Risks to the Egyptian Military

A facade of pseudodemocratic institutions, representative structures, and legitimating principles overlay the rather sophisticated institutional infrastructure of Egypt's authoritarian political order. With the political system rigged to serve the interests of the state elite, however, the existence of these pretenses of democracy is curious. With the means of political control generally effective and the distributional advantages of the political system seemingly secure, why bother? As is the case in Algeria and historically in Turkey, the veneer of democratic institutions and practices does, in fact, provide a range of benefits to Egypt's military establishment and its civilian allies.

Legitimacy and Political Insulation

Although the Free Officers came to power in 1952 with little in the way of a coherent ideological program, they were vested with a common set of core beliefs about Egypt's situation at midcentury and the country's future potential.[43] The cornerstone of these ideas was nationalism, on which the other components of the officers' vision were based—notably economic development and social justice. The immediate result was the development of rhetoric in which the military conceived of itself as the vanguard of a vast movement of the Egyptian masses seeking national freedom and dignity. As their political project developed over the course of the mid-1950s, the officers established institutions and structures to match this discourse, which were intended to endow their self-described revolution with greater legitimacy. The existence of a parliament, elections, and judiciary seemingly narrowed the gap between objective reality and the leadership's democratic rhetoric.

These institutions and structures do, to some extent, function. Although the People's Assembly does not exercise significant influence on high state policy, it does maintain a measure of power in areas related to agriculture, local administration, youth, and the interests of its primary constituency—the bourgeoisie.[44] The Egyptian judicial branch has often fought to retain much of the independence with which it was endowed in various founding documents. Indeed, it was this independence that compelled the Egyptian leadership to rely more heavily on the Supreme State Security Court and military tribunals.[45]

In the summer of 2000, for example, the High Constitutional Court declared the election law that had governed the balloting for the 1995 parliamentary elections to be unconstitutional, thereby forcing the dissolution of the People's Assembly and a new election. At the same time, the court also struck down the infamous NGO law (Law 153/1999), which would have severely compromised the efficacy of the nongovernmental sector, on procedural grounds.[46] That key institutions such as the People's Assembly and the judiciary command a measure of authority permits the leadership to make the not entirely erroneous claim that the political system functions in accordance with its founding documents.

Egypt's democratic facade also provides a certain amount of flexibility to the political order. There is often some confusion about the nature of authoritarian systems. Unlike their totalitarian counterparts, authoritarian regimes have neither the ideological nor the institutional wherewithal to thoroughly penetrate society. The presence of pseudodemocratic institutions and representative structures permits authoritarian regimes like Egypt's to diffuse, co-opt, and/or deflect political opposition. For example, Nasser responded to the demands of a significant cross section of society in the aftermath of June 1967 with a call for a deepening of democratic practice (the March 30 Program) that was subsequently followed with a "permanent constitution" as institutional scaffolding to this initiative. In the 1980s the accommodation between the government and the Muslim Brotherhood was part of an effort to contain the organization through the pseudodemocratic institutions and structures of the state. As Gehad Audah has written, the Muslim Brotherhood "would channel the quest for political reform and liberalization of the political system through state political institutions (to be defined to include political parties, professional associations, and Parliament)."[47] President Mubarak and his allies calculated that the Brotherhood's political participation would significantly reduce the willingness of the group's activists to express themselves through popular demonstrations and strikes—activities the authorities worried would cause political instability.

The Egyptian officer corps derived additional interrelated benefits from the political system's democratic facade, which were borne out of the military's unhappy experience after June 1967. The ease of Israel's victory that June humiliated the officer corps. Adding to their sense of shame and betrayal was the antipathy with which many Egyptians held the officers for the military's apparent failure to defend the country.[48] The result was the immediate retrenchment of the military establishment, which relinquished its significant role in the day-to-day governance of Egypt in favor of a mission that focused almost exclusively on preparing for another round of warfare with Israel. Though the circumstances of 1967's crushing defeat forced the officers to accept an alteration in their role, the military achievement associated with the destruction of Israel's heavily fortified Bar Lev line along the East Bank of the Suez Canal in October 1973 vindicated those changes. The officers have grown comfortable with arrangements in which one of their own remains the head of state and a range of pseudodemocratic institutions and representative structures insulate them from politics.[49] Unlike the period following the 1967 defeat, any public dissatisfaction with the prevailing state of politics is generally directed at the prime minister, the cabinet, or the bureaucracy. In addition, with its limited connection to the day-to-day politics and administration of the state, the officer corps has been able to focus its attention on the development of a modern, technologically advanced fighting force.

Empowering the Democratic Facade

Like in Algeria, Egypt's democratic facade poses significant risks to the military establishment and its allies within the state elite. Over the course of the last 50 years, the Egyptian leadership has distinguished itself for its ability to outmaneuver, co-opt, or outright repress its opponents. Although the Muslim Brotherhood has been subject to repression, it has nevertheless demonstrated imperviousness to co-optation and significant staying power. Moreover, it has proven to be adept at taking advantage of opportune moments to use the pretenses of democracy to advance its agenda.

The capacity of the Brotherhood to harness Egypt's democratic facade throughout the 1980s and early 1990s was made possible by the assassination of President Anwar Sadat in October 1981. While the military and police forces engaged in a severe crackdown on extremist groups, the new leader, Hosni Mubarak, sought to release the political pressure that had been building in the last year of Sadat's life. Mubarak freed activists from across the political spectrum who had been imprisoned during the summer of 1981 for their opposition, real or perceived, to a variety of government policies, and he voiced a commitment to greater democratization.[50]

Included among the released prisoners were members of the Muslim Brotherhood, who were openly and harshly critical of Egypt's relations with the United States, the country's accommodation with Israel, the excesses of *infitah* (economic opening), policies relating to women's rights, and the dismal state of politics.[51] Yet, in what seemed to be a return to the early 1970s, the new president reached an accord with the Muslim Brotherhood. The organization, which had apparently eschewed violence as a means of political change since the 1970s, would become an ally, albeit an unofficial one, in the government's battle against Islamist extremist organizations such as al-Jihad, whose members were responsible for Sadat's assassination, and the Jami'at Islamiya.[52] Although Mubarak refused to legalize the Muslim Brotherhood or its flagship publication, *ad-Dawa*, the Ikhwan (Brothers)—whose own democratic

credentials were decidedly uncertain—were given official sanction to preach, organize, and mobilize in an effort to undermine the ideological appeal of those who
sought to wage war on the Egyptian state.[53] The goal was to use the considerable
appeal of the Brotherhood to foster "the emergence of [an] Islamo-conservative,
urban, lower middle class [to] increase social stability and make possible the integration of less wealthy and potentially more turbulent groups through employment,
services, and charitable activities created by their socio-economic network."[54] A key
aspect of this strategy was, however, the military-political elite's calculation that even
as the Brotherhood was authorized to pursue social and political activities, the organization would nevertheless remain subject to state control. For its part, the Ikhwan
stood to benefit from this accord, which gave official sanction to aspects of the
organization's social, economic, and political agenda.[55]

The Egyptian leadership's efforts to establish an accommodation with the Ikhwan,
coupled with the relatively open political environment, allowed the Brotherhood to
harness the country's democratic facade to engage in a rhetorical assault on the
government and state elite. In the process of this bid to advance its agenda, which led
to the gradual accumulation of the Brotherhood's political power, the organization
encroached upon a series of the military establishment's core interests. Though the
risks to the parochial and institutional interests of the officer corps were clear, there
was no exclusionary or even repressive response from the military establishment and
its allies.

Although Egypt's military-political leaders grew concerned over the Brotherhood's efforts, there is evidence to suggest that they believed the organization's continued presence in the political arena served their own overall objective, which was to
drain away support for violent Islamist extremist groups. Moreover, given that members of the military enclave are not perfect assessors of politics, the decision not to
repress or exclude the Brotherhood may have been a miscalculation based on the
belief that it was in no position to realize the reforms it advocated. The unintended
consequence of this accommodation was, however, the increased political prominence and power of the Muslim Brotherhood.

Economic Interests

Over the course of its history, the Muslim Brotherhood has consistently called for
the reform of the Egyptian economy. There has been a movement away from the
organization's statist vision of the late 1940s and early 1950s toward a position that is
more friendly to private enterprise, but a number of key themes first articulated in the
post–WWII period remain.[56] Besides standard Islamist concerns regarding the aboli-

tion of *riba* (usury) and the encouragement of *zakat* (charity), the Ikhwan's economic program has revolved around two core axes: economic independence and economic development. The former is regarded as no less than a prerequisite to political independence and the latter as a means to achieve social cohesion, thereby ensuring national unity. Perhaps the Ikhwan's most authoritative contemporary statement on the condition of the Egyptian economy came in March 1987 with the public consummation of the organization's pact with the Socialist Labor Party (Hizb al-Amal al-Ishtiraki) and the Liberal Party (Hizb al-Ahrar), though the latter played a relatively minor role in this partnership. The Electoral Program of the Labor Party List—it remained illegal for the Brotherhood to participate in its own name—was the basic policy platform of the three-way coalition, which became known as the Islamic Alliance (al-Tahaluf al-Islami).[57]

The program emphasized that Egypt's growing economic dependency on foreigners, specifically non-Muslims, should be reversed for the sake of national independence and social justice: "In confronting the world today and the hegemony of the great powers, it is necessary that there be mutual support between the private and public sectors for the sake of future development and an equitable reliance on imports and local production. It is necessary to unify the role of the two sectors in accordance with social welfare and the protection of the national economy from foreign penetration."[58]

The call for the unification of the public and private sectors should not be misunderstood as an effort to return to the statism of the 1950s and 1960s but rather as a call for greater coordination between the two sectors in the service of Egypt's development goals. The Ikhwan and their allies asserted that the government needed a "corrective understanding of *infitah*," so that the policy "supports independence and not dependency and [places Egypt] on the path of increasing production rather than consumption provoking desires for commodities."[59] The Brotherhood's proposals did not favor autarky, however. Instead, the organization's economic vision sought to emulate the rapid development of the "Asian Tigers." As a result, the electoral program of the Islamic Alliance called for restrictions on imports, protection of key industries, limits on debt, and carefully targeted foreign direct investment.[60] By criticizing *infitah*, a hallmark of Egyptian economic policy, the Brotherhood and its political partners were suggesting that the military-political elite had compromised both the country's wealth and its independence, key components of the officers' revolutionary legitimacy.

The Alliance's program was equally critical of the apparent failure of the Egyptian leadership to foster social justice. In a nod to the liberal streak that ran throughout the Ikhwan, the program called for the implementation of policies that would serve as "incentives for investment" and encourage the development of a "national consciousness of investment as a religious duty" in an effort to achieve full employment and ameliorate problems associated with Egypt's generally low standard of living. In addition, as part of its prescription for overcoming the significant wage-price gap confronting workers and peasants, the Islamic Alliance called for an end to fiscal irresponsibility. This included ending practices such as *seigniorage*—a tool to finance budget deficits that produces inflation—and "ostentatious government spending . . . on celebrations, receptions, cars, vacations, and the children of government officials," which only contributed to revenue shortfalls.[61]

The complaint concerning official profligacy was part of the Brotherhood's ongoing appeal against widespread corruption in government circles. This was nothing new for the Ikhwan (or any of the other opposition political forces such as they were), but since it was enjoying an environment of official toleration, the Brotherhood did not refrain from widely publicizing its position. In an unsolicited policy memo to President Mubarak, the Brotherhood's Supreme Guide at the time, Hamid Abul-Nasr, indicated that "lowered moral standards and values" inexorably led to Egypt's economic malaise.[62] The Islamic Alliance's electoral program built on this theme in a section titled "Spreading Virtue and Closing the Gates of Corruption," which called for an end to corruption in the state and public sectors through the application of *shari'a*.[63] The implication of this was clear: Despite the official commitments of the government embodied in Article 2 of the constitution identifying Islamic jurisprudence as *the* source of Egyptian law, the state elite had willfully neglected Islamic principles, which had deleterious effects on the quality of governance and directly contributed to corruption. According to the Brotherhood, the implementation of *shari'a* would remedy problems associated with payoffs, compromise the ability of the elite to employ *wasta* (connections) as a means of procuring government contracts, require an explanation for rejected bids, and lift the secrecy surrounding investigations conducted under the auspices of the Central Auditing Organization and the Organization of Administrative Oversight.[64]

The Brotherhood's economic vision and its criticism of prevailing conditions and practices posed a potential risk to the economic interests of the officer corps, which by the mid-1980s extended to an impressive array of industries and initiatives. Like their counterparts in Algeria, members of Egypt's senior officer corps positioned themselves at the nexus of the state and private sectors in order to reap the benefits of both. The military establishment sought to capitalize on Sadat's much-vaunted *infitah,* particularly the benefits associated with foreign direct investment and the potential rent streams it produced. Besides financing for projects like Field Marshal Abu Ghazala's foray into domestic car manufacturing—an initiative his partner, General Motors, initially considered less than prudent—there were lucrative opportunities to become consultants to, and representatives of, foreign corporations. In contrast to either the Algerian or Turkish officer corps, however, the Egyptian military establishment became directly involved in manufacturing and the provision of services. This economic activity included everything from weapons production and procurement to the manufacture of appliances and footwear, agriculture, food processing, and services related to aviation, security, engineering, land reclamation, and tourism.[65] The finances for these enterprises, reportedly rife with corruption, were cloaked in secrecy.[66] Notwithstanding the military establishment's efforts to portray the economic interests of the armed forces as an integral element of the country's economic and social development, there is evidence to suggest that the ostensible budgetary benefits of these activities were misrepresented. As Robert Springborg notes, Egypt's military enterprises were subsidized to such an extent that these business activities were an actual drain on the overall state budget.[67]

Although the Muslim Brotherhood's rhetoric concerning the exigencies of economic independence, the amelioration of significant gaps in standards of living, and the state elite's exploitation of the country's economic institutions had potentially negative consequences for the military's economic activities, it provoked little direct reaction from the officer corps or its allies. Despite their rather robust interests in Egypt's economic arrangements, the senior officers tended to keep a low public profile on matters related to economic policy, preferring to leave these matters to technocrats within the government. Nevertheless, senior officers have sought to defuse opposition criticism with their own emphasis on economic development and independence.

In a 1988 interview with the weekly magazine *al-Musawwar,* Field Marshal Abu Ghazala reasoned that Egypt's strategic relationship with the United States was an important component of long-term economic development. Washington's military and economic aid would, he argued, help develop Egypt's defense industrial base further, which would in turn spur economic growth and thus render Cairo less dependent on Washington.[68] On social issues, the military maintained that its various projects through the National Service Projects Organization, including infrastructure rehabilitation and development, agricultural expansion, and water purification, were dedicated to resolving persistent problems of inequality and providing the bases for economic progress.[69] In 2004, the senior command signaled its support for economic reform. Implicit in this support was the belief that economic development would infuse the political system with greater legitimacy, but the officers also warned that reform should not disrupt social cohesion, providing an opportunity for "certain groups" (the Muslim Brotherhood) to profit politically from the suffering of average Egyptians.[70]

State and Political Apparatus

The functioning, or more precisely the shortcomings, of various components of Egypt's political apparatus was the second broad front in which the Ikhwan reproached the government. Making use of various aspects of the country's democratic veneer, the Brotherhood sought to hold the members of the state elite accountable for the apparent disparity between political principle and practice. For example, in a 1990 column titled "Valuable Freedom," the Brotherhood's Supreme Guide invoked the legitimating principles of freedom and democracy so characteristic of Egypt's founding texts to elaborate this gap: "Freedom is dear and it is preferable for you to avoid your nation's anger and riots. It cannot be imagined that any people will remain under subjugation and repression after hearing and witnessing surrounding nations achieve their freedom and dignity . . . A nation's power is derived not from material power, but from the entire citizenry's liberty, the people's trust in the government, and the government's trust in the people. A government that lacks the people's trust due to the government's dominion, subjugation, and denial of the people's rights and freedoms has no weight among states."[71]

The Brotherhood not only exploited the democratic discourse that had prevailed since the Free Officers' coup, but it also directly challenged the leadership on the state of the electoral system, the status of the judiciary, questionable legal statutes, and the constitution itself.[72] In this way, the Brotherhood was asserting that the Islamists were the true wardens of democracy, not the members of the military-political complex who were merely defenders of an increasingly inappropriate status quo.

Recognizing that they had much to gain from free and fair elections, the Brotherhood included this issue in their ongoing critique of the way Egypt's political apparatus performed. Shortly after the 1984 elections, which brought ten members of the Ikhwan to the People's Assembly, then Supreme Guide Umar Talmasani suggested the result did not reflect the true strength of the organization. Talmasani told an interviewer from the London-based weekly *al-Majalla:* "I think if matters had proceeded normally, all the Brotherhood candidates would have won."[73] Subsequently, the Ikhwan and their partners called for the government to maintain neutrality and guarantee freedom in general elections. Moreover, the Islamic Alliance sought the creation of an independent judicial body under the auspices of the High Judicial Council to supervise the elections and establish "durable" penalties for election fraud. The Brotherhood's program also called for the establishment of a mechanism through which the elections to the People's Assembly could be appealed.[74]

In 1990, even after the promulgation of a new electoral law, which in some ways satisfied the objections the High Constitutional Court raised when the justices declared previous electoral laws unconstitutional, the Brotherhood nevertheless took the leadership to task for perceived shortcomings. The creation of 222 new constituencies designed to favor the NDP's chances of obtaining a two-thirds majority, the continued absence of guarantees against fraud, and the ongoing state of emergency led the Ikhwan to declare that the government's commitment to democracy was merely rhetorical, compelling opposition groups to boycott the October-November parliamentary elections.[75] This boycott was part of a more general demand calling on the government to repeal laws that contradicted not only *shari'a* but also Egypt's legitimating principles related to democracy and individual rights and freedoms.[76] As Supreme Guide Talmasani declared during the Ikhwan's efforts to secure legislative representation, "We want more freedom to the point where a citizen can stand up and, without fear, tell the ruler, 'You have erred.'"

Finally, the Brotherhood sought to alter a number of aspects of the constitution. Although Article 5 formally established Egypt's multiparty system, the Brotherhood and its electoral allies indicated that the constitution was essentially geared toward a single-party system and thus lacked coherence and suffered from contradictions. The Islamic Alliance also called for constitutional changes that would provide for the direct election of the Egyptian president and vice president(s).[77] In an effort to rein in the power of the presidency and establish closer executive accountability to the People's Assembly, the Brotherhood and its partners sought to transfer the power of the purse from the executive to the People's Assembly. Although, in accordance with Article 115 of the constitution, the parliament was vested with the power to ratify the state budget, it was prohibited from making changes to the plan without the approval of the government. The Alliance's electoral program proposed altering this balance of power by granting the assembly power to modify the budget without executive branch approval.[78]

The Ikhwan's appeal sought nothing less than the empowerment of key components of Egypt's political facade: truly free and fair election, direct election of the head of state, greater balance between the executive and the legislature, and the elimination or alteration of restrictive aspects of Egypt's legal system.[79] These proposals could expose the military-political elite to significant risks and eviscerate its means of political control. It was left to President Mubarak—a fellow officer—to respond to the Brotherhood's demands. In the late 1980s, President Mubarak was given to reiterating the virtues of Egyptian democracy while emphasizing a particularly consensual role for the opposition. According to the president, "If the ruling party is in reality the executive authority within the government, then the opposition parties are in reality the partner in building stability."[80] The president also sent sharp rebukes to convey that dissent was inappropriate in Egyptian politics: "What next, when some heedless people seem to be expressing a well-studied political line aimed at division, and voicing alien wishes that have no place in a democratic rule . . . I do not wish to give a name to such calls, but shall merely say that they are devoid of any substance, voiced by those who only represent themselves or their own cravings . . . "[81] One officer recalling this period echoed Mubarak when he affirmed, "The military is a bulwark against extremism and these people [the Brotherhood] were not interested in democracy. We must be careful that extremism does not disrupt our economic development and progress."[82] Although the military-political leadership had in the past placed itself at risk to protect certain elements of the state and political apparatus, the activities of the Brotherhood, like those of the Front Islamique du Salut (FIS) in Algeria, resulted only in rhetorical ripostes.

Nationalism, Foreign Policy, and Security Policy

Analysts have tended to underscore the Brotherhood's opposition to Egypt's foreign and defense policy, but in the 1980s and 1990s the organization also called into question the government's internal security practices. Rather than risk direct collision with the internal security agencies attached to the Ministries of Interior and Defense, however, the Ikhwan sought to place the government on the defensive by emphasizing the rule of law and the independence of the judiciary. Although members of the judiciary were widely regarded to have tenaciously guarded their independence, the Brotherhood believed that the judiciary's position was tenuous.

The Islamic Alliance's 1990 electoral program cited budget control, judicial appointments, the increasing use of the Supreme State Security Court and military tribunals, and other mechanisms at the disposal of the executive which compromised the efficacy of the judicial system.[83] It called for the abolition of both the "emergency courts" (Supreme State Security Court) and the Socialist Public Prosecutor, which operated with virtual impunity outside the purview of the "regular" judiciary. Further, the Brotherhood sought to ban the practice of appointing justices to positions within the government, thereby protecting against the politicization of judicial authority; to strengthen the right of appeal; and to transfer the responsibility of prisons to the Ministry of Justice.[84]

Another target of the Brotherhood's demands in the area of domestic security was repeal of the Emergency Law and the retrial of all those convicted under its statutes in Egypt's regular court system. Still, the Ikhwan did not limit their criticism to Law 162/1958 but called for the repeal of all "disreputable laws shackling public and personal freedoms and [those] that contradict the constitution and human rights."[85] The practical effect of the continuation of these laws and other restrictive statutes,

Brotherhood spokesmen warned, was the inevitable radicalization of Islamist-oriented political activists who would conclude that they could only effect change through violence.[86]

In the realm of foreign and defense policy, the Brotherhood has a long history of challenging the government. The Ikhwan's willingness to ask questions about Egypt's relations with Israel, and by extension the United States, cast aspersions on the officers' nationalist narrative.

Initially, the Brotherhood and the military establishment shared the same nationalist terrain. Their first major confrontation in this area developed over the October 1954 Anglo-Egyptian agreement, which contained provisions allowing British forces to return to the Suez Canal zone in the event of aggression against members of the Arab League and Turkey.[87] The ultimate betrayal of Egyptian nationalism, however, was Sadat's trip to Jerusalem in 1977 and Egypt's subsequent peace treaty with Israel. For the Brotherhood, which had been one of the earliest organizations to call attention to the perceived dangers of Zionism to Arab rights and Islam's patrimony in Palestine and whose members had participated—by many measures valiantly—on the battlefield in the war of 1948, the settlement with Israel was "shameful" and "illegitimate." What in the West was regarded as a bold initiative to claim peace for the Egyptian people, reclaim all of their occupied territory, and set them on a course of prosperity, was, to the Ikhwan, an abrogation of the military-political elite's duty to protect Egypt, its Muslim character, and Islam itself.[88]

In the Mubarak era, the Brotherhood kept up its drumbeat of criticism concerning Egyptian-Israeli relations, though in a seemingly more solicitous manner than it had done during the Sadat period. Throughout the 1980s and the 1990s, the Ikhwan availed themselves of various components of Egypt's democratic facade to express dissatisfaction with Cairo's "equivocation" in its relations with Jerusalem. In a February 1987 article in *ash-Sha'ab*, Supreme Guide Abul-Nasr insisted that a tougher line with the Israelis on the Palestinian issue must be a crucial component of Egypt's defense policy: "Egypt's security . . . is totally linked to the security of Palestine, as Egypt has often been invaded across its eastern border. It is in the homeland's interest to have a sisterly state that will cooperate with Egypt through thick and thin."[89] Moreover, the leadership's failure to do otherwise, according to Abul-Nasr, betrayed not only Egypt's historic position as the guardian of Arab and Islamic interests but also its national honor. The Islamic Alliance's 1990 electoral program took a similar position. In an effort to further demonstrate that the Islamists would better protect Egypt and the Arab/Islamic world, the Brotherhood advocated freezing the country's obligations under the Camp David accords due to Israel's consistent violation of that agreement.

The Brotherhood's criticisms became more vocal with the convening of the Madrid peace conference in October 1991. On the eve of that conference, the Brotherhood's leader used *ash-Sha'ab* as a platform to warn its readers that participation at Madrid was no less than a "sell out." The efforts of the conference's primary sponsor—the United States—were not geared toward forging peace between the Arab states and Israel but were an "effort to preempt any attempt for a possible renaissance of the [Islamic/Arab] nation to recover its vitality and unity."[90] By dint of their close partnership with Washington, particularly in the Arab-Israeli peace process, members of Egypt's military enclave were complicit in this plot, according to the Ikhwan.

U.S.-Egypt relations were a recurrent theme of the Brotherhood's counternarrative. Concomitant with the negotiations to separate Israel and Egypt on the battlefield in 1973 and the fitful negotiations over the terms of peace during the 1970s was a dramatic expansion of U.S.-Egypt relations.[91] The Brotherhood, however, regarded the strategic relations between the United States—Israel's patron—and Egypt as a threat: "The danger of the special relationship with America in light of its strategic agreement with Israel based on obvious bias toward Israel damages our national security and thus is all the more reason to refuse to grant it [the United States] facilities and military bases for its forces or tolerating joint maneuvers on our soil . . ."[92]

Moreover, the Ikhwan and their allies advocated a more effective use of the military's resources in an effort to "support and strengthen the Egyptian army to be our armor in confronting our enemies," implying that Egypt's military-to-military and overall strategic relations with the United States precluded this from becoming a reality.[93] Clearly, the Brotherhood sought to harness the pseudodemocratic institutions and representative structures of the Egyptian political order to drive home what the Islamists perceived to be the shortcomings of the U.S.-Egypt relationship. In the process, the Ikhwan implied that they were the most appropriate sentry of Egyptian security, a direct affront to the officers' nationalist narrative.

Concern over U.S.-Egypt ties was heightened in 1991 as Cairo aligned itself with Washington in the effort to repulse Saddam Hussein's invasion of Kuwait. In general, the Ikhwan supported neither Baghdad's claims to Kuwait nor Egypt's participation in the U.S.-led international diplomatic and military coalition to force Iraq's withdrawal from Kuwait. Like Algeria's FIS, the Ikhwan were ideological competitors to the secular Ba'athism of Saddam Hussein, but the Brothers recognized that the Iraqi leader possessed a certain mystique. According to Brotherhood spokesman Maamoun Hudeibi, Saddam "has become a symbol of resistance for having resisted a formidable coalition" and in doing so "has the people and their conscience."[94] Hudeibi described the confrontation with Iraq as "a colonial war" and asserted in an interview with *Le Monde*, "The problem is not Saddam, in fact it is his power . . .

bombing does not constitute 'the means to liberate Kuwait, but the annihilation of Iraq.' "[95] Hudeibi's references to colonialism, "the people," and the devastation of allied attacks on Iraq represented a harsh, if entirely implicit, criticism of the Egyptian military, which, with 35,000 combat troops in the Gulf, maintained the fourth largest contingent in the area (after the United States, Great Britain, and Saudi Arabia).[96] The implication was that Egypt's military-political elite, whose own nationalist narrative was based on resistance to foreign penetration and the will of the people, were pursuing a course of action that ran counter to these nationalist principles.[97]

The Ikhwan's efforts to question the nationalist credentials of Egypt's state elite in the areas of defense and security policy elicited a mixed response from the military establishment. In the 1980s, Field Marshal Abu Ghazala sought, with some success, to defuse the Islamist critique of the military. The defense minister made a number of overtures to the Brotherhood through an emphasis on his and his family's piety, in particular the fact that his wife wore *hijab*. In addition, Abu Ghazala stressed that the mission and worldview of the military conformed to Islamic principles.[98] Subsequently, Abu Ghazala and his successors, Yusuf Sabri Abu Talib and Mohamed Hussein Tantawi, touted the efforts of the armed forces to achieve military self-sufficiency and to develop a credible deterrent to maintain regional stability, thereby neutralizing the Ikhwan's grievances, at least to some extent.[99] In general, however, the military establishment sought to remain aloof from the criticism, though officers such as General Ahmad Fakhr, a deputy to Abu Ghazala who was authorized to speak in the name of the military establishment, did respond. Fakhr rebuked the opposition's efforts to discuss delicate elements of defense policy (including the strategic relationship with the United States) claiming such a discussion would jeopardize national security.[100] In this way, the military was sending a clear signal to the public: the Brotherhood was irresponsible when it came to the country's security.

Response to the Brotherhood's criticism of Egyptian policy during the Gulf War was more forceful. In order to deflect charges that Egypt was complicit in colonial aggression against an Arab and Islamic nation, senior officers such as Major General Mohamed Ali Bilal, commander of the Egyptian forces in the Gulf, emphasized the ostensibly sacred aspect of the armed forces' mission in the Saudi desert—to protect the holiest of Islamic lands from invasion.[101] For his part, President Mubarak lashed out at the Brotherhood in an effort to undermine the nationalist and religious legitimacy of the Islamist position. In a February 1991 speech at al-Azhar University— Islam's oldest and most venerated institution of higher learning—marking the anniversary of Mohamed's ascension to heaven, Mubarak protested: "Some people cast doubt on our position and attempt to provoke the sentiments of simple people against our policy, exploiting hollow slogans and fabricated arguments that are not based on sound logic, straight religious principles, or good behavior. What is worse is that they are exploiting religion to propagate their fake claims and deviationist obscurantism. They have nothing to do with religion. Sometimes they concentrate on the presence of foreign forces in the Arab region, alleging their aim is confined to demanding the evacuation of these forces from the region, forgetting that the reason for the presence of these forces was the Iraqi president's aggression against Kuwait and threat to Saudi Arabia and the Gulf."[102]

Clearly, the Ikhwan's efforts to encourage and participate in a public review of defense and security policy caused consternation among military and political leaders. Still, from the perspective of the military-political leadership, the Brotherhood's challenge required little more than a rhetorical response, particularly as the leadership still relied on the Ikhwan to limit the popular pull of extremist groups.

Regime Maintenance and the Military Enclave's Perception of Threat

By 1992, the Muslim Brotherhood's ability to leverage Egypt's pseudodemocratic institutions held out the potential for the Islamists to alter the country's political order, which meant that the military-political elite almost certainly would crack down on the organization and its activists. The early-1980s bargain that the military-political elite struck with the Brotherhood, which offered the Islamists an official imprimatur for their cultural and social activities in exchange for their assistance in reducing the appeal of extremist organizations, did not necessarily play out as the leadership expected. The consequence of the accommodation was not containment of the Islamists, as Mubarak and his advisers had intended, but a significant increase in the organization's political power.

Consider, for example, the Brotherhood's infiltration of Egypt's institutions of higher learning, the training ground for future influential segments of society—doctors, lawyers, engineers, journalists, and teachers, to name just a few. Because campuses, particularly those located in Upper Egypt, were prime recruiting grounds for extremist organizations, the leadership gave the Brotherhood free rein to organize university students in an effort to weaken the appeal of the extremists of the Jami'at Islamiya and al-Jihad. Already influential within institutions of higher education, the Brotherhood established control over the boards of a variety of student unions. Its influence even extended to the faculty and university administration. Over the course of the early 1990s, for example, the Brotherhood gained control of the faculty clubs at the state-run universities located in Zaqaziq, Asyut, and Cairo.

In addition, the Ikhwan became influential in the elected university councils.[103]

Control or significant influence within the universities provided the Ikhwan yet another venue from which it could carry out its mission to transform Egyptian society. There were also the Ikhwan's electoral successes in the 1980s, which made the Brotherhood the largest opposition group in the Majlis ash-Sha'ab. These outcomes were noteworthy not because the Brothers could necessarily have a substantive effect on state policy but because they demonstrated an unrivalled ability to organize and mobilize. As Muslim Brotherhood spokesmen indicated at the time, the organization's entry into the Majlis ash-Sha'ab provided the Ikhwan a platform to preach their powerful counter-narrative.

By 1991–1992 the Brotherhood had captured the boards of Egypt's most prestigious professional syndicates, including the associations representing doctors, dentists, teachers, engineers, and pharmacists. The results of the September 1992 balloting for seats on the board of the national bar association demonstrated the Ikhwan's political power. The bar had long been a bastion of regime supporters who played a minor, but significant, symbolic role in Egypt's democratic facade. However, the Brotherhood's control of 14 of 25 seats indicated that the state's military-political elite could no longer expect the lawyers' guild to offer its professional and ostensibly moral approval to legislation and decrees.[104] Although the Brotherhood made up only about 15 percent of the membership of many of the syndicates, its members were able to win positions on their governing boards through a combination of their ability to mobilize, voter apathy, and protest votes.[105] Egypt's generally weak party system made the professional associations, which were not as tightly controlled as the parties, an indicator (however crude) of the political sentiment of a potentially influential segment of society. Moreover, control of the syndicate boards gave the Brotherhood additional resources—such as newspapers, magazines, and newsletters—with which to advance its agenda.[106]

The Ikhwan's success establishing a majority on the board of the bar association coincided with an increase in extremist-related violence directed against tourists in Egypt in late 1992. These attacks provided a convenient pretext for the military-political leadership to end the accommodation it had maintained with the Ikhwan over the previous decade. Beginning in late 1992, Brotherhood activists and leaders were arrested in a series of security sweeps. Although the leadership sought to link the Brotherhood to extremist organizations, the Interior Ministry's spurious evidence suggests that the political violence of Jami'at Islamiya provided a convenient justification to exclude the Brotherhood because it had "gradually appropriated public space [and] created new models of political leadership and community."[107] The crackdown on the Ikhwan was based on the perception that the Brotherhood, if left unchecked, could be a threat to the political order.[108]

Events surrounding the October 1992 Heliopolis earthquake brought these dynamics into sharp relief. In the immediate aftermath of the temblor, Brotherhood activists from several professional syndicates—primarily the doctors' and engineers' associations—proved far more adept than state organizations, even the armed forces, at bringing relief to those left homeless and in need of medical attention. Within two weeks of the event, however, paramilitary security forces tore down the makeshift medical tents of the Ikhwan-affiliated doctors, and other Islamist relief workers were forced to suspend their activities.[109] Through a combination of its previous representation in the People's Assembly (it had boycotted the 1990 polling), control of professional syndicates, social activism, and ability to frame the prevailing discourse, the Brotherhood was in a unique position from which it could credibly question the prevailing political order.[110] The military-political elite perceived this threat, and Mubarak and his allies put an end to the official forbearance of the Ikhwan.[111] To take any action other than exclusion—for example, continued accommodation—would risk the military establishment's entire position in Egypt's political system and the political order itself. In an interview with *Der Spiegel,* the Egyptian president continued to link the Ikhwan with violence and underscored the military-political elites' perception of their threat: "[The Muslim Brotherhood] is an illegal organization that is behind most of the activities of the religious troublemakers. Have a look at what happened in Algeria. I advised the former president not to permit any religious parties. He flung my advice to the winds. Now Algeria is in trouble." Indeed, in 1992, Egypt's military-political leadership was concerned about a scenario unfolding in a manner parallel to events in Algeria ten months earlier.[112]

Mubarak was, of course, quite correct—the FIS, like the Ikhwan, was a religious party. Yet the ostensible religious commitment of both organizations was almost beside the point. The Brotherhood's religious character was the basis of the group's prestige, but the threat to the officer's regime lay not in its advocacy of Islamic principles but in its ability to harness the pseudodemocratic institutions of the state for actual political gain. Such gain could provide impetus for the development of conditions more conducive to the implementation of the Brotherhood's agenda and, in the end, regime change.

This dynamic is eerily similar to that of Algeria and Turkey, though the Ikhwan had neither won a majority in parliament (as FIS had in Algeria) nor become the senior partner in a governing coalition (as Refah had in Turkey). Still, the defenders of the Egyptian regime determined that the Brotherhood could not be left in a position of power, and official toleration of the Brotherhood came to an end with arrests, trials before the Supreme State Security Court, and ultimately (beginning in

1995) military tribunals. As one retired, high-ranking officer commented, the issue with the Brotherhood was "all about the chair"—his euphemism for power.[113]

In addition to the arrests, the leadership undertook a series of initiatives to ensure that neither the Ikhwan nor any other potential political opposition group could effectively harness Egypt's democratic facade to advance their agenda or gain power. In addition to the continuation of the Emergency Law, a series of laws and decrees were promulgated to close areas of the democratic facade that the Brotherhood had exploited, making it difficult for any opposition group to operate. In the immediate aftermath of the 1992 earthquake, for example, the authorities promulgated Military Decree 4/1992, which made it illegal to receive unauthorized financing from abroad. The decree had a potentially significant effect on the Brotherhood's ability to carry out its social service programs, as financing from individuals and organizations located in the Gulf countries, where the Ikhwan had extensive connections, was placed under government surveillance.

President Mubarak then turned his attention to the syndicates, which had become influential instruments to propagate the Ikhwan's agenda. Law 100/1993—the Law to Protect Democracy in the Syndicates—was an effort to dilute the Brotherhood's influence over these professional associations. The statute required 50 percent of an organization's registered members to vote in a board election for the results to be valid.[114] The military-political elite found other ways to bring the syndicates into line. For example, through accusations of financial irregularities, two of Egypt's most prestigious professional organizations—the engineers' syndicate and the bar association—were placed under judicial supervision.[115]

Mubarak and his allies also sought to depoliticize Egypt's universities. Recognizing that professors and university administrators had become part of the Brotherhood's ability to mobilize, the government issued the Egyptian Universities Act of June 1994, terminating the relative autonomy that Egypt's universities had enjoyed. Although deanships were previously elected posts, under the new law the government-appointed university presidents were granted the prerogative to select faculty members for these positions. Similarly, university councils were placed under the control of those closely aligned to the government.[116]

The depoliticization effort was not limited to Egypt's campuses, however. President Mubarak and his allies within the military-political leadership determined that the Ikhwan would not have the opportunity to replicate the success of the FIS in capturing local and municipal elections. Law 26 of 1994 transformed local officials into government-appointed functionaries. The election of mayors, deputy mayors, and members of local councils, a process that dated back to the Nasser period, was terminated in May 1994. Local elections were set to return to Egypt in 2006 but were abruptly cancelled in February of that year.

Finally, the parliamentary elections of 1995 were a crucial test of whether the Ikhwan would be permitted to return to Egypt's electoral process. Initially, 150 Brotherhood-affiliated candidates were permitted to campaign and mobilize support for the November balloting. But in September, 49 of the Ikhwan candidates were arrested and an additional 15 were remanded in October, all to be tried before military tribunals. The official reasons for the arrests were familiar: allegations of links to extremist groups and accusations of incitement against the government. The combination of arrests, polling day repression, and fraud kept all but one Ikhwan-affiliated candidate from gaining seats in the Majlis ash-Sha'ab. Although 19 members of the Brotherhood entered parliament in 2000 as independent candidates, the organization remained under considerable political and legal pressure. Routine security sweeps put both grassroots activists and some of its most prominent members in prison.[117]

The Muslim Brotherhood–affiliated independents secured 88 seats in parliamentary elections staged in late 2005. The Ikhwan were once again the largest opposition group in the People's Assembly. This demonstration of political power resulted in further state pressure on the organization, leading to arrests and detention of its members. Despite the unprecedented number of Islamists in parliament, their ability to affect the political system remains limited because the ruling NDP continues to maintain a decisive, albeit somewhat diminished, majority in the legislature.

Ironically undertaken in the name of democracy, the continuing repression of the Ikhwan and other opposition groups points to a profound feature of the Egyptian political system—stability. Within this nondemocratic regime, the press, opposition political parties, and a rather well-developed sector of nongovernmental organizations engage in furious debates and political contestation. Yet, the institutional setting, which can be traced back to the Free Officers and serves to benefit their descendants, blocks the path to progressive political development in favor of a stable but flexible authoritarian order.

CHAPTER FIVE

Turkish Paradox

Islamist Political Power and the Kemalist Political Order

In November 2002, the Islamist-based Adalet ve Kalkinma (Justice and Development, or AK) Party swept into power, gaining an absolute majority in Turkey's parliament and precluding the need to form a coalition government. Although the scale of AK's victory was unprecedented, there had been an Islamist-led government in Turkey's officially secular political order. In 1995, Necmettin Erbakan's Refah (Welfare) Party, which had never garnered more than 12 percent of the vote, stunned political observers both within and outside Turkey with its 21.4 percent tally in national legislative elections. This strong showing gave the party the largest bloc—158 seats—in the 550-seat Grand National Assembly and set off a wave of political turmoil and intrigue that left the country adrift with a caretaker government for the better part of a month.

Under Turkish law, the president of the republic selects the leader of the party with the largest number of seats in parliament to form a government. Refah's victory so unnerved the Turkish establishment that President Süleyman Demirel, with the active encouragement of the General Staff, broke with this precedent. Demirel called upon Mesut Yilmaz, leader of the Motherland Party, and former prime minister Tansu Çiller, who led the True Path Party, to form a blocking coalition. Together these right-of-center parties secured 38.9 percent of the vote. In time, however, the formal agreement establishing the government could not contain the personality differences of Yilmaz and Çiller. The Motherland–True Path coalition fell in June 1996. Left with little choice, President Demirel reluctantly turned to Erbakan to form a government. After considerable back-room deal-making in which Erbakan reportedly promised to shield Çiller from any potential corruption investigations stemming from her turn at the prime ministry two years prior, Turkey's first Islamist-led government (known as Refahyol in Turkish after the two parties Refah and Doğru Yol that made up the coalition) came into existence on July 3, 1996.

The development of Islamist political power is a paradox in Turkey's secular political system. Indeed, over the course of the last 40 years, the guardians of that system—the officers of Turkey's military enclave—have intervened in politics four times to remove governments that the military's senior command deemed anathema to the interests of the republic. Islamist or Islamist-leaning political parties and politicians were suppressed as a result of the coups of 1960, 1971, 1980, and the "postmodern" or "soft" coup of 1997. Despite six decades of competitive multiparty elections, a legislature that generally functions above the level of a rubber stamp, and the participation and leadership of Islamist parties, the logic of regime stability in Turkey has been nevertheless strikingly similar to that of Egypt and Algeria—until recently.

Evolution and Character of the Regime

Although the antecedents of some of the institutions of modern Turkey can be traced to the Ottoman Empire's last century of existence, specifically the reforms of the *Tanzimat* period (1839–1871) and those associated with what is referred to as the First Constitutional Period (1876–1909), there is no denying that the establishment of the Turkish Republic in 1923 represented a dramatic break from the *ancien régime*. The leadership of the nationalist movement that ultimately proclaimed the republic was composed of military officers, the most prominent of whom was Mustafa Kemal and his close associates General Ismet Inönü, Marshal Fevzi Çakmak, along with officers such as Kazim Özalp, Fuat Bulca, Kemalettin Sami, Kazım Karakebir, and Ali Fuat Cebesoy.[1] That the founders of the Turkish Republic were predominantly military officers should not come as a surprise given that the new political order was established in the aftermath of World War I. Following the defeat of the German-Ottoman axis, Kemal and his coterie of nationalist officers successfully routed the Greek, British, French, and Italian forces that had occupied sections of Anatolia and effectively undermined the political authority of the Sultan.[2] Indeed, Kemal directed the Turkish Grand National Assembly (TGNA), the legislature of the provisional government, to eliminate the sultanate before the republic was even officially proclaimed.[3] This bold move was, however, only the opening ploy of a political project in which Kemal and his fellow officers—with the assistance of a burgeoning nationalist elite comprising lawyers, journalists, and members of the bureaucracy taking shape in Ankara—set out the ideological and institutional foundations of the new republican order.

The political power and legitimacy of the sultanate rested, by many measures, on the exalted place the Ottoman rulers held in the Islamic world. Not only were the sultans political leaders, but since the 16th century they were also caliphs, who, as the spiritual leaders of the *ümmet* (Turkish for *umma*), commanded resources from the Balkans and the Fertile Crescent through the Levant and stretching into North Africa. And while the dominant narrative of Kemal's reforms indicates that he perceived the problems of the Ottoman dynasty and backwardness of Anatolia to be the result of religious obscurantism and superstition, it is clear that the measures undertaken between the mid-1920s and mid-1930s were calculated to forestall the use of Islam as an instrument of political opposition to the new republican political order.

In addition to a variety of social changes, including the use of Latin script, European numerals, and last names; the adoption of the Gregorian calendar; and the criminalization of the fez, beginning in 1924, Kemal and his officers oversaw a series of initiatives that were more directly related to politics. For example, the new republican elite saw to the abolition of the caliphate; the office of Şeyh 'ül-Islam (Sheikh al-Islam), which played an important role in Ottoman administration; the Ministry of Religious Affairs and Pious Foundations; and the *medrese* (*madrasah*), which served as schools for religious learning and indoctrination throughout the Ottoman period. The following year, Sufi brotherhoods, known as *tarikats*, were outlawed and their lodges closed.[4]

The efforts to relegate religion to the realm of personal conscience were, of course, part of a broader endeavor to forge a nation-state within the Anatolian rectangle. When Kemal and his fellow officers—many of whom were imbued with the ideals of European nationalism—established the republic, they sought to reorient the values and allegiances of the inhabitants of Anatolia. Instead of a Muslim community loyal to a political-religious establishment that derived its authority and legitimacy from Islam, the founding officers of the republic envisioned a new Turkish man whose affinities were to a nation and state in which the political class derived its legitimacy from its adherence to progressive ideals and science.[5]

Though they had civilian collaborators, the military establishment played the most prominent role in forging the new Turkish state and implementing Kemal's reforms. For example, in the early years of the republic, officers manned administrative posts, assumed dual roles as both field commanders and governors, and served as delegates in the Turkish Grand National Assembly. They accounted for 20 percent of the TGNA and held one-third of its most important posts. The commanders were also well represented in a cabinet composed of members of what was essentially the ruling party, the People's Party (later renamed the Republican Peoples Party, or CHP).[6] Indeed, like their counterparts in Egypt and Algeria, Turkish commanders were intimately associated with the founding of a new political order. And, as in those two countries, the linkage between regime and military would have consequences for Turkey's political development.

Democratic Institutions, Representative Structures, and Legitimating Principles

The Kemalist account of Turkish history indicates that Atatürk, which Kemal took as a surname in 1934, and his associates—both civilian and military—sought the development of a democratic political order for the new republic. Indeed, the Turkish political system has long resembled a democratic polity. Even before the establishment of the republic on October 29, 1923, the parliament of Turkey's emergent nationalist forces approved the Law on Fundamental Organizations, which served as the rudimentary institutional base for what its authors envisioned as a democratic and secular polity. Toward that end, the first of the republic's founding texts located sovereignty "without condition or reservation with the nation" and indicated that the system of state administration rests with the Turkish people who "direct [their] own destiny."[7] In addition to these legitimating principles related to democracy and sovereignty, the Law on Fundamental Organizations identified the Grand National Assembly as the sole representative of the people and the executor of both legislative and executive power.[8]

On April 20, 1924, the Turkish Grand National Assembly ratified the republic's first constitution, which emphasized liberty, equality (both before the law and among citizens), and various freedoms closely associated with liberal democracies, including those of thought, speech, association, and the press.[9] Article 2 of the 1924 constitution identified Islam as the religion of state. This article was included in apparent recognition that religion would remain an important cultural touchstone for a vast number of Turks and thus provide an additional legitimating principle that served both to inoculate opposition to Kemal's project from religious notables and to evoke loyalty to the new republic.[10]

The 1924 constitution also provided the legal basis for the Turkish Grand National Assembly and defined its powers as the republic's legislative branch. In addition to establishing the legislative competence of the TGNA, Article 5 vested the legislature with executive power: the assembly was given authority to elect the president of the republic who, in turn, was responsible for selecting the council of ministers. Locating the executive within Turkey's legislative branch was part of an effort to check the personalized power and despotism that had come to characterize the Ottoman sultans. Moreover, under Article 26, the founders of the republic granted the TGNA wide-ranging powers to "enact, modify, interpret, and abrogate laws," ratify treaties, declare war, approve the state budget, print money, approve contracts, authorize amnesty, and commute sentences. The assembly was invested with oversight and investigatory powers, including the prerogative to appoint members of the Council of

State, which was charged with adjudicating administrative disputes and claims as well as rendering opinions on draft laws and contracts.[11] In addition, the constitution provided for an independent judicial authority, whose members were enjoined from undertaking any obligations that could compromise their judicial responsibilities.

In 1928, the text of Article 2 of the constitution, which identified Islam as the religion of state, was replaced. Having defeated the Sultan and outmaneuvered the remaining opposition to the republican project, Kemal and his associates no longer needed to appeal to the religious conservatives of the deeply nationalistic Anatolian heartland. Moreover, the article clearly contradicted Kemal's intention to render religion the province of individual conscience. The new version of Article 2 identified "republicanism, nationalism, populism, étatism, secularism, and revolutionism" as the pillars of Turkey's political system.[12]

In the 36 years between the promulgation of the 1924 constitution and the 1960 coup d'état, two critical events took place. First, in 1938 Mustafa Kemal died. His long-time deputy, Colonel Ismet İnönü, succeeded him in a peaceful transition to power. Second, in January 1946, four members of the establishment-based Republican People's Party (CHP)—Celal Bayar, Refik Koraltan, Fuat Köprülü, and Adnan Menderes—established the opposition Demokrat Partisi (DP), spurred in part by their opposition to the CHP's proposed land reform program. After 18 months of debate within the CHP, President İnönü agreed to recognize the DP in July 1947. At the time, however, neither the DP nor the CHP sought to amend the constitution or pass a political parties law that would explicitly provide for a multiparty system.

The constitution of 1924 remained in force until the coup d'état of May 27, 1960. Within a short time after their intervention, the officers of what was called the National Unity Committee (NUC) quickly established a Constituent Assembly charged with drafting a new constitution. The Constituent Assembly's document, which was ratified on July 9, 1961, more fully elaborated a series of legitimating principles emphasizing democracy. The preamble of the new constitution said Turkey would be "[g]uided by the desire to establish a democratic rule of law based on juridical and social foundations, which will ensure and guarantee human rights and liberties, national solidarity, social justice, and the welfare and prosperity of the individual and society . . . " The preamble was, of course, supplemented with a succession of articles emphasizing individual equality and freedoms of thought and faith, expression, demonstration, and association. The 1961 constitution placed legislative power in the hands of the elected representatives to the TGNA, which was transformed into a bicameral body consisting of a House of Representatives and a Senate of the Republic. The prerogatives of the Turkish parliament remained generally the same as those elaborated in the 1924 constitution, though there was one notable change. The multipartyism that had become a regular feature of Turkish politics since 1946 was institutionalized.[13]

In a further effort to enhance the quality of Turkey's democratic practices, Article 75 charged the judiciary with the task of overseeing elections through a body called the Supreme Election Board composed of magistrates from the Court of Cassation and the Council of State. There were also several provisions intended to buttress the firewalls between politics and the judicial branch that the 1924 constitution had established. For example, Article 132 expressly prohibited members of the government, civil service, or parliament from communication with magistrates "in connection with the discharge of their judicial duty." Most important, however, the constitution of 1961 established a Constitutional Court with the power of judicial review—a critical check in the balance of power between the different branches of government.[14]

On September 12, 1980, the military under General Kenan Evren effectively nullified the 1961 constitution with its third coup d'état (the "coup by memorandum" occurred in 1971) in 20 years.[15] Like the officers of the National Unity Committee in 1960, the officers of the National Security Council (as the new junta was known), convened a Constituent Assembly to draft a constitution for the Turkish Republic.[16] The new constitution, which the public ratified in November 1982, upheld a variety of liberal democratic principles. For example, the document specified that sovereignty lies with the nation and "that no individual or body empowered to exercise it on behalf of the nation shall deviate from democracy based on freedom, as set forth in the Constitution and the rule of law instituted according to its requirements."[17] The democratic principles outlined in the preamble—freedom and rule of law—were bolstered throughout the text in formal articles. And, like Turkey's previous constitutions, there were provisions outlining personal rights related to religion, thought, expression, and association, as well as freedom of the press.

The centerpiece of Turkey's democratic institutions remained the TGNA, which was once again identified as the repository of the nation's sovereignty. Its official functions differed little from those outlined in the previous constitutions—drafting, enacting, and repealing laws, supervision of the Council of Ministers, approving the draft budget, ratifying international treaties, and so forth. In keeping with the precedent set in the 1961 constitution, the Turkish judiciary, through the Supreme Election Council, was charged with overseeing elections to ensure that polling was conducted fairly and in an orderly fashion. Moreover, in an effort to ensure that appeals, investigations, and complaints of voting irregularities would not succumb to politicization, Article 79 stipulated that the decisions of the Supreme Election Board were final. As a result, petitioners were barred from appealing to the TGNA for redress. The independent nature of the Supreme Election Council reflected the provisions of political neutrality and independence the constitution set out for the judiciary as a whole. For example, the 1982 constitution stipulates tenure and income guarantees for judges and leaves all disciplinary proceedings related to magistrates to the Supreme Council of Judges and Public Prosecutors. With the principles and institutions of democratic governance in place, the National Security Council oversaw the return of multiparty elections and ultimately the return of civilian leadership in 1983.

The Authoritarian Reality

The political and social institutions of any given polity are likely to reflect the interests of the founding elite and its successors. Turkey is no exception. The military and civilian elite that founded the Turkish republic may have fervently believed that its reforms were in the best interests of Turkish society, but the result was nevertheless a political system skewed heavily in its favor. Indeed, Kurds and conservative Muslims grew restive and even violently opposed to the nationalist elite's project once it became clear that their interests would not be adequately represented in the institutions of the republic.[18] Unwilling to alter their vision, Kemal and his associates sought to ensure the durability of their project against meddling from ethnic minorities and religious conservatives. Not incidentally, they also reinforced the power of the military and its nationalist allies. To be sure, between 1924 and 2002 there were many changes in Turkey's institutional setting, including the development of multiparty politics, free and fair elections, and a legislature that was something more than a rubber stamp. Yet these modifications did not change the well-defined contours of Turkey's authoritarian regime.

In the early years of the new republic, Turkey's authoritarianism was reflected in the 1924 constitution, which lacked effective checks and balances, and in the composition of the TGNA. Though the Republican People's Party—a creature of the military establishment and its civilian allies—was not intended to be a vanguard party in the same manner as Algeria's Front de Libération Nationale or Egypt's Liberation Rally, the party maintained unrivaled control of the assembly for the first 27 years of the republic's existence. In 1924, some members of the Grand National Assembly, unhappy with what they considered to be the growing authoritarianism of the republic, founded the Progressive Republican Party and mounted a lone opposition in parliament. The party was banned in 1925 and its leaders brought to trial before what were called Independence Tribunals. These were justified through the Law on the Maintenance of Order (1925), which gave the government the authority to repress political dissent.[19] Consequently, with political opposition stifled and the TGNA vested with both legislative and executive power, the constitution became the blunt instrument of a one-party state.

There were other enduring authoritarian qualities in the first decades of the republic. Although Turkey's founding texts endow Turks with basic freedoms and rights, these liberties have often been simultaneously limited either through provisions in the very same document or restrictive implementing legislation. Like in Egypt and Algeria, the strategic use of the phrase "within the limits of the law" was employed in order to constrain certain freedoms, specifically freedom of the press, in the 1924 constitution.

After the March 12, 1971, coup, the officers directed the Grand National Assembly to amend various aspects of the 1961 constitution that the General Staff had deemed too liberal and thus a threat to social cohesion. The amendments effectively limited freedoms of expression, conscience, and thought and as a result could be used as justification to subdue political opposition. A decade later, though the officers banned a number of leading civilian political figures, it nevertheless seemed that they might loosen restrictions on the political opposition. Article 68 of the 1982 constitution granted Turks the right to establish political parties. Yet clauses within the very same article, as well as Article 69, actually restricted this right. For example, although political parties were identified as "indispensable elements of the democratic political system," which may "be founded without prior permission," parties were prohibited from advocating policies that "conflict[ed] with the indivisible integrity of the State with its territory and nation, human rights, national sovereignty, and the principles of the democratic and secular republic."

The Kemalist elite broadly interpreted such provisions to punish their political opponents, primarily political groups associated with Kurdish causes and Islamist-oriented parties. Moreover, Article 69 prohibited parties from establishing links with "associations, unions, foundations, cooperatives, and public professional organizations in order to implement and strengthen their party policies, nor shall they receive material assistance from these bodies."[20] The implementing legislation that followed these constitutional provisions, the Political Parties Law of 1983, reflected these restrictions faithfully.[21]

The Turkish penal code complemented the constitutional and legal restrictions on political parties with additional limits that outlawed mixing religion and politics. Article 163 criminalized the establishment of organizations that would disseminate "propaganda directed at transforming the fundamental order of the state based on religious principles."[22] Additional provisions specifically prohibited the exploitation of religion for political purposes and enjoined Turks from "openly incit[ing] people to enmity and hatred by pointing to class, racial, religious, confessional, or regional differences."[23] While these regulations were not surprising given the secular context of Turkey's political system, the Turkish elite has a tendency to construe restrictions on religion and politics rather broadly. Consequently, the criminal code was employed as an instrument to repress political opponents. Both Islamist leader Necmettin Erbakan and his one-time deputy Recep Tayyip Erdoğan were convicted of crimes under the penal code and were banned for various periods from participating in the political process. In 1998, the Diyarbakır Security Court found Erdoğan guilty of inciting religious enmity and sentenced him to ten months in jail and prohibited him from participating in politics. Erdoğan's crime was reciting a Ziya Gökalp poem to an audience in the southeastern town of Siirt, titled "Soldier's Prayer," which read: "The minarets are our bayonets, the domes are our helmets, mosques are our barracks, the believers are soldiers / The Holy army guards my religion Almighty, our journey is our destiny, the end is martyrdom." There is some controversy whether Erdoğan paraphrased the first stanza of the poem, but that does not diminish the irony of his arrest and subsequent conviction. Gökalp was not an Islamist firebrand but rather one of the leading theoreticians of nationalism during the Young Turk period (1908–1918).

Although Turkey's founders initially vested the Grand National Assembly with both legislative and executive power, over time its executive authority was enhanced. The 1961 constitution, often hailed as the most liberal of these texts, is a prime example of the officers' efforts to retain their primacy in the political system. Crafted by a coalition of officers, members of the CHP, Kemalist intellectuals, and members of the small Republican Peasant Nation Party, the constitution was a response to the unhappy experiences of the military establishment during the decade that the Demokrat Party dominated Turkey's parliament (1950–1960).[24] During this period officers worried that Adnan Menderes's governments were retreating from Kemalist reforms, promoting officers who were loyal to the Demokrats, undermining the officers' political influence by reducing the number of officers in Cabinet posts, and overseeing a decline in the real wages of the officer corps.[25] The new constitution separated the executive from the legislature and strengthened the powers of the presidency and, by association, the prerogatives of the bureaucracy at the expense of the parliament. These reforms were intended to limit the potential power of any political formation that might, like the Demokrats, endeavor to alter the way in which state resources were distributed and/or offer a seemingly viable counter-narrative to Kemalism.

Yet it was the 1982 constitution that had the most significant effect on the balance of power between the legislature, judiciary, and executive. In particular, the officers of the junta significantly upgraded the president's powers. The powers included the capacity to call the parliament into session; promulgate laws; resubmit draft legislation to parliament; accredit representatives of Turkey and receive those of foreign states; call new elections for the Grand National Assembly; issue decrees with the force of law; appoint rectors of universities; and name members to the State Supervisory Council, Higher Education Board, and various parts of the judiciary.[26] The State Supervisory Council, which was attached to the Office of the Presidency, was charged with overseeing the functioning of the government and could, at the request of the president, conduct investigations into all public bodies, including "public professional organizations, employers' associations and labor unions at all levels, and public benefit associations and foundations."[27]

Finally, the formally institutionalized influence of the military establishment also contributed to the authoritarian nature of Turkey's political order.[28] In 1949, the Supreme Council of Defense was established to coordinate policy and facilitate communication between the armed forces and the government. Comprising senior military officers and several civilian ministers, this body was the forerunner of the National Security Council (MGK), which was established under Article 111 of the 1961 constitution. The MGK was charged with "communicat[ing] the requisite fundamental recommendations to the Council of Ministers with the purpose of assistance in the making of decisions related to national security and coordination."[29] According to Feroz Ahmad, the officers of the NUC intended that "national security" be broadly defined so that the military, through the MGK, would have an opportunity to present its views to the civilian leadership on a wider range of issues than those associated with national defense.[30] The year following its formal establishment, the power of the MGK was enhanced when its military representatives were permitted to attend cabinet preparatory sessions, thereby allowing them to directly influence deliberations of the Council of Ministers.[31] The 1982 constitution further enhanced the influence of the MGK, enjoining the government to "give priority consideration to the decisions of the National Security Council concerning the measures that it deems necessary for the preservation of the existence and independence of the State, the integrity and indivisibility of the country, and the peace and security of the country."

Moreover, under the Law on National Security of 1983, the MGK "determines the necessary measures preserving the constitutional order, providing for national unity and integrity, orienting the Turkish Nation around the national ideals and values by uniting around Kemalist Thought [and] Atatürk's Principles and Reforms."[32] This clause—among a variety of others, including the service codes of the armed forces and the texts of the 1961 and 1980 constitutions—indicates the military establishment's determination to uphold its self-endowed right to intervene in politics based on wide-ranging criteria. As one officer candidate explained: "We are opposed to anybody, no matter whether they are there by the grace of the ballot box or the votes of the National Assembly, who attempts to violate Atatürk's principles. We have a right to act to this end in the interests of our people, and for their protection."[33] This autonomy was bolstered through an additional set of constitutional provisions. The 1961 constitution, for example, separated the Turkish General Staff from the Ministry of National Defense. As a result, the chief of the General Staff is formally subordinate to the prime minister but not the civilian minister of defense. At NATO ministerial meetings it is common practice for the chiefs of staff to sit behind their ministers of defense with the sole exception of the Turkish officer who has traditionally sat next to the Turkish defense minister. Moreover, the 1961 constitution made members of the National Unity Committee ex officio members of the Senate of the Republic and exempted the officers from any liability for actions taken during the NUC period. The 1982 constitution carried similar provisions and exempted the military from the oversight of the State Supervisory Council and the judiciary. For example, officers dismissed from the armed forces had no legal recourse to appeal the decision of the senior command.

As in Egypt and Algeria, the informal power of the Turkish military establishment extends to a range of policy and issue areas beyond national defense and security. In Turkey, the origin of these institutions lies in the prominence of the military establishment in the founding of the republic and is a consequence of the military's formal role as the guardian of the political order. Overall, the development of civil-military relations has conformed to Kemal's vision in which the officers of the armed forces eschew involvement in politics but retain a prominent position from which they can influence policy and the political process.

During the first three decades of the republic the power of the military establishment was not based on formal legal institutions but rather on the influential positions many officers occupied—most prominently, the president of the republic. Although Article 40 of the 1924 constitution placed the armed forces under the auspices of the Grand National Assembly, these powers were delegated to the presidents of the republic who, during the first 27 years of the republic's existence, were Mustafa Kemal and Ismet Inönü, the two leading members of the Turkish military enclave. Others such as the chief of staff, Marshal Fevzi Çakmak, exercised significant influence within the Council of Ministers, though he was not formally a member of that body. And, as noted above, officers occupied many seats within the TGNA, though they were prohibited from command positions during their tenure in the legislature.

The military's role in the selection of six of Turkey's nine post-Kemal presidents highlights how informal institutions function in Turkish politics. Marshal Çakmak's support for Ismet Inönü helped secure his ascension to the presidency after Kemal's death in 1938. And in 1961, just as they were preparing to hand the reins of power back to civilians, the officers of the NUC informed the politicians that they expected their leader, General Cemal Gürsel, to be elected president once a new Grand National Assembly, which formally chooses the president of the republic, was seated. In the spring of 2000, Hussein Kıvrıkoğlu, chief of the General Staff, informed parliamentary leaders who were responsible for selecting the next president that while the senior command did not have a particular person in mind, the officers preferred the candidate to possess certain qualities of character—integrity, a commitment to Kemalism, and strong leadership. While these attributes were far from objectionable, Kıvrıkoğlu's very public pronouncements effectively ended the presidential aspirations of Mesut Yilmaz, leader of the Anavatan Partisi (Motherland Party), for whom the military establishment had displayed thinly veiled contempt in a series of public statements. The General Staff was opposed to Yilmaz due to alleged financial irregularities during his tenure as prime minister in 1997–98 and his willingness to publicly question the military's role in forcing the Refah-led government from power in 1997.

The informal power of the Turkish military establishment has conditioned Turkey's civilian leaders to a basic, if unwritten, rule of Turkish politics: Politicians must ensure that they and their followers do nothing to elicit the ire of the military establishment and its collaborators among the state elite. In the late 1990s, Bülent Ecevit, leader of the Democratic Left Party, consistently implied that one of his best attributes as prime minister would be his ability to maintain good relations with the General Staff. When in 1998, the Turkish press reported that Ecevit was, in his capacity as deputy prime minister, trying to influence personnel changes in the armed forces, he flatly denied the reports and stated: "I have never done so even when it was my duty as prime minister in the 1970s. I would never do such a thing today."[34] When Recep Tayyip Erdoğan sought a return to politics in 2001, he reportedly met first with military officers bearing the message that he had mended his ways. The platform of Erdoğan's AK Party makes obvious efforts *not* to draw the attention of the military establishment; consequently the party lacks any discernible difference from other right-of-center parties already present in the political arena.[35] For all the seeming dynamism of Turkish politics, the informal power of the military that conditions politicians' behavior has been successful in producing parties remarkable for their conformity. There is very little that distinguishes right-of center factions from those on the left. And, as Hakan Yavuz has noted, politicians have asked questions about the sources of power, legitimacy, and authority in the Turkish system only at significant political risk.[36]

Despite practices such as multiparty competitive elections, the political system continued to include authoritarian characteristics well into the late 1990s. As is the case in Egypt and Algeria, formal and informal institutions rigged the political system in favor of the senior command and its civilian allies. These groups enjoyed the distributive advantages of the prevailing institutional setting. Turkish counter-elites have continually sought to participate in the political arena to rectify this imbalance but until the early 2000s were unable to alter their situation.

The Benefits and Risks of the Democratic Facade

The officers of the Turkish military benefit from Turkey's amalgam of democratic practices and quasidemocratic institutions in three closely connected areas. First, these attributes of democracy conform well to the rhetoric of the Kemalist project, the centerpiece of which involved efforts "to raise Turkish society to the level of civilization" (in this case, the democratic and secular West). For the officers and their civilian allies, the seeming convergence between principle and practice helps to reinforce the legitimacy of the regime.[37] Over the last four decades, the military establishment has on occasion countenanced the open defiance of the Turkish people. For example, even though the 1960 coup d'état was undertaken, at least in part, to place the Republican People's Party back in power, the military establishment did not intervene when the Turkish public overwhelmingly supported the Adalet Partisi—a successor to the deposed Demokrats—in the October 1961 polling. Similarly, the junta of the 1980–1983 period did not obstruct the transfer of power when, in the first post-coup general elections, Turgut Özal's Motherland Party soundly defeated the center-right and center-left parties created as part of the junta's project of political engineering. The legitimacy of a political order in which a rhetorical commitment to "democracy" has figured so prominently would have been compromised had the military not honored the outcome of elections in 1961 and 1983. The resemblance of Turkey's political system to a functioning democracy is critical to eliciting the loyalty of the public.

Second, the officers use Turkey's pseudodemocratic institutions to insulate themselves from politics. For the military establishment, the second largest armed forces in NATO, it is critical that the officers are shielded from the vicissitudes of politics in order to maintain the military's professionalism.[38] The existence of a national parliament, competitive elections, and alternating government coalitions represents an indispensable buffer between politics and the military enclave, permitting the commanders to focus their attention on matters related to military modernization and national defense. Without ever having relinquished the right to stand sentry over the political order, the military officers have sought to leave politics and day-to-day governance to civilians.

Third, the pseudodemocratic institutions give the military the respect and admiration of large majorities of the Turkish people. Although the officers are responsible for the political order, the presence of institutions resembling a democratic polity effectively shields them from any public dissatisfaction. Consequently, the military establishment has, in general, remained above reproach.[39] Moreover, given the widely held perception that Turkish politicians—with a few notable exceptions—are incompetent, venal, and thoroughly corrupt, the military's influence and various interventions are regarded as stabilizing factors in politics.[40] In the end, the consistent high regard with which the public holds the military establishment and the apparently positive manner in which the public views the military's potential to intervene in politics has led the officers and their spokesmen to conclude that the role of the military is entirely appropriate.[41]

Refah Partisi and the Accumulation of Power

While pseudodemocratic institutions offer considerable advantages for the officer corps, they also expose commanders to significant risk. Many Turks have internalized Kemalist claims concerning the "secular and homogenous" character of Turkish society, yet Kemalism has been vulnerable to challenges from religious Muslims and the Kurdish minority.[42] Islamist politicians have historically resisted co-optation and have sought to exploit Turkey's formally democratic institutions, representative structures, and legitimating principles to advance their political agenda. Yet in the 1990s the military enclave permitted the activists of Refah to remain in the political arena in the apparent belief that the officers could—through a combination of restrictive rules, decrees, laws, structures, and informal institutions—control and contain the Islamists.

Some scholars and analysts as well as journalists have devoted much attention to what they see as the primary problem in Turkish politics: the conflict between the forces of secularism, which the officers of the armed forces represent, and those of Islamism. Turkey's senior commanders often to express their opposition to Islamist-oriented political groups in terms of a secular-religious dichotomy.[43] Yet the relationship between the military establishment and Islam has historically had far more nuance than these characterizations suggest.

The officers and their civilian allies have long sought to harness Islam in an effort to achieve their own objectives. In Turkey's war of independence, Kemal tapped into the power of Anatolia's religious notables to mobilize the masses against the sultan and the forces of the remnant Ottoman Empire. Both the officers of the National Unity Committee of 1960–61 and the military junta of 1980–83 saw Islam as an instrument to counter the growing power of the Left. The junta that took power in 1980 believed that Islam was not only an effective answer to what they perceived to be a leftist/communist threat, but also a means to depoliticize Turkish society through the Turkish-Islamic Synthesis.[44] Accordingly, the military establishment began a vigorous program of mosque building, the expansion of *imam-hatip* (preacher) schools, and the inclusion of religious education in the public school curricula. These apparent deviations from the Kemalism to which the officers and their civilian allies have always affirmed their allegiance reflect what Umit Cizre Sakallioğlu refers to as the "double discourse of the Turkish state."[45] Refah and its leaders were the unintended beneficiaries of these policies. As a result, by the 1990s, the party was in a position to exploit effectively Turkey's democratic practices and quasidemocratic institutions in an effort to offer Turks an alternate vision for society—and in the process place the Islamists in power.[46] Like the Front Islamique du Salut (FIS) in Algeria and the Muslim Brotherhood in Egypt, to varying degrees Refah's counter-narrative encroached upon the core interests of Turkey's military enclave.

Economic Interests

In the post–World War II period, Turkey has experienced two periods of unprecedented economic growth. The first occurred in the 1960s and was a consequence of a policy of import-substitution industrialization (ISI). The benefits of ISI were short-lived, however. By the 1970s, state-directed development could not sustain the growth rates of the 1950s and 1960s. Gross domestic product continued to grow, but the rate of growth slowed considerably and imports continued to outstrip exports, leading to yawning gaps in current account balances. Import-substitution industrialization also involved the establishment of a large state-owned sector. These enterprises were established with both economic and political rationales, which often trumped sound economic management.[47] The second era of prosperity resulted from efforts to correct the distortions of ISI as General Kenan Evren and his colleagues who led the 1980 coup oversaw the implementation of a neoliberal structural adjustment program.[48] By the late 1980s and early 1990s, however, Turkey's economic reform program lost momentum as privatization waned, productivity fell, and inflation took its toll on investors as well as the average Turk. In general, prior to Refah's ascension to power in the summer of 1996, the party's economics related attack on the government could be broken down along three broad fronts. Although Refah advocated such standard Islamist economic prescriptions as prohibitions against usury and calls for greater Islamic economic cooperation, it also criticized monopolies in the Turkish economy, deficiencies related to social justice, and the elite's ostensible betrayal of economic nationalism.

The small businesses and merchants who formed the core constituency of Refah's immediate predecessor, the National Salvation Party, expanded rapidly with the liberalization of the 1980s. By the 1990s, with the help of financing from Saudi Arabia and other Gulf countries, Turkey's Islamist business sector included financial services firms, insurance companies, consumer products concerns, and medium- to large-sized holding entities. Refah and its supporters did not have a problem with capitalism, but they did oppose state support for what the party's literature and spokesmen derisively referred to as "monopolies."[49] Though the firms to which Erbakan and his colleagues were referring did not necessarily meet the technical criteria of monopolies, they were large holding companies, located primarily in Istanbul and its environs, and were the recipients of state largesse that tipped the competitive balance in their favor. Added to this Turkish version of corporate welfare was the economic bureaucracy's tendency to discriminate against companies that were not associated with the Association of Turkish Industrialists and Businessmen (TÜSIAD), further contributing to an uncompetitive economic environment.

In response, conservative businessmen in Anatolia established the Association of Independent Industrialists and Businessmen (MÜSIAD). Although not officially affiliated with Refah, given the constitutional prohibitions against such linkages, the leaders of MÜSIAD-member firms nevertheless represented one of Refah's most influential constituencies. Using the discourse that had become so closely associated with the Turkish government and its leader—American-trained economist Tansu Çiller—the Refah leadership sought to highlight the unfair practices that benefited TÜSIAD members at the expense of its own constituency.[50] For example, the first section of a 1995 Refah publication outlining its Just Economic Order (*Adil Ekonomik Düzen*) called for government policies that were "genuinely pro-private sector":

> The free market system and price mechanism are constituted completely freely on the basis of supply and demand. Demand drives production. In the Just Order the price mechanism works freely. There is no central planning institution that may influence the operation of this mechanism adversely.

> One of the responsibilities of the state is to prevent monopolization . . . In the Just Order every entrepreneur benefits from state services. There is no discrimination among individuals and corporations . . .

> The existing order is not an honest order. If the state takes anyone's side, then it would necessarily limit the will and the consent of someone else. In the present order credits are issued only to a handful of rich people and the amount of credit available is limited. As a result, private enterprise has become a right available to only a certain social segment, and monopolies have formed. Consequently the existing order is a monopolist order rather than a private enterprise order.[51]

Refah's criticisms of this "monopolist order" was a signal to MÜSIAD members not only that their interests would be looked after if the Islamists came to power but also that Refah would be a steward of a "genuine capitalist system," which did not exist in Turkey.

Refah also sought to underscore the Islamist commitment to social justice—an area where the Turkish government had been, official policy to the contrary, largely negligent. Whereas the party's antimonopoly rhetoric was quite obviously directed at its constituency within the Islamist business sector, its social justice appeals were intended to secure the loyalty of the urban poor who inhabited the shantytowns (*gecekondular*) that developed in and around Turkey's major urban centers, primarily Istanbul, Izmir, Adana, and Ankara. Yet beyond party rhetoric in tracts like *Adil Ekonomik Düzen* and statements by Erbakan and his associates, Refah activists exploited freedoms of speech, organization, and the press formally guaranteed under Turkey's constitution to great advantage. The party was able to elicit the loyalty of what Ernst B. Haas calls the mobilized, but unassimilated, masses.[52] Throughout the 1990s, Refah's highly motivated and disciplined activists visited the nation's poorest sections offering a myriad of services and benefits including health care, job training, tutoring, food, and fuel.[53] Its activities in the shantytowns demonstrated that the Islamists had the wherewithal and organizational skills to match rhetoric with practice—something sorely lacking among all of Refah's adversaries, particularly the right-left governing coalition at the time.[54]

Refah's harshest criticisms of government policy focused on the lack of economic development nationwide. Successive governments, it maintained, had betrayed their nationalist credentials as they sought to harmonize Turkey's economy with the West. Refah was not reflexively opposed to the development of the country's foreign economic relations; however, its leaders believed that developing more extensive ties with Europe and the United States placed Turkey at a distinct disadvantage. Erbakan and other spokesmen publicized their case on this issue through the relative freedoms that Turkey's institutional setting afforded them, just as they had done with the problems relating to monopolies and the lack of social justice. Upon the completion of Turkey's Customs Union negotiations with the EU in early 1995, Erbakan informed his party's parliamentary deputies in a public forum: "Turkey's entry to the Customs Union without being a member of the European Union, the decision-making body of the trading bloc, would amount to accepting to live in the servants' quarters next to the doghouse in the garden of a manor."[55] This type of rhetoric was consistent with the principles of *Adil Ekonomik Düzen*, which conjures national pride in Turkey's vast economic potential, unrealized only because of the predatory behavior of foreign economic actors and the complicity of the country's prevailing elite. According to

Refah's theoreticians, Turkey's relationships with international financial institutions, Europe, and NATO have done little more than undermine Turkish industry, force the country to purchase expensive imports, and accumulate crippling debt.[56] Refah's leadership was clearly seeking a middle way, in which it could incorporate the principles of "genuine capitalism," social justice, and the rhetoric of self-sufficiency to convince Turks that the Islamist camp was the proper custodian of the nation's economic well-being.

Once the coalition between Refah and the right-of-center Doğru Yol Partisi came to power in July 1996, Erbakan outlined a policy carefully couched in the discourse of both populism and neoliberal orthodoxy. When presenting his government's program to the TGNA, a constitutionally mandated prerequisite for a vote of confidence, Erbakan stated: "In a bid to realize the leap in development expected in the economic field, the major goal of our government will be—speedily, in a planned manner, with enthusiasm, belief, and courage—to remove the obstacles blocking the path to development; prevent waste; increase productivity in all fields; develop our resources; launch a production mobilization; enable the restructuring of the state; ensure speedy and efficient state services; and, in short, protect the interests of our villagers, workers, civil servants, shopkeepers, the unemployed, the retired, the needy, merchants, industrialists, exporters, and all producers."[57]

Erbakan called for increased incentives for savings and investment, a more realistic calculation of tax rates, a balanced budget, increased autonomy for the central bank, more effective privatization policies, greater independence for agricultural cooperatives, and development of infrastructure to meet Turkey's growing energy needs. He also promised to "render the Customs Union effective" and ensure that its implementation was "based chiefly on the principle of mutual interests." At first blush Erbakan's policy statement seems like it could have been written at the headquarters of the International Monetary Fund, but against the backdrop of the party's economic program, the Islamist leader's monologue was actually a caustic—though predominantly implicit—critique of the economic distortions that the policies of previous governments had fostered. In particular, Erbakan's commitment to remove obstacles to development, restructure the state, strive for greater efficiency, endow the central bank with greater independence, and revise Turkey's trade agreement with the EU was aimed directly at the economic interests of the officer corps.

From the founding of the republic, the exigencies of both economic development and national defense placed the officer corps in a leading position in the economy. The armed forces had played a critical role in the development of Turkey's infrastructure due to its relatively advanced organizational and technical capacities in relation to other state organizations. It also developed intimate links with Turkey's relevant economic actors during both the period of ISI and the relative liberalization that began in the 1980s. These reforms had been accomplished primarily through the Army Mutual Aid Association (Ordu Yardimlaşma Kurumu, OYAK).[58] OYAK, which is exempt from taxes and duties, derives its income from a 10 percent mandatory contribution from its members. This income is, in turn, invested in a large number of industrial and financial ventures, including the automotive, cement, electronic, construction, food, petroleum, tourist, and financial services industries.[59]

Unlike in Egypt or Algeria, the economic activities of the Turkish armed forces through OYAK or other military-related business activities do not generate streams of rent that personally benefit the senior command. Yet, there are significant implications to the military establishment's having become embedded in the national economy. First, although officers may not necessarily enjoy access to rents, they still benefit through professional opportunities in both public and private enterprise.[60] Second, the direct relationship between the military establishment and leading Turkish industrial companies (Koç, Sabancı, and Eczacibası, for example); the 30 companies that comprise the Foundation for the Strengthening of the Turkish Armed Forces; and U.S., European, Israeli, and Russian defense contractors represents a significant stake in the way business is conducted in Turkey.[61] Consequently, the military establishment has a compelling interest in sustaining Turkey's prevailing economic arrangements. In this context, Refah Partisi's economic program, notably its intention to level the playing field for its constituents, eliminate waste, revise the tax system, and place greater emphasis on economic relations with Turkey's neighbors to the south and east was clearly a challenge to the military's core economic interests. Yet despite the potential threat this posed to the military establishment—particularly in the area of weapons acquisition—Refah's activities and policies elicited little reaction from the officers other than increased surveillance of the party's activities through an intelligence cell located within the General Staff called the Western Study Group.[62]

Foreign and Security Policy

Refah Partisi also held an alternative vision of Turkey's security and foreign policy. On the domestic front, the most immediate security issue confronting Turkey was the nationalist insurrection of the Kurdistan Worker's Party (PKK), which had been underway since the mid-1980s in the southeastern portion of the country. Because the PKK and its leader, Abdallah Ocalan, claimed to speak on behalf of Turkey's entire Kurdish population, the conflict raised many uncomfortable questions concerning Kurdish and Turkish identity.

Though Erbakan and other Refah spokesmen often laced their statements and public appearances with a distinct Turkish nationalism, particularly when addressing core constituencies in central Anatolian cities like Konya, Kayseri, and Erzurum, the Islamists nevertheless saw political opportunity in the Kurdish issue. Erbakan proposed nothing less than a redefinition of Turkish nationalism in an effort to resolve the country's most vexing internal security problem. Beginning with the party's 1993 annual conference, Refah's leadership, while firmly denouncing the terrorism of the PKK, indicated that the underlying cause of this phenomenon and Kurdish nationalist agitation in general was the fundamental nature of Turkish nationalism, which refused to recognize ethnic differences among the inhabitants of Anatolia.[63] Erbakan told supporters in the predominantly Kurdish city of Bingol in 1994:

> All parties except Refah are parties of falsehood. They are all almost the same. They are
> minions of the infidel powers. What did they say to the people of this country? Follow us
> and give up your religion. They harmed both religion and the nation. When starting
> school in the morning assembly, the children of this country used to begin with "in the
> name of God." You changed that and made them say: "I'm Turk, I'm brave, I'm hard-
> working." On the other hand, when you said that, a Muslim of the Kurdish origin may
> feel it is within his right to say: "Oh really, in this case I am a Kurd, I'm more brave, I'm
> more hardworking." In the near future, when the Turkish Grand National Assembly is
> controlled by Muslims, everyone will get his equal right without any bloodshed.[64]

Muslim solidarity was Refah's prescription for the problem of PKK violence, and by extension the problem of Kurdish nationalism. Looking back to what he alleged was an era of Muslim solidarity during the Ottoman period, Erbakan believed the renewal of this brotherhood was the means through which to ameliorate ethnic tensions among the inhabitants of the Anatolian rectangle. This "neo-Ottomanism" would regard Kurds as an honored ethnic group within a society in which religious, rather than nationalist or ethnic, cohesion would be the means to equality, economic development, and ultimately the social integration of the southeast.[65]

Once in power, Refah's rhetoric on the Kurdish issue was toned down significantly, largely in an effort not to alienate other, more nationalist, elements of the party's complex constituency. At the party's sixth annual conference held in October 1996— the first after it had become the senior partner in the coalition government—Erbakan promised that the army would stamp out PKK terrorism and assured the party faithful that emergency rule in the southeast would soon be lifted and villagers permitted to return to their homes. Though references to Islamic brotherhood and the shortcomings of Turkish nationalism were no longer a part of Refah's discourse, Erbakan nevertheless expressed interest in exploring a nonmilitary solution to the

PKK problem. As prime minister, Erbakan directed Fetullah Erbaş—a Refah deputy of Kurdish origin—and another Islamist deputy, Ismail Nacar, to meet with leaders in the southeast to discuss how hostilities might be brought to a conclusion.

Refah also sought changes to Turkey's foreign relations policy. The Islamists proposed a loosening of relations with the United States, Europe, and Israel in favor of stronger ties with Pakistan, Egypt, Malaysia, Indonesia, and Iran, which the Refah leadership considered Turkey's natural partners. Turkey's historic relationship with the West was one of subjugation, in which its national interests were rendered secondary to those of its ostensible partners. Such arguments, which Refah emphasized in campaigns and literature in the early and mid-1990s, sought to demonstrate the vast difference between the principled position of the Islamist party and that of its establishment rivals, who were consistently derided as "imitators" of the West. Erbakan told the assembled delegates at Refah's fourth party conference in October 1993 that the dire situation in Bosnia was a consequence of these circumstances: "While Iran and Pakistan offered to send planes, the representatives of the imitator regimes in Turkey blocked the initiative saying that 'America would not like it.' . . . As a result, they just watched the destruction of a very important Muslim state from the sidelines . . . Had the Refah Partisi been in power, the Serbs would not be able to assault Bosnia."[66] To the Islamists, Turkey's efforts to become a full partner with the West not only brought Turks very little in terms of material benefits but also forced Turks to abrogate their sacred responsibility to fellow Muslims.

Refah proposed the establishment of an Islamic United Nations, Islamic common market, Islamic single currency, integrated Islamic defense arrangements, and an organization dedicated to cultural cooperation in an effort to fend off the predations of the West. Ankara's traditionally Western-oriented foreign policy kept Turkey—perhaps indefinitely—at the gates of Vienna, but Refah's policy of international Muslim solidarity would rectify this humiliating situation and place Turkey in a position of international leadership. Although cooperation with the West would not come to an end, the relationship between Ankara and its NATO and EU partners would be based firmly on what the Islamists believed to be national interests and the mutual respect born of international power.

As soon as they assumed government leadership in the summer of 1996, Prime Minister Erbakan and his advisers sought to align Turkish foreign policy with Refah's agenda, though Erbakan never repudiated NATO, the Customs Union with the EU, or Turkey's relations with the IMF. Still, even though the foreign ministry was in the hands of Refah's non-Islamist coalition partner, the True Path Party, Erbakan sought to improve Turkey's relations with other Muslim countries. In October 1996, at a development conference held in Istanbul, Erbakan proposed the establishment of the

M-8 (Muslim Eight, sometimes referred to as the D-8), comprising Turkey, Indonesia, Pakistan, Iran, Bangladesh, Malaysia, Egypt, and Nigeria, as an alternative to the G-7 of leading industrial countries.

Even before his suggestion for this new multilateral forum, however, Erbakan had been developing a set of bilateral relations different from those associated with Ankara's traditionally Western-oriented foreign policy. Erbakan's first foreign trips were not to Brussels, Paris, London, or Rome but to Tehran, Cairo, and Tripoli.[67] The prime minister's trip to Iran barely a month after winning a confidence vote in the TGNA was noteworthy. Previously Turks had cast a wary eye toward their neighbor to the east, concerned that Iran posed a threat to Turkish secularism. Yet Erbakan's visit with Iranian president Hashemi Rafsanjani resulted in an agreement worth $18 billion committing Tehran to supply Turkey with 190 billion cubic meters of gas over a 23-year period beginning in 1999. The contract represented a significant step toward meeting Turkey's estimated energy needs.

Erbakan also visited Syria's Hafez al-Asad. The attempted rapprochement with Syria actually represented less of a break from past policies than the rapprochement with Iran. Successive Turkish governments throughout the late 1980s and 1990s had attempted to persuade Damascus to remove its support for the PKK through conciliation. Support for the PKK was linked to Syrian charges that Turkey's Southeastern Anatolia Project was diverting Euphrates River water, violating Damascus' riparian rights. Erbakan's apparently more forthcoming position regarding Turkish-Syrian relations sought to ameliorate both problems.

Refah's position on security and foreign policy presented a challenge to Turkey's military establishment, which had generally assumed the critical role in the development and implementation of both. This role was not at all surprising given (1) the military's primary vocation—protecting Turkey from both internal and external enemies; (2) the formal institutions of the state that gave the officers pride of place in foreign and security policy; (3) the officers' self-image as the best-equipped state organization; and (4) the decidedly low opinion with which the commanders generally held civilian leaders.[68] As a result, senior officers tended not to brook any civilian differences on key security and foreign policy issues.[69]

Of course, there were exceptions to this rule. During the first Gulf War, President Turgut Özal proved to be Turkey's key foreign policy actor as he pressed for a second front along the Turkish-Iraq border. Although Turkish troops never invaded Iraq, Özal's actions resulted in the resignation of Chief of Staff Necip Torumtay over the president's apparent violation of the conventions of decision-making in Turkish security policy. In the late 1980s and early 1990s, Özal's prestige—both in Turkey and abroad—insulated him from the military's manipulation and interference. Once he passed from the scene in 1993, past patterns of civilian-military relations reemerged. Rather than the gradual acquiescence of the military establishment to the civilian leadership as some analysts such as William Hale, Metin Heper, and Aylin Gunëy had expected as a result of the Özal period, the officers remained committed to retaining their autonomy.[70]

The imbalance of power between the officers and civilians led the latter to relinquish responsibility for security policy to the military. The problem of Kurdish separatism in the southeast brought this situation into sharp relief. As Henri J. Barkey and Graham Fuller have written: "Since President Özal's death . . . the civilian leadership has abdicated its share of the responsibility for devising and implementing policies toward the southeast. By directing the army to spearhead policies to cope with the problem, the civilian leadership has abandoned other policy instruments, leaving armed force the sole implement for dealing with the southeast problem."[71] Given the well-developed freedom of action that the military enjoyed, particularly in the southeast, the military establishment did not welcome Refah's suggestions or interference.[72] The Erbaş and Nacar missions undertaken at the behest of Erbakan to explore the possibility of a peaceful resolution to the conflict were unsuccessful due to the military's abiding opposition.

The Refah-led government's posture toward Iran and Syria challenged the military's assessment of the threats facing Turkey, an area that had previously been restricted to the officers of the General Staff and the National Security Council. Throughout the 1990s, in periodic statements on Turkey's internal and external defense policy, the combined expertise of both the General Staff and MGK determined —not entirely without reason—that both Iran and Syria posed significant threats to Turkey's national interests. Erbakan's overtures to Tehran and Damascus threatened to upset the officers' primacy in national security decision-making.[73]

Although the officers refrained from responding directly to Refah's vision for Turkish foreign policy, they undertook actions to demonstrate that they retained a position of primacy in this area. For example, two senior generals joined Erbakan on his visit to Tehran shortly after the establishment of the Refahyol government. Although it is not unprecedented for representatives of the armed forces to travel with the prime minister, the presence of such senior officers was an apparent indication that the military establishment would keep vigilant watch over Erbakan and his associates so that the conduct of Turkish-Iranian relations would not overstep the bounds of what was acceptable to the General Staff.

The military establishment also took a series of steps to demonstrate its autonomy. The first related to Turkish-Israeli relations. Historically, Erbakan and his associates tended to engage in either crude forms of anti-Zionism and anti-Semitism (a phenomenon largely alien to Turkey) or affected a studied ambiguity on the question of Turkish-Israeli ties that betrayed the Islamists' opposition to the relationship. Prior to early 1996, those relations consisted of diplomatic ties, tourism, trade, and coopera-tion in the area of counterterrorism. In February of that year, however, just two months after Refah became the largest party in the TGNA, the military establishment dramatically upgraded Turkey's relations with Israel. The General Staff—without consultation with the civilian leadership—completed a "military cooperation and training agreement" with its Israeli counterpart. The announcement of the accord, which provided for intelligence sharing, border security, port visits, and the use of each country's airspace for training, coincided with a series of high-level military visits between the two countries.

Turkish-Israeli ties continued to develop under the guidance of Turkey's military after the establishment of the Refahyol government, even as Erbakan sought to de-velop closer ties with the Arab and Islamic worlds. In the end, the military establish-ment's efforts to turn the Turkish-Israeli relationship into a test of wills between the officers and the Islamists ended in the military's favor. Erbakan was, for example, forced to abandon a campaign commitment to revisit Turkish-Israeli ties.[74] In a more dramatic demonstration of their independence in the area of national security how-ever, in May 1997 the military invaded northern Iraq in an operation intended to root out PKK guerillas without bothering to notify Erbakan or any other member of the government until after the fact.[75] Clearly the officers were willing to countenance Refah's efforts in the realm of security and foreign policy precisely because the mili-tary retained and reinforced its autonomy in this critical area.

State and Political Apparatus

Refah also criticized aspects of Turkey's state and political apparatus that the party leadership believed contributed to authoritarianism. According to Haldun Gülalp, Refah intellectuals envisioned a society of "multiple legal orders" in which the state's primary role would be to ensure the autonomy of each. Turks would be free to pursue their lives and vocations under the system that matched their own individual beliefs. This was a response to what Refah perceived were prevailing political-social circum-stances in which "the few pushed their views on the many."[76] In practice, however, Refah and its leadership took a less radical approach to the problems they believed to be plaguing the state apparatus and the political system's deficit of development, democracy, and human rights.

Refah proposed extending greater power to local and municipal governments.[77] Ankara would retain its primacy in security and foreign policy, administration of justice, and the development of macroeconomic policy but would otherwise merely help local and municipal administrations coordinate the provision of social services to the public. If implemented, the proposal promised to benefit Refah in two ways: First, by highlighting the dismal performance of successive governments to provide critical social services, the Islamists hoped to recruit new activists and voters. Second, the shift in resources necessary for the provision of health, education, and welfare benefits to local and municipal governments—many of which were under Refah control—would, despite the Islamists' rhetoric about clean government, permit Erbakan and his associates to develop further the Refah political machine through patronage.

The Islamists told voters that if national elections resulted in a Refah victory, the new government would directly empower citizens through the use of referenda to determine national policy. This proposal was a key part of Refah's counter-narrative, which afforded Turks greater political openness than under prevailing conditions. In a meeting with columnists from the newspaper *Milliyet* just a week before the 1995 elections, Erbakan declared: "There will be democracy. There will be no more quarreling with the country's people, religion, and history. We will adopt decisions together with the people. The people will have the right to ask for referendums."[78] The Islamist leader's call for consensual decision-making implied what many Turks and close observers of Turkish politics already understood: notwithstanding the state elite's public commitment to democracy, Turkey was run by a relatively small group of people, the most influential of whom were military officers. According to Refah, referenda would allow the people to be heard.

The Islamists also pledged that a Refah government would revise the MGK in an effort to further liberalize Turkish politics. Erbakan told the same group of columnists from *Milliyet* that, if elected, his government would retain the council but that it would "function in accordance with the national view." This statement represented an aggressive challenge to the military establishment on two levels. First, it implied that the decisions and recommendations emerging from the MGK and its military-dominated secretariat did not conform to the convictions of the majority of Turks. Second, Erbakan's allusion to "national view" (*milli görüs*) was a reference to the guiding principles of Refah. In essence, Erbakan was explicitly proposing that the Islamists supplant the military's competence in national security affairs.[79] Erbakan even questioned the quality of Turkish democracy: "The council adopts its decisions without consulting the National Assembly, the government, or the people's right to know. It adopts its decisions in a darkened room. That makes it the darkroom administration."[80] To shine light into this darkened room, Refah proposed the inclusion of opposition groups in MGK deliberations.

Refah's proposed alterations to particular aspects of Turkey's state apparatus con-
stituted a threat to the interests of the military establishment. In principle, the officers
advocated democracy and had become adept in the discourse of democratic transition, yet in practice they were more interested in preservation of the Kemalist order.
As one Turkish military officer related, "We want to protect democracy, but the
civilians have proved to be so incompetent, we are left to do their job. We have made
practical decisions to solve problems. We do not want the fundamentalists to undo
everything we have achieved."[81] This outlook, which was particularly sensitive to any
perceived deviations from the Kemalist narrative, conformed more closely to a desire
for effective administration rather than political liberalization and democratization.
Refah's proposals not only potentially hindered the administrative efficacy that the
officers desired, but they also threatened to complicate the military establishment's
ability to influence, observe, and at times control political developments. The use of
referenda and the devolution of power to local and municipal governments would
remove the decision-making from elites in Ankara whom the military could easily
manipulate or intimidate.

The military's response to these proposals was, in essence, to change the subject.
Rather than allowing Refah's initiatives to gain momentum among the public, the
military establishment sought to manipulate society. Much of the military's discourse
between Refah's 1994 victories at the local and municipal level and the forced disintegration of the Refah-led government in 1997 emphasized the party's alleged "reactionaryism" (*irtica*). Just months after Refah's victories in Ankara, Istanbul, and other
municipalities, the chief prosecutor of the Ankara state security court (a mixed
military-civilian court), asked Hayri Birler of the *Turkish Daily News:* "Can you
imagine—let's suppose fanatic fundamentalists come to power during an election in a
democratic atmosphere? Will they ever give up power again? There is no question
about it. And what happens if we do not take this measure [to protect the secular
order]? They will go to the polling centers after making use of propaganda and
emerge as the ruling party. Will they or won't they take measures to prevent the use of
the ballot box for their opponents to come to power in the future? Everyone knows
exactly what the reply to this is."[82] The chief prosecutor's rhetorical questions reflected the general tenor with which the officers and their allies dealt with Refah's bid
for power.

Moreover, the military took highly publicized measures to ostensibly protect the
secular nature of the political order. Shortly after the establishment of the Refah-led
government, for example, the contents of a General Staff briefing warning that "extremist religious activities [were being] directed toward the destruction of Atatürk-
ism and the secular and democratic order" were leaked to the press.[83] This disclosure

was intended to heighten fears concerning Refah's true intentions. Yet, as alarming as this warning seemed to be, the officers did not move against Refah. Despite its demonstrated capacity to intervene in the political arena at will, the Turkish military establishment regards this action as a last resort.[84] The military's attempts to heighten concern about fundamentalism were part of an effort to forestall intervention in the belief that the Islamist-led coalition would falter under public pressure or that Refah would constrain its own agenda to ensure its legal place in the political arena.

Nationalism and Kemalism

Finally, the Islamists attacked the government and Turkish elite on the issues of nationalism and Kemalism. Refah's strategy was to convince the public that the Islamists were the true custodians of nationalism and the appropriate heirs to Kemal's legacy. On the issue of nationalism, Refah's critique came in two forms. The first suggested that the ethnic nationalism that was a consequence of Atatürk's vision of a homogenous nation-state had done Turkey a disservice. As noted, Refah prescribed coexistence within a religious framework to end the debilitating war in the southeast and the alienation of parts of the Kurdish population.[85] To the Islamists, the division between Turk and Kurd was unnecessary in a society where only two-tenths of the population was not Muslim.

Second, although the Islamists chastised their secular-oriented counterparts for perpetuating a worldview that unfairly discriminated against their co-religionists, they also portrayed themselves as staunch defenders of both Turkey's unique civilization and the country's national interests. The tactic sought to outmaneuver the Islamists' political adversaries, who, according to Erbakan and his associates, willingly engaged in self-abnegation to please Turkey's partners in the West despite their rhetorical commitments to uphold nationalism.

For the Islamists, the complicity of the military establishment with Western powers had short-circuited Turkey's natural development and precluded the achievement of its vital national interests. As the party sought to harness the country's seemingly democratic institutions in pursuit of power, Refah's leadership unfailingly suggested that the elite's drive for Westernization had sacrificed key aspects of Turkish culture, reflected a "defeatist psychology," and was "an insult to the Turkish nation." For example, Turkey's role in the Bosnian conflict was not one of a responsible NATO member and aspirant European Union member but a shameful example of the elite's dishonorable fealty to the West.

Refah did not consider this to be a critique of Kemalism but rather a condemnation of what the Islamists believed to be significant deviations from Atatürk's vision.

The Islamists upbraided the forces claiming the mantle of Kemalism for betraying the principles upon which the republic was founded. In an interview with the German magazine *Der Spiegel*, Erbakan explained that Turkey's Islamists were the true inheritors of Kemal's legacy:

> DER SPIEGEL: In a minute you [Erbakan] are going to tell us that Refah is not a Muslim party, but a . . .
>
> ERBAKAN: . . . political party in the tradition of state founder Atatürk; that is true. Do you know what Mustafa Kemal Atatürk did when he was president from 1923 to 1938? He declared independence; he did not amass debts, but tried to advance the country by its own strength; he industrialized Turkey. Instead of traveling across the world, he thought about our great history. He said that Turkey would be at the forefront—by means of science and rationalism.
>
> DER SPIEGEL: Unlike you, state founder Atatürk banned religion from official affairs and politics.
>
> ERBAKAN: No, no again you are wrong. He prayed in the mosque, he opened parliamentary sessions with prayers, along with sheikhs and *hodjas,* religious scholars. If Mustafa Kemal lived today, he would be a member of Refah.[86]

Erbakan and his associates consistently sought to convey the notion that the Turkish elite had misapprehended Kemal's principles, insisting that Refah, not the establishment, "represent[ed] the values that emerged during the war [of independence]."[87] To reinforce this account, Erbakan tended to reference the role of Islamic notables—such as Sutcu Imam and Ridvan Hoca (Hodja) and their followers—in the battle against the Greeks and the World War I allies. According to Refah, Islamists were not only well equipped to pursue Atatürk's lofty goals of independence, industrialization, and modernization, but they were also the only political force that truly upheld the significance of Islam in the republic's founding. This issue had tremendous potential to resonate deeply with Refah's constituency, particularly the large and growing reservoir of urban poor who responded to the party's brand of "vernacular politics" (which framed Refah's political program in a discourse that conformed to cultural norms).[88]

Whereas the FIS and Muslim Brotherhood asserted that their respective governments had strayed from their professed duty to uphold the principles of Islam, Refah condemned its opponents for misinterpreting secularism. Rather than the respect for Muslim practices and religious neutrality that, according to the Islamists, Kemal had advocated, the elite had pursued a Jacobin-like *laïcisme* that sought to control religion and limit public expressions of religiosity. Consequently, on Refah's agenda was the amendment of Article 24 of the 1982 constitution, which contained provisions for "freedom of conscience, religious belief and practice" but also placed religious instruction under the sole purview of the state and prohibited "exploit[ation] or abuse [of] religion or religious feelings, or things held sacred by religion, in any manner whatsoever, for the purpose of personal or political influence, or for even partially basing the fundamental, social, economic, political, and legal order of the State on religious tenets."[89] To the prevailing elite, Article 24 was the hallmark of Kemal's reforms and critical to the political system's secular orientation. Refah highlighted the hypocrisy of circumscribed religious freedom and placed the party on the front lines of the battle over Western-style secularism. Party leaders ranging from Erbakan to General Secretary Oguzhan Asiltürk, widely regarded as a hardliner, and Abdullah Gül, the architect of Refah's foreign policy platform and a self-described moderate, proclaimed that they merely wanted to give Turks the same religious rights as citizens of the United States, Switzerland, Great Britain, and other Western democracies.[90] Turkey was unique among its Western partners, Erbakan claimed, because the state "prevents people from carrying out their mode of worship."[91] Using the personal freedoms outlined in Article 24, Refah was calling the government—and by extension the dominant elite—to account for what the Islamists perceived to be a significant gap between principle and practice.

Socialization at military high schools, academies, and war colleges inculcated officers with the sense that the armed forces were the vanguard of the Turkish nation and that the commanders were duty-bound to uphold Kemal's principles. Consequently, the officers tended to evaluate Turkey's civilian politicians against the military's own commitment to Kemalism and nationalism—a comparison in which the civilians generally paled.[92] As a result, Refah's discourse, which subtly suggested that the Islamists were Turkey's appropriate stewards in these areas, drew a strong—though not exclusionary—response from the officers.

The officer corps sought to undermine the Islamists' claim to be Turkey's true nationalists and authentic Kemalists by warning of the potentially dire consequences of a Refah victory at the polls. Relying on their dominant narrative of the republic's history, the military establishment reminded Turks that the officers, as the direct descendants of Mustafa Kemal, stood between the progressivism that characterized modern Turkey and a return to the religious reactionaryism of the Ottoman state. On the eve of the 1995 polls, General Ismail Hakkı Karadayı, chief of the General Staff, sought to influence—however implicitly—voters when he proclaimed that the "Turkish armed forces are the greatest insurance of the Turkish republic, which is a democratic and secular state."[93]

Other responses from the military tended not to be as diplomatic as Karadayı's.

Generally conveyed anonymously through Turkey's establishment press, statements from senior officers accused Erbakan and his cadre of seeking to reverse the enormous progress the republic had made since its founding and sought to tie Refah to "religious fanatics" throughout the Middle East.[94] Turkey's neighbor, the Islamic Republic of Iran, was a convenient and oft-used bogeyman. The officers' efforts gained traction not only among the Turkish elite but also the general public. During the winter of 1996–1997, many Turks turned off their lights for one minute every evening at 8:30 in what was called "one minute of darkness for enlightenment" in protest against Erbakan and Refah. This demonstration of the public's support for secular principles gave the General Staff room for maneuver when the officers did eventually apply pressure to push Refah from the prime ministry. Yet in the first six months of the Islamist-led government, the officers' response to Refah remained largely indirect.

Regime Maintenance and the Military Enclave's Perception of Threat

Refah's counter-narrative regarding economics, foreign and security policy, Turkey's state apparatus, and Kemalism and nationalism was a threat to Turkey's senior commanders. Still, their opposition to establishment policies did not bring the military out of the barracks. The officers and their civilian allies successfully checked the Islamists' national political agenda to the extent that none of Erbakan's goals in these areas were ever achieved. Yet Refah's effort to pack the Turkish bureaucracy with Islamist activists was one area where the party met with success.

The military enclave saw this activity as a grave threat to the Kemalist political order.[95] If there was any continuity between the Ottoman state and the Turkish Republic, it was the critical role that the bureaucracy played in implementing, nurturing, and buttressing the respective political projects of the ruling elite.[96] Immediately after the founding of the republic, military officers manned key bureaucratic posts; over time, however, as the new republican bureaucracy took shape, civilian officials infused with Kemal's ideals took up positions in the ministries and agencies of the Turkish state. The bureaucracy grew indispensable to the functioning and maintenance of the Kemalist political order. Ultimate responsibility for the regime still lay with the officer corps, but the military establishment's desire not to rule directly meant that the bureaucracy would be the first line of defense against any perceived deviation from the officers' conception of the appropriate path of political development.

In practice this arrangement required a degree of ideological cohesion that was, in general, confined to senior members of the bureaucracy.[97] Although the judiciary—including prosecutors—vigilantly guarded against perceived departures from the Kemalist project, the same cannot be said of the education, religious affairs, and even internal security bureaucracies. The infiltration of dedicated counter-elites into the structures of the state was therefore a continuing cause for concern for the military elite and its civilian allies, which was one reason senior commanders were so apprehensive about the establishment of the Islamist-led government.[98]

This concern was not without merit. Although Erbakan denied any intention to place Refah activists in key bureaucratic posts, protesting that he did not even change the staff of the prime minister's office, the Islamists undertook several initiatives that contradicted his denials.[99] The first actually sought not to deposit party activists in the civil service but to foster the allegiance of those people already staffing the bureaucracy. One of Erbakan's first acts as prime minister was to announce a 50 percent across-the-board pay raise for Turkey's corps of civil servants.[100] Second, within a month of taking office, Erbakan and the new political leadership sought to place long-time party activists at the heads of several important ministries, government corporations, and organizations, including the Ministry of Energy and Natural Resources, Ministry of Industry and Trade, Ministry of Public Works and Housing, Administration for Religious Foundations, Turkish Electricity Corporation, National Electric Distribution Corporation, Pipeline and Petroleum Transport Corporation, and the Turkish Scientific and Technical Research Organization.[101]

Third, Refah not so subtly sought to push judges and middle-level bureaucrats whom the party suspected to be hostile to the Islamist agenda out of their posts. The party schemed to have secular-oriented judges transferred to rural areas (which the Islamists believed would likely result in resignation or retirement) and replaced with jurists believed to be more receptive to Refah's worldview. Non-Islamist bureaucrats whose jobs were protected under civil service laws were forced to undertake meaningless tasks—such as counting cars at busy intersections—to encourage retirement so that Refah activists could fill the vacated positions.[102] These efforts did not leave the military bureaucracy untouched, though Refah did tread more lightly in this area. Unable to place party officials within the Ministry of National Defense over the General Staff's objections, Erbakan set up a "study group" within the prime ministry to examine the way the military did business and acquired weapons systems.[103] This was entirely consistent with Erbakan's assertion in August 1996 that his government would play a role in "determining the needs of the Turkish Armed Forces" and ensuring that "the defense industry . . . operate[s] in accordance with national goals."[104] In the context of Turkish civil-military relations at the time, however, this was an unprecedented assertion of the civilian leadership's prerogative. Since the mid-1940s, Turkey's procurement process has subordinated the civilian-led Ministry of National Defense to the General Staff.[105]

Indeed, it was the perception that Refah was positioning itself to capture the Turkish state through the strategic infiltration of the bureaucracy that led to what is euphemistically referred to as the 28th of February Process. Packing the bureaucracy was a tactic that Turkey's political parties, including Refah's antecedent, the Milli Selamat Partisi (National Salvation Party, MSP), had perfected. Yet unlike the MSP, Refah was the senior partner in the governing coalition and as a result was in an unrivalled position to place its activists throughout the bureaucracy. If Refah successfully packed Turkey's vast civil service, the Islamists could maintain significant influence on government policy for many years to come, regardless of the party's electoral prospects.

The seriousness of the challenge was not lost on the military elite. According to a retired officer, Refah's strategy to penetrate the Turkish bureaucracy was a key component in the "battle over money and who has the right ideology to guide society and the state."[106] The senior command feared not only that the distribution of resources could be directed away from the traditional recipients of state largesse—the Kemalist elite—in favor of the Islamists' constituency but also that Islamist-affiliated bureaucrats could potentially alter or not bother to implement laws, regulations, and decrees that were crucial components of the regime's institutional infrastructure. Another officer, who was privy to the deliberations within the General Staff during this time stated: "The dark forces of reactionaryism were dangerous. They wanted to undo everything that Turkey has achieved through infiltration of the state."[107] Just a day before the council's February 28th meeting, the officer-dominated MGK secretariat released a statement indicating that "civil organizations" (Refah) sought to establish an Islamic state through a combination of terror and political activity within the state sector.[108] The connection between Islamism and terror in the Turkish context is, in general, unfounded. Yet the military's assertions to the contrary created an atmosphere conducive to undermining Refah.

The 28th of February Process (also referred to as the blank or postmodern coup), which was the result of National Security Council Decision #406, represented a simultaneous effort to exclude Refah and ensure that Turkey's institutional setting remained rigged in favor of the military and its allies. This was to be accomplished through less a renovation of Turkey's institutional setting than a reemphasis of existing laws, regulations, and decrees. Promulgated in the name of protecting secularism and Kemalism from the forces of religious reactionaryism, Decision #406 was designed to ensure the integrity of the military-founded regime. The most important of its 18 "recommendations" were:

- The modification of laws to ensure that the principle of secularism is upheld (recommendation 1).
- Greater state control over the Islamic education sector, which had become an important feeder into the civil service (recommendations 2–4).
- Prohibition on the use of religious facilities for political purposes (recommendation 5).
- Control of "media groups that oppose the Turkish Armed Forces" (recommendation 7).
- Prohibition of military personnel who have been expelled for anti-secular activities from employment in the bureaucracy or other areas of the public sector (recommendation 8).
- Prevention of "extremist infiltration" into the Turkish Armed Forces, the universities, judiciary, and bureaucracy (recommendation 9).
- Swift action taken against those who have contravened the Law on Political Parties, the Penal Code, and the Law on Municipalities (recommendation 12).
- Prevention of resolution of Turkey's political problems based on the *ummet* (religious community), rather than the *millet* (nation) (recommendation 17).[109]

The actions of the MGK were designed to place Erbakan and his associates in the unenviable position of having to choose between devotion to their own principles and the wrath of the military establishment. For Erbakan to implement the military's recommendations would have contravened much of what he and his party championed (at least rhetorically) and no doubt would have damaged Refah's prestige. Yet to do anything but implement the recommendations would invite further confrontation with the senior military command. In practice, Erbakan split the difference. He signed Decision #406, but in an implicit challenge to the democratic credentials of the military establishment, the prime minister asserted that he would only implement the MGK's recommendations if the Grand National Assembly approved.

Rather than placing tanks and troops in the streets, as had happened in Algeria, or pursuing mass arrests of their antagonists, as in Egypt, the Turkish military leadership engaged in a public campaign to undermine the government they were duty-bound to serve. Between March and June 1997, representatives from the business community, the judiciary, academia, women's groups, trade unions, and the media were summoned to military installations in Ankara and Istanbul for a sophisticated multimedia program warning that the government's foot dragging was placing Turkey's secular order in jeopardy.[110] This created a seemingly overwrought public concern about Islamic militancy, which provided the officer corps public support for its inherently undemocratic efforts to undermine the Refah-led government.

In conjunction with these activities, the Ankara State Prosecutor filed charges against Refah and the party leadership for violating the Political Parties Law and the Turkish Criminal Code. The military's political, legal and public pressure, along with no small amount of maneuvering on the part of Erbakan's ostensible coalition part- ner, Tansu Çiller, ultimately resulted in the prime minister's forced resignation and an end to the government on June 18, 1997. Subsequently, in January 1998, Refah was banned for violations of the Political Parties Law and the Penal Code. For his part Erbakan was (once again) barred from politics along with a number of other Refah leaders including Recep Tayyip Erdoğan.

Yet the dissolution of Turkey's first Islamist-led government and the closure of Refah did not represent an end to the 28th of February Process. In an effort to preclude any future challenges to their regime, the General Staff vowed that this process would last "1,000 years if necessary." Since the fall of the Refah-led govern- ment, members of the military enclave have ensured that the most important recom- mendations of Decision #406 were implemented. As a result, in accordance with recommendations 2–4, for example, the Turkish government has either taken control or increased its supervision of "trade courses," private dormitories, and pensions associated with religious orders. The judiciary has filed cases against 12,071 individ- uals who failed to comply with Law 2584 related to the management of student dorms.

Turkish children were now required to attend eight uninterrupted years of school- ing and Qu'ran schools came under the supervision of the Ministry of National Education. Students enrolled in *imam-hatip* schools have been exposed to a curricu- lum that actually limits the number of hours devoted to study of the Qu'ran and includes a greater emphasis on "secular subjects" such as math and science. Recogniz- ing that the education system, including the Islamic schools, was an important feeder into the Turkish civil service, the emphasis the military establishment placed on education in its recommendations was part of an effort to train new cadres that share a worldview compatible with that of the Kemalist elite.

The Ministry of Interior also began, in 1998, investigating local officials for alleged ties to fundamentalist activity, and in 1999 Prime Minister Bülent Ecevit issued a circular requiring senior officials within the civil service to crack down on "all man- ifestations of fundamentalist activity at all levels of government." By the end of that year, some 3,000 bureaucrats had been punished for alleged ties to Islamist groups. Despite these efforts, the senior command remained gravely concerned that Islamist infiltration in the bureaucracy continued to threaten the political order. As a result, in August 2000, Chief of Staff Kıvrıkoğlu demanded that the Ecevit government issue a "decree with the force of law" providing for the immediate dismissal of those civil servants alleged to have ties to fundamentalism. Kıvrıkoğlu's actions actually precipitated a mini-political crisis as the Turkish president, Ahmet Necdet Sezer, opposed the decree, but in the end, despite modifications to the military's proposal, the officers were able to force suspect members of the bureaucracy from their positions as they had done so routinely with fellow officers accused of ideological predispositions toward fundamentalism. Moreover, in June 2001 the courts shuttered Refah's successor party, Fazilet (Virtue), which represented the largest opposition group in the TGNA, for its alleged activities as a "center of anti-secular activity."[111] In this way, the authoritarian institutions of the state successfully headed off what the Kemalist elite perceived to be a potentially significant threat to Turkey's prevailing political order.

The European Union and a Kemalist Reformation

The scale of the Adalet ve Kalkinma (AK) Party's electoral success in November 2002 was remarkable even for those who expected the Islamists to prevail. Yet, as significant as AK's demonstration of electoral power was, it pales in comparison to what the party has achieved since coming to office. Given the organic connection between the senior officers and the Kemalist regime, it is extraordinary that an Islamist party has been able to undertake critical wide-ranging and thoroughgoing institutional changes to the Turkish political system. It is possible that analysts have overstated the historic influence of the military or that the senior officers of the General Staff have always been committed democrats, but the long-standing pattern of coups d'état and authoritarian politics belie these types of assertions. Rather, the Kemalist reformation that began in Turkey with the AK victory is directly related to the role of the European Union. In a paradoxical way, Turkey's recent transition, which is by no means complete, occurred despite, not because of both the military establishment and the Islamists.

Since the elections of November 2002, the Turkish Grand National Assembly has passed no less than seven comprehensive legislative reform packages and a variety of major constitutional amendments under the auspices of two AK governments. The changes fall under broad categories of judicial, human rights, economic, minority rights, and foreign policy reforms. Although many of these legislative changes are uncontroversial, many compromise the authoritarian core of Turkey's military-founded regime.

In an effort to expand personal freedoms and rights, Turkey's mixed civilian-military state security courts were abolished, an entirely new penal code was established, the death penalty was banned under all circumstances, and amendments to the anti-terror law made it more difficult to prosecute Turks based on speech alone. Freedom of the press was also strengthened through a constitutional amendment. Prohibitions on broadcasting and teaching in Kurdish were lifted. Each of these reforms chipped away at the ability of Turkish elites (officers or civilians) to undermine their political opponents. Political rights were also significantly expanded. The new AK-dominated parliament amended Articles 76 and 78 of the constitution, which made it more difficult to ban a political party or a politician from the political arena. This paved the way for AK's charismatic leader, Recep Tayyip Erdoğan, who, as noted above had been banned from politics and sentenced to prison for ostensibly inciting religious strife in 1998, to return to politics.[112]

The reform packages even included a series of changes that either diminished the General Staff's vaunted autonomy or compromised the channels through which the military has historically influenced politics. Under December 2003 amendments to the Law on Public Financial Management and Control, for example, the military's extrabudgetary funds, specifically the Defense Industry Support Fund, were made subject to oversight and control. This change also strengthened the capacity of the civilian-controlled Under Secretariat of Defense to identify priorities for defense expenditures. Until these changes, the civilian leadership of the Ministry of National Defense and its various agencies merely carried out the procurement wishes of the General Staff. Moreover, a constitutional amendment in the spring of 2004 rescinded the military's exemption from Court of Auditors oversight.

The AK-dominated Grand National Assembly also made several changes to various government boards through which the military exercised its influence. Military representatives were removed from the Higher Education Board and its High Audio-Visual Board. Established after the 1980 coup, the senior command used these boards to ensure Kemalist orthodoxy by prohibiting anything other than official interpretations of Islamism (reactionaryism), Kurdish nationalism (separatism), and socialism in university curricula and the media.

By far the most significant alterations to the military's capacity to impose its will on civilian politicians were made to the National Security Council. The composition of the MGK first was taken up in a constitutional amendment in October 2001. This amendment tipped the number of representatives in favor of civilians. The MGK's recommendations are, however, based on consensus rather than voting—an arrangement that continued to favor the military. Given the past patterns of relations between the military leadership and civilian politicians and the superior preparation of the officers on the MGK, there was little reason to believe that having more civilians around the table would undermine the military's influence. In fact, recognizing that "civilianizing" the MGK was little more than a cosmetic change, the military signaled its willingness to accede to this change a year before the amendment was adopted.[113]

In January 2004, the Turkish parliament began the implementation of legislative changes pertaining to the MGK that had been passed the previous summer. Unlike the 2001 revisions, the new regulations significantly altered the composition, functioning, and competence of the National Security Council, reducing the number of officers serving on the council to one—the chief of the General Staff. In addition, a civilian was to be appointed secretary-general of the MGK, a position that was always reserved for a senior officer.[114] Previously the officer who served as secretary-general of the council was subordinate to the chief of the General Staff. The civilianization of the position serves to bypass the military's most senior officer and subordinates the secretary general to the prime minister and the president. The Grand National Assembly also reduced the frequency of council meetings from monthly to bimonthly unless the MGK is requested to convene at the behest of the prime minister or the president of the republic.

The new regulations significantly downgraded the power of the MGK and the MGK secretariat. Article 118 of the 1982 constitution directed the government to "[g]ive priority consideration to the decisions of the National Security Council," but under the seventh reform package, the duty of the MGK was redefined as "[r]eaching advisory decisions regarding the designation, determination and implementations of the state's security policies within the prescribed frameworks, determining a method for providing the necessary coordination, and reporting these advisory decisions to the Cabinet Council." Moreover, the MGK secretariat, which the military staffed, was stripped of its executive powers. Consequently, the secretariat no longer had the capacity to conduct its own national security investigations. One way the new regulations ensured that the officers adhered to the regulation was budget control. The funds allocated to the secretariat were placed under the exclusive control of the prime minister. Finally, the new regulations lifted the veil of secrecy on the decrees that "governed the activities of the National Security Council General-Secretariat."[115]

The practical effect of these reforms on Turkey's four-decade effort to join the European Union was dramatic. In October 2004, the Commission of the European Union found that the institutional changes that the Turks had undertaken had met the EU's Copenhagen criteria, which laid out clear benchmarks that Ankara had to meet in order to begin membership negotiations. As a result, the Commission recommended that the European Council start accession talks with Turkey, which subsequently began in 2005. Although the speed and thoroughness of Turkey's reform program were surprising, the truly extraordinary aspect of this episode was the response of the military establishment. With the exception of the MGK secretary general, General Tuncer Kilinc, and his adviser General Mustafa Agaoğlu, who expressed concern about "annihilating" the council, the senior command made no moves to slow down, deflect, or derail the process.[116] This is not to suggest that the relationship between the officers and the government has been completely harmonious. There have been sharp differences between the General Staff and Erdoğan over the status of graduates from *imam-hatip* schools, *hicab,* and other perceived efforts to inject religion into the public sphere, but the military establishment remained quiescent as Erdoğan and his government pushed reforms through the Grand National Assembly.

Turkey's significant progress toward more democratic politics since AK came to power in 2002 defied expectations of what was possible in the Turkish political system. In early 2004, Günter Verheugen, the EU's Commissioner for Enlargement, who was often perceived to be less than enthusiastic about Ankara's potential accession, called Turkey's reform efforts "impressive." After the Refah episode and the 28th of February Process, to say nothing of the three previous coups d'état, it seemed unlikely that an Islamist government and parliament would be able to raze the institutions of political control that were so important to the military establishment. There was, however, one important difference between the Turkish political settings of 1997 and 2002. In those five years the EU became a critical factor in not only Turkish foreign policy but domestic politics as well. At the European Council's Helsinki summit in December 1999, the EU offered, and the government of Bülent Ecevit accepted, an invitation to become an applicant for accession. Although Turkey's association agreement with Europe dates to 1963 and Ankara signed a Customs Union agreement with Brussels in 1995, the agreement at Helsinki was the first tangible sign that Turkey might eventually be accepted as a member within Europe's exclusive club.

The European Union has often been duplicitous in its relations with Turkey, but the requirements for EU membership offer great hope for the consolidation of liberal democracy in Anatolia. The combination of material and political benefits associated with EU membership created a vast constituency in support of the reforms Europe demands. As the process unfolded, both Prime Minister Erdoğan and his foreign minister, Abdullah Gül, asserted that the rapid pace of reform legislation and subsequent implementation were directly related to Turkey's EU candidacy. Beyond the details of the government's reform drive, the EU project produced something much more profound and important for the country's future political trajectory—a shift in the interests and constraints of its most important political actors, Islamists and officers.

Islamists who once railed against the West now view membership in the EU as a critical component of Turkish political development. Thinly veiled hostility toward the West characterized Erbakan and the Islamist politicians of his generation, but the younger generation of Islamists also engaged in anti-Western discourse. Abdullah Gül, who was the first AK government's prime minister and an architect of the reform drive told the daily *Milliyet* in February 1995: "We cannot remain silent in the face of unfair behavior. We hope they [Europe and the United States] will be more understanding when they realize the support we have from the people. If the Western countries have usurped our interests and rights, then we will naturally make an effort to take them back, even if that means that their interests will be harmed. We are convinced that they will not want to lose everything they have, so they will adopt a rational approach."[117]

Yet the promised benefits of EU membership encouraged Gül, Erdoğan, and their followers in AK to discard the anti-Western shibboleths of the past and portray themselves as the Islamic analogue to Europe's Christian Democrats. Given the widely held anti-Western sentiment within the Islamist camp since it became formally politically active in 1969, the current pro-European posture of Turkey's Islamists is a striking shift.

After decades in which Turkey's Islamists were forced to confront the state's vaunted means of political control, the leaders of AK came to see membership in the European Union as the best means to forge a Kemalist reformation. As a member of the European Union, the Turkish state would have to do away with its system of *laïcité* (*laik* in Turkish), which not only inserts the state into religious affairs but also places restrictions on various aspects of religious practice, in favor of a system that guarantees freedom of religion. The potential resolution of the religion issue, as well as related difficulties associated with freedoms of conscience and association, encouraged Islamists to not only join, but also lead a coalition of big business; cosmopolitan elites, who have long considered themselves European; and ordinary Turks looking forward to greater prosperity in support of EU membership.

Although the promise of EU membership altered the incentives of Turkey's Islamists, it has also placed constraints on the country's other primary political actor—the General Staff. One of the most important and controversial aspects of the Copenhagen criteria was the EU's demand for an alteration of the military's relationship to the Turkish political system. Consequently, the military establishment found itself in a decidedly awkward position. If the officers had opted to oppose the EU reform program, it would have exposed their devotion to central Kemalist tenets such as modernization and democracy as a fraud and confirmed what the Islamists had been saying for the better part of the previous decade, that they were the appropriate stewards of a democratic, modern, and secular Turkey. The potential fallout of such a scenario should not be underestimated. Since the founding of the republic, the prestige of the Turkish military has been based in large measure on the officer corps' claim to be a vanguard of modernization. For the Islamists to supplant the officers as the perceived agents of Westernization would not only represent an astonishing irony but also risk a breach with the majority of Turks who overwhelmingly support the political reforms Europe demands. The result would be a significant diminution of the prestige of the officer corps, which would simultaneously enhance that of the civilian leadership, rendering it more difficult for the officers to act autonomously, influence the political arena, or defend the political order.

Ultimately, the commanders chose to consent to certain aspects of the EU reform program in the belief that they could control the process. Between AK's election in 2002 and the EU Commission report in 2004 recommending that Turkey begin accession negotiations, a variety of senior officers made public statements about their country's "special circumstances," suggesting that the EU was making too many demands on Ankara and implying that the reforms should be slowed down.[118] Yet the officers miscalculated the cascade of events resulting from the EU adjustment program that developed beyond their own capacity to manage the political arena. For example, the momentum of the first several reform packages and the external and internal political pressures to continue the process made it more difficult for the officers to subvert or preclude additional reforms—changes to the National Security Council—that significantly diminished, although did not completely undermine, the military's ability to influence, manipulate, or intercede in politics.

It seems clear that although the national security state in Turkey is deeply embedded, European Union demands have forced significant and promising political change in Ankara. The officers do retain features of their autonomy and influence. The General Staff, for example, remains outside the control of the civilian minister of defense, and the officers maintain their almost exclusive prerogatives on promotions and retirements within the officer corps. More importantly, the Internal Service Act (1961), which lays out the service codes of the armed forces, remains intact. Article 35 of the Internal Service Act establishes the basic mission of the Turkish military, which is defense of the republic and the "Turkish Fatherland." Article 85 states that the "Armed Forces shall defend the country against internal as well as external threats, if necessary by force."[119] Given the past patterns of civil-military relations, it may be some time before the officer corps is fully subordinated to the civilian leadership and relinquishes its self-endowed right to intervene in politics, but the changes that the EU's incentives and requirements have wrought have clearly created conditions more conducive to the deepening of democratic practices in Anatolia.

CHAPTER SIX

Toward a Democratic Transition?

Weakening the Patterns of Political Inclusion and Exclusion

The problems of authoritarian stability and democratization in the Middle East have been hotly debated topics among political scientists, historians, and area specialists. The tenor and tone of the scholarly studies on these issues tend to oscillate from expectations prevalent in the early 1990s that the Middle East was on the verge of a democratic breakthrough to the deeply pessimistic commentary of the latter part of the decade. The disparities in analytical optimism suggest that, in part, current events drove these accounts rather than a systematic understanding of authoritarian systems in the Middle East. The close reading of contemporary Egyptian, Algerian, and Turkish politics provides insights into the nature and staying power of authoritarian political orders. Understanding the theoretical concerns behind these cases helps extend the argument beyond Egypt, Algeria, and Turkey. It also suggests approaches useful to policy-oriented analysts who want to know how external actors can promote political change in military-dominated political systems.

Limiting Formal Politics in Authoritarian Systems

Analyses of authoritarian systems often note that these political orders feature *rule by law* as opposed to *rule of law*, which is a central feature of democratic systems. Yet this dichotomy fails to take into account the powerful effect unwritten codes, norms, and principles have on politics, especially through informal institutions. A careful examination of Egyptian, Algerian, and Turkish constitutions past and present reveal many features found in liberal democratic polities. Yet, informal institutions, which are rooted in past practices and balances of power that shape the expectations and behavior of individuals, deprive formal institutions of content and meaning.

Perhaps the best way to illustrate the power of informal institutions is by way of a nonpolitical example. Consider the *seeming* chaos of Cairo traffic. Like in most densely populated cities of the world, Cairo has traffic lights, stop signs, speed limits, and clear rules for passing cars. These formal institutions are almost universally ignored, producing what the uninitiated individual might assume to be nothing short of anarchy. Yet Cairo's drivers know when to go, when to stop, and when to pass based on a set of unwritten, yet widely accepted, norms and principles. Viewed from this perspective, there is order in the mess of Cairo's traffic.

In the same way, informal institutions are critical to regime maintenance for authoritarian elites. When formal mechanisms of control fail to contain political challenges, informal institutions have proven decisive in deflecting, defusing, and undermining these challenges. The power of informal institutions to limit formal politics introduces additional complexity to democratic political change. Formal institutional change that provides for greater freedoms, accountability, and rule of law may indicate democratic development, yet it offers insufficient evidence to draw the conclusion that a given political system has made the transition from authoritarianism to democracy. The substantial institutional changes that Turkey has undertaken since 2002 have clearly made that country more democratic, but the informal institutions of Turkish politics afford the General Staff ample means to influence and, if necessary, to intervene in the political arena.

The debate about Middle East elections following the dramatic gains of the Muslim Brotherhood in Egypt in November 2005 and the victory of the Islamic Resistance Movement (known more commonly by its acronym, HAMAS) in Palestine is oddly ahistorical. Elections have been held regularly in many Middle Eastern countries since the 1970s. These elections are generally staged to fill the seats of national legislatures, which convene regularly and engage in often vigorous debate. Yet these states are neither democratic nor is there any indication that leaders in the Middle East are committed to a democratic future for their societies. Under these circumstances, what accounts for the presence of pseudodemocratic institutions in authoritarian political systems? Why would authoritarian leaders bother staging elections and convening a parliament in the first place? Paradoxically, authoritarian leaders derive political advantages from institutions that look democratic, but that are actually devoid of content and meaning.

The elaborate facades of democracy common to many authoritarian political systems serve two primary purposes: First, they are an integral part of regime defense; second, particularly in the cases of military-dominated regimes, they protect the leadership from involvement in politics and day-to-day governance. On the normative level, the presence of pseudo- or quasidemocratic institutions allows authoritarian leaders to claim that they are living up to their oft-invoked principles about democratic governance with practice. The political theater of Egypt's ruling National Democratic Party's program of "New Thinking and Reform Priorities" and official Algerian statements highlighting the large number of political parties participating in elections are prime examples of the effort on the part of nondemocratic elites to elicit popular support through pseudodemocratic institutions. Elections, parliaments, human rights commissions, and formally independent judiciaries represent some of the principle means through which authoritarian leaders co-opt, deflect, and delegitimize their political opponents.

At the same time that pseudodemocratic institutions are an important component of regime stability, they do pose a certain risk to nondemocratic leaders. Although analysts have never taken the seemingly democratic laws, rules, and regulations of authoritarian regimes very seriously, dedicated counter-elites have. Opposition groups in authoritarian settings have consistently sought to leverage pseudodemocratic institutions to their advantage. In the Egyptian, Algerian, and Turkish stories, this is the friction point between the Islamists and the military establishment that rules but does not govern. The Muslim Brotherhood, Front Islamique du Salut (FIS), and Refah each sought to give content and meaning to institutions that the military and its civilian allies preferred remain hollow. Much has been written about the confrontation between Islamists and defenders of the state in the Muslim world, but that work has generally failed to recognize that what was unfolding was primarily a battle over control of a certain set of state institutions.

An understanding of this political contest highlights another crucial analytic insight from the Egyptian, Algerian, and Turkish cases. Predicting precisely when a military might exercise its influence in the political arena either through coup d'état or some other mechanism is difficult. Prior analyses of militaries and politics contain some general notion of "interests," but they do so without clearly deriving and delineating those interests. The evidence demonstrates, however, that in the case of Egypt, Algeria, and Turkey, the senior command is unwilling to permit opposition groups to gain control of institutions that would pave the way for a fundamental alteration of the military-founded political system.

This realization implies that military-dominated political systems are likely to be stable. That does not mean that ideological battles will not take place in authoritarian systems or that stability implies stasis. The historical record clearly indicates otherwise. Yet even though Turkey initiated multiparty elections in 1946, the Egyptians in 1976, and the Algerians in 1989, it did not indicate a transition to democracy. Moreover, the political agitation in many parts of the Middle East between 2004 and 2006 demonstrates that many in the Arab world want political change. Although these outpourings of popular support for more open and accountable governance may be exhilarating to watch, they tell analysts very little about the stability of the political systems in question.

Even as Arab societies organize to demand more freedom, justice, and, ultimately, dignity, the overarching authoritarian institutions remain intact throughout the Middle East. Although authoritarian leaders have often made changes to these institutions—whether under internal or external pressure—these alterations have never been intended to allow for more democratic politics. Rather, such revisions are only a guise of reform aimed at satisfying some demands for change, while shoring up the authoritarian political system. Analysts will know that democratic change is under way in the Middle East, when, for example, political parties laws actually permit people to organize, national assemblies can exercise oversight, extraconstitutional security courts and laws are abolished, and citizens are endowed with the tools to hold their leaders accountable. Until both the formal and informal mechanisms of political control are razed rather than merely revised, authoritarianism will likely remain a fact of life in the Arab world.

Patterns similar to those in Egypt, Algeria, and Turkey can be found in countries both within and outside the greater Middle East—in Tunisia, where military-security generals dominate; Indonesia, where a former senior military officer is president and the military's subordination to civilian leadership during the presidency of Megawati Sukarnoputri was tenuous; and Pakistan, whose military leader has, since he came to power in a coup d'état in October 1999, consciously sought to replicate some of the key authoritarian institutions and structures of the Turkish Republic. All three states have also encountered difficulties accommodating the demands of Islamist counter-elites and their constituencies for political representation and power. Pakistan, in particular, mirrors the political development in Egypt, Algeria, and Turkey.

The partition of the Indian subcontinent that produced the new state of Pakistan in 1947 had a profound effect on the Muslim officers of the British Indian Army who were to become the leadership of the Pakistani military. Throughout the colonial period, British training emphasized civilian rule and the subordinate position of the military. Although independent Pakistan's military academies and staff colleges did not jettison these principles, the exigencies of building the new state led the officers to revise their understanding of the military's proper role in the Pakistani political system. Pakistan's officers saw themselves as the critical component of modernization and institutionalization, no less state survival. Subsequent socialization of the officer corps emphasized the importance of the armed forces to the country's development and produced a military establishment that saw itself as the "special expression of Pakistan."[1]

Quite like Turkey's officers who seized power in 1961 and 1980, Pakistan's president, General Pervez Musharraf, has sought to enhance the political role of the Pakistani military establishment through constitutional mechanisms. In August 2002, for example, Musharraf issued a Legal Framework Order, which served as the legal apparatus through which he went about altering Pakistan's constitution by fiat. These institutional changes enhanced presidential powers at the expense of the National Assembly. As a result, Musharraf and any future president would have the right to dissolve the legislature, reject the prime minister's nominations to the country's highest courts, and select provincial governors, which endowed the president with the power, albeit indirectly, to dissolve provincial assemblies. The Legal Framework Order also undermined legislative prerogative, as it was used to confer constitutional legitimacy to all acts and decrees of the military government and extended Musharraf's term as president for five years.[2]

In the starkest parallel with the Turkish officer corps, Musharraf established a National Security Council (NSC) that would serve as the primary means for the officers to oversee Pakistani political development. The council comprises the president, the chairman of the Joint Chiefs of Staff, the service chiefs, the prime minister, the leader of the opposition, the speaker of the National Assembly, and the chairman of the Senate. Given the prevailing patterns of civil-military relations in Pakistan, the military dominates this formal advisory body. Moreover, Pakistan's NSC is guided by a purposefully expansive definition of national security that channels the military's influence into "strategic matters pertaining to the sovereignty of the state; and matters relating to democracy, governance and inter-provincial harmony." This provides the military with the legal pretext to exert its influence in arenas outside its professional competence. Parliamentary affairs, national education, and the development of the national economy all fall under the NSC's—and thus the military's—purview.

Pakistan's commanders have developed a network of formal and informal institutions that limits political challenges and ensures the officers' political order. As is the case with Egypt and Algeria, pseudodemocratic institutions are a critical component of the country's military-dominated regime. Groups offering alternative visions of Pakistan's future have sought to advance their agenda through this democratic facade. Similar to Egypt in the 1980s and 1990s, when the political-military leadership entered into an unspoken alliance with the Muslim Brotherhood for the elites' own political ends, General Musharraf tacitly supported an Islamist coalition, the United Action Front, in the 2002 legislative elections. At the time, the president and his fellow officers regarded the Pakistani Muslim League-N, which was affiliated with Musharraf's nemesis Nawaz Sharif, and the Pakistani People's Party as more potent challengers than the Islamists. So long as the Islamists do not threaten the integrity of the system that ensures the predominance of the military establishment, they will remain participants in the political arena.

Overall, the configuration of pseudodemocratic institutions, the power of informal institutions to limit the formal political arena, and the prevailing worldview of the officer corps suggest strongly that Pakistan's military is unlikely to consent to substantive democratic reforms. The policy implications of this insight are fairly straightforward. For those most concerned with Islamabad's ability to be a reliable ally in the war against al-Qa'eda and its affiliated networks, Pakistan's military-dominated political order will likely remain stable. This does not bode well, however, for the other primary component of U.S. policy in the Middle East and South Asia— support for democratic political change.

Breaking the Syndrome of Authoritarian Stability

Turkey's experience beginning in 2002 indicates that the logic of regime stability can be weakened, opening the possibility for the development of more democratic political systems. Although this type of change is ultimately the result of internal political contradictions and problems, the European Union's approach to Turkey was decisive in altering the interests of and constraints on important political actors, helping to make the Turkish transition possible. It is fashionable, particularly among Arab elites, to say that democracy cannot be imposed from the outside, but the lessons of EU-Turkey relations indicate that the United States and France can play a role facilitating conditions more conducive to democratic change in Egypt and Algeria. First, it is important to underscore exactly what is necessary to weaken the logic of regime stability.

What Is Necessary

For almost six years, Egyptians have openly speculated about who might succeed Hosni Mubarak as president. History would suggest that, like Mubarak in 1981, an officer will assume the presidency to fill any future vacancy. Indeed, this is the expectation of a variety of current and former Egyptian officials and analysts. Yet there are persistent rumors that Mubarak has sought to place his son, Gamal, in a position to succeed him. The younger Mubarak has assumed high-profile positions as the assistant secretary-general of the National Democratic Party and the head of the party's policy secretariat, represented his father on overseas trips, and publicly spoken out— albeit ambiguously—on the need for political reform.

If Gamal, who has no military experience, were to take over the presidency, it would represent a crucial institutional change to Egypt's political order. For the first time in the modern era, the military establishment would be separated from the presidency. Obviously, the civilianization of the Egyptian presidency is necessary for democratic change, but it is not sufficient in itself. A civilian president may augur a more politically active and autonomous military. Mubarak's close association with the military has rendered Egypt "coup-proof."[3] Given the influence of the officers, Gamal, or any other civilian who assumed the presidency, would need to cultivate ties to this most important constituency. As a result, a civilian president would be constrained from pursuing policies independent of the military. For example, the officers would likely oppose any reforms or policy shifts that would impinge upon the military's well-developed economic interests or separate Egyptian foreign policy from the Arab consensus. The narrow band through which a civilian would be forced to operate by a more autonomous military would likely only reinforce the logic of regime stability.

Whereas the EU-required reforms have considerably reined in the power and influence of the Turkish General Staff, the relatively untroubled (by Turkish standards) relationship between the officers and the civilian government between 2003 and 2006 also appears to be related to a gentlemen's agreement between Prime Minister Erdoğan and chief of the General Staff Hilmi Özkök. During this time, both men made strenuous efforts to minimize the antagonism between the military and the Islamist government of Adalet ve Kalkinma. Yet the ability to sustain these circumstances was based in part on personality. In August 2006, General Yaşar Büyükanıt replaced Özkök as chief of staff. Under Büyükanıt, who is regarded as a more traditional officer than his predecessor, it is entirely possible that the relationship between the government and the military might become more fractious.

The purpose of highlighting Egypt's "Gamal scenario" and drawing attention to the improved, but still unsettled, state of civil-military relations in Turkey is to underscore how institutional innovations would bridle the military establishment and sufficiently compromise the officers' ability to influence the political arena over the long term. Significant changes are under way in Turkey, and reform may be in the offing in both Egypt and Algeria, but absent institutional controls on the military establishment, the officers in all three settings will likely remain dominant. Moreover, an array of informal institutions—not just a single factor—preserve the power, prestige, and influence of the Egyptian, Algerian, and Turkish officer corps. Although far from an easy task, the likelihood of weakening these unwritten codes and norms over time would be greater if channels through which the military has been able to influence politics were closed; the officers were prevented from engaging in activities not strictly related to defense and national security; the military establishment was bound to the civilian leadership; civilians maintained the means to override the officers; and the prevailing ethos of the officer corps that justifies their influence and intervention was altered.

To use Turkey by way of example, dissociating the military from politics means deepening the Kemalist reformation that began in 2002 and resulted in significant changes to the National Security Council in 2004. Yet to finally resolve the "military question" in Turkey, the following institutional innovations are required:

1. Subordinate the General Staff to a civilian minister of defense regardless of that individual's party affiliation.
2. Empower the Council of State and other parts of the judicial branch with the authority to overrule the Supreme Military Council.
3. Overhaul the internal service codes of the armed forces, which justify the military's intervention in politics.
4. Alter the curricula at military academies and staff colleges to emphasize the supremacy of civilian leadership in policymaking.

All of these points, but particularly three and four, require reinterpretation of several key components of Kemalism—notably those that simultaneously admonish the officers from engaging in politics but justify their guardianship of the political system. Moreover, a reconsideration of Kemalist notions of secularism, citizenship, and the rule of law would also be a vital component of this project. These types of changes would require a sustained national dialogue over many years. Although transforming Turkey's deep-rooted national security state (as well as those of Egypt and Algeria) is a difficult task, these proposed changes can create conditions more favorable to civilian supremacy and improve the chances that the political reform under way will be durable.

What Will Not Work

How can conditions more favorable to institutional change and civilian supremacy develop in Egypt and Algeria? Given its long history of military involvement in politics and recent successful transitions to democracy, Latin America offers a heuristic from which to pursue questions concerning the prospect for democratic change in Egypt and Algeria, as well as enriching the process in Turkey.

It is an overgeneralization to suggest that the Latin American experience has been overwhelmingly positive. While Argentina, Peru, and Chile have institutionalized civilian supremacy, Ecuador, Guatemala, and Venezuela feature some of the same dynamics as the military-dominated states of the Middle East.[4] Moreover, while

Brazil is often—correctly—cited as a positive example of military subordination, President Luiz Inácio Lula da Silva has sought to use the military in a variety of nonnational security-related functions to advance his ambitious social agenda. Nevertheless, as the literature on transitions to and from democracy clearly indicates, cases like Chile, Argentina, Peru, and Brazil underscore the importance of pacts and "democracy with guarantees" as the appropriate means to bring autonomous military establishments to heel.

While these arrangements have had relatively positive results in Latin American states, they may be less relevant to the Middle East. In military-dominated states such as Egypt and Algeria, the officers either seem impervious to pacts or partake in implicit pacts that essentially preserve the influence and prestige of the military. This is not to suggest that pacts that constrain the power of the officers are impossible in these settings but rather that under current conditions the military establishments of Egypt, Algeria, or Turkey have not been compelled to seek such arrangements. Indeed, the Algerian officer corps rejected the St. Egidio agreement, which contained the basic building blocks of a pact, in 1995 because it would have recognized the FIS as a legal party. In Egypt and Turkey there are implicit pacts including officer recognition of the importance of Islamist social activism and the acceptability of certain kinds of Islamist political activity. Chapter 4 emphasizes the implicit pacts the Egyptian leadership entered with the Muslim Brotherhood in the early 1970s and once again in the early 1980s. Egypt's Islamists were accorded wide latitude in the cultural, educational, and social spheres so long as they made no effort to accumulate political power. Of course, once the Brotherhood violated the terms of this implicit pact, they were repressed.

What has historically distinguished Egypt, Algeria, and Turkey from Latin America is the officers' determination *not* to be directly involved in day-to-day politics and governance. This insulates commanders from the consequences of a given government's mistakes and provides the military establishment with a greater margin for error when forced to manage the political arena. In Chile, Argentina, and Brazil the officers' involvement in politics and governance corroded the cohesion of the military establishments. In addition, poor economic management—with the exception of Chile—and ongoing repression further undermined military rule. The combination of these factors provided incentives for the officers to seek ways to remove themselves from the political arena, as long as their interests were ensured. These pressures were particularly acute in Argentina after the military junta was discredited in the aftermath of the Falkland/Malvinas defeat. To be sure, the Egyptian armed forces also suffered a crushing defeat in June 1967, but there is an important difference between Egypt and Argentina. Although Israel's victory stirred popular protests against Nasser and the Egyptian government, the exigencies associated with Israel's occupation of the Sinai made the military indispensable and thus a demilitarization of Egypt impossible. The success of the armed forces in crossing the Suez Canal and bloodying the Israeli Defense Forces in October 1973 significantly restored the prestige of the Egyptian military.

Civilian supremacy over the military has also developed in the wake of major domestic upheaval. Prior to the fall of the Shah, the Iranian officer corps exhibited similar features to their contemporary counterparts in Egypt, Algeria, and Turkey— prestige, prerogatives in policy areas not strictly related to national security and defense, and ultimate responsibility for the defense of the regime. Yet years of the Shah's meddling in the military's affairs to ensure against a coup so compromised the cohesion and professionalism of the officer corps that the military could not act decisively and with a sense of purpose even during a period of grave crisis. After the Shah departed Iran in early 1979, the military establishment was left adrift and was unable to preserve the regime.[5] After rounds of purges, the remnants of the Iranian military who once answered to the royal court became subordinate to Iran's *mullahs*. There is little reason to believe that the Egyptian, Algerian, and Turkish armed forces would collapse in moments of crisis, however. The senior commanders of all three militaries have worked assiduously to prevent civilian interference and have demonstrated an ability to act coherently, decisively, and autonomously when they perceive danger to their regimes.

To be sure, pacts or the deterioration of the coherence of the armed forces are entirely plausible in the Egyptian, Algerian, and Turkish contexts. The pacted transitions of Latin America and the disintegration of Iran's imperial armed forces were arguably the consequences of errors, which, in the former cases encouraged military officers to seek a way out of the political arena and in the latter caused the military to collapse. Still, building theories based on the prospects that at some point military officers will make a mistake offers little that is helpful to understanding the conditions under which authoritarian systems unravel. For policymakers, waiting for officers to make an error or for some event to precipitate the collapse of the military leadership is no policy at all and may be detrimental to securing vital national interests.

The Limits of Civil Society, Economic Development, and Punitive Policies

Promotion of democracy in the Middle East by the United States—when it has been done at all—has been too focused on building civil society, the alleged transformative effects of economic development, and punitive measures. Democracy in the

Middle East is unlikely to hinge, as it seems to have done in Eastern Europe, on the activities of civil society organizations and activists. U.S. policymakers and analysts express a particular Tocquevillian view of civil society as an agglomeration of private, voluntary organizations that have the capacity to assert the rights of individuals and groups, but there is a less heroic perspective on civil society that emerges from Antonio Gramsci's writing in *The Prison Notebooks*. As noted in Chapter 1, Gramsci viewed civil society as an outer perimeter of defense for a hegemonic state. In the context of the support civil society groups gave the Algerian military when the officers nullified the FIS electoral victory in 1992 or the cooperation between labor unions and the state in countries such as Tunisia and Egypt, his insight seems more accurate. Moreover, Gramsci scoffed at the notion that the state would permit itself to be willfully disarmed. Of course, civil society organizations in the Middle East provide important services to people in need, but both the nature of civil society and the extreme circumstances under which they operate make it unlikely that these groups will be a linchpin of democratic development. U.S. policy aimed at promoting and strengthening civil society seems misplaced.

Along with this faith in the power of civil society, much of U.S. democratization policy in the Middle East rests on the erroneous belief that economic development inexorably leads to progressive political development. Whereas economic development *correlates* with democracy, it does not *cause* democracy.[6] Nevertheless, the Partnership for Progress and a Common Future with the Region of the Broader Middle East and North Africa (a G8 initiative that was launched in 2004 to promote political change in the Arab world), the Middle East Partnership Initiative, and a variety of U.S. Agency for International Development programs are predicated on the assumption that economic development produces new entrepreneurs, who will subsequently demand greater political openness because liberal polities are superior environments in which to pursue their business activities.

This dynamic has not occurred in the Middle East. When Arab leaders have pursued policies to alter their economies—for example Egypt's much vaunted *infitah* (opening) of the late 1970s or Algeria's version of the same in the 1980s—the result has been the liberalization of the economy without the institutionalization of market economies or the emergence of democracy. While economic development has given rise to new classes of entrepreneurs, these individuals have not demanded democracy. The companies and individual members of various Arab Chambers of Commerce and regional business councils, for example, operate within the ambit of the Egyptian and other Arab states. As a result, these businessmen have been easily co-opted because their fortunes remain tied to the state, which continues to be the primary economic actor in many Arab countries. This pattern illuminates how difficult a transition to democracy may be even in situations where economic development has been relatively successful, casting doubt on common claims that economic growth is a prerequisite of political change.[7]

Washington has also employed a range of punitive measures in the region to force change. Libya, Iran, and, of course, Iraq were subject to military, economic, and diplomatic sanctions in an effort to contain these rogue regimes and, it was hoped, to compel Muammar Qadhafi, various Iranian leaders, and Saddam Hussein to alter their behavior. Although sanctions were generally successful in containing these leaders, there is no evidence that this policy lever compelled the Libyans, Iranians, or Iraqis to pursue more responsible foreign policies or open up their domestic politics. The overall record indicates that sanctions tend to be counter-productive. Saddam Hussein was particularly adept at manipulating nationalist sentiment to resist this type of external pressure and interference. Given the sanctions' spotty record in coercing political change, there is little reason to anticipate that the Syria Accountability Act (2004) will be effective in encouraging Syrian President Bashar al-Asad to end his support for Hizballah, renounce Syria's quest for weapons of mass destruction or, in the interests of political reform, dismantle the national security state he inherited from his father.

Of course, the ultimate punitive policy instrument is war. As its codename suggests, Operation Iraqi Freedom was intended, in part, to foster democracy in Iraq and by extension the Middle East. Although the January 30, 2005, Iraqi elections provided momentum for grassroots demands for change in the Arab world, it is unlikely that the "new Iraq" will be a catalyst for political liberalization and democracy in the region. Regardless of the outcome of the political process in Iraq, few in the Middle East believe that the U.S. invasion and subsequent nation-building project is a model for democratic development.

Since the Middle East became the focus of U.S. foreign policy in 2001, even Washington's regional friends have come under increased scrutiny. Along with the Syria Accountability Act, Congress has sought to pressure countries like Egypt and Saudi Arabia to pursue political reform. The Lantos amendment to the fiscal year 2005 Foreign Operations Appropriations Act—named for its sponsor Rep. Tom Lantos (D-CA), who heads the Congressional Human Rights Caucus—proposed a 25 percent reduction in military assistance to Cairo, shifting that money to economic support.[8] Lantos argued that Egypt confronts no significant military threat and U.S. funding would better serve the Egyptian people through economic development and political reform. Although the reasoning behind the proposal was sound, the amendment caused an uproar in Cairo as Hosni Mubarak's government portrayed the proposal as a "cut" in U.S. aid designed to weaken the country, thereby manipulating nationalist sentiment and mobilizing resentment toward the United States. Clearly, the United States and other countries need a fresh strategy to promote democracy in the Middle East beyond promoting civil society, economic development, and the application of sanctions to modify behavior.

Not a Turkish Model, but an EU-Turkey Model

Chapter 5 explains how the European Union's accession requirements have proven decisive in creating the conditions under which Turkish soldiers have taken at least one boot out of the political arena. The overwhelming public support for EU membership in Turkey placed the officers in a quandary. For fear of losing their longstanding prestige among the public, the officers were unable to either oppose or control institutional changes that diminished their capacity to intervene in politics. There is an opportunity for U.S. and French policymakers to learn lessons from the European Union. To be sure, unlike the EU's Turkish project, neither the United States nor France would want to offer Egypt and Algeria membership in their own exclusive clubs. The French attempted to incorporate Algeria into France between 1830 and 1962 with disastrous consequences for both countries. While the push-pull dynamic between Brussels and Ankara is quite different from Washington and Cairo or Paris and Algiers, the substance of the EU's approach—based almost exclusively on incentives—is integral to the Turkish program of reform. Although the durability of Ankara's recent political liberalization remains to be seen, the country's current evolution is directly linked to its aspirations for EU membership.[9] Considered from this perspective, Turkey itself is less a model for the Arab states than EU-Turkey relations are for U.S. or French officials interested in democracy promotion.[10]

The combination of clear political benchmarks combined with incentives is a potent force that can alter interests and impose new constraints on important political actors. The United States, France, and others should pursue a policy of "conditionality" in an effort to promote political change among their strategic allies. Scholars working in the field of international political economy and experts on foreign aid tend to believe that conditionality's effect is limited. In fact, the international political economy literature finds that World Bank conditionality has been generally more effective in promoting economic reform than in encouraging political liberalization. This theme is taken up in the research on foreign aid. Thomas Carothers, for example, argues that foreign aid only succeeds in promoting reform if governments are already receptive to undertaking political and economic change, implying that conditionality is a weak method of altering the incentives of state elites. Yet Carothers, Gordon Crawford, Olav Stokke, and others emphasize the punitive aspects of conditionality, in which extreme asymmetries are exploited to achieve a particular outcome by denying recipients aid.[11] There may be no getting around the imbalance of power between donor states and recipients, but this problem could be ameliorated if aid is structured as an incentive. After all, Libya's decision to relinquish its weapons of mass destruction program in 2003–2004 was based, in part, on incentives, as was Ukraine's decision to abandon the nuclear weapons it had inherited from the Soviet Union in the early 1990s.

Given the importance of U.S. largesse to both Egypt's economic and military modernization, changes to the way these funds are dispersed can make aid to Cairo a significant lever to encourage reform. Cairo receives an annual contribution of $1.3 billion from the United States earmarked for the operation and modernization of Egypt's military and an additional $450 million in economic support funds, with no reciprocal commitment from Egypt to the United States. An incentive-based approach would work differently. Washington could actually offer up to $2.3 billion in military aid. In keeping with current policy, the first $1.3 billion would *not* be subject to any conditions. Egypt's access to an additional billion dollars would be based on Cairo's willingness to embrace a range of institutional reforms that would result in greater transparency, government accountability, political inclusion, and individual liberties. On the economic side of the ledger, the United States would offer the Egyptians an additional $500 million. Access to this aid would require reform of laws governing foreign investment and banking as well as change in trade and monetary policy.

The question remains, however, whether the Egyptians would be willing to accept such an arrangement, especially if the core of their approximately $2 billion aid package remained intact. Just as the decision to accede to the Copenhagen criteria was ultimately up to the Turks, the same is true for Egypt's leadership and the prospect of additional U.S. aid. Washington's financial assistance to Cairo, when adjusted for inflation, has actually decreased by more than half since 1979, so the Egyptians might find the incentive of additional money too difficult to resist, especially as U.S. funding is the critical component of Egypt's ongoing program of military modernization. Not only would the potential infusion of $1.5 billion rebalance Egypt's overall aid package and return this assistance to its original level, but it would also have the added political benefit of bringing Egypt's aid closer to parity with Israel, which receives a base of $3 billion from the United States.

Adding incentives to the U.S.-Egypt relationship would have the benefit of placing constraints on the military through the revision of the very institutions that reflect the power and influence of the military establishment. To be sure, Washington would be giving the Egyptian armed forces *additional* aid, but it would be concomitantly requiring that the military submit to fundamental political change. For its part, additional economic aid holds the potential to alter the interests of Egypt's business community—a thoroughly co-opted constituency of the country's leadership. The removal of trade barriers, changes to banking and investment laws, rationalization of subsidies, and a meaningful commitment to privatization could be undertaken in exchange for supplemental economic assistance that would slash public debt, reduce unemployment, and open the national economy to the global marketplace. Business elites would thus no longer be obliged to the Egyptian state for their livelihoods, increasing the possibility that they would, in turn, demand additional reforms to reinforce economic as well as political change: rule of law, anticorruption measures, and transparency in government decision-making.

Finally, an incentive-based approach to Egypt would highlight some of the contradictions and problems of the regime. In the month prior to the 1999 presidential election, Egypt's cities and towns were festooned with banners imploring citizens to vote yes for President Mubarak, "*min agli-l-istiqrar w-al tanmiya*" (for the sake of stability and development). This phrase is emblematic of the Mubarak era in which the president and successive governments have promised the public that stability would lead to prosperity. In addition, the National Democratic Party often invokes its goals of "deepening and strengthening democracy."[12] Yet the political system has delivered political and economic stagnation rather than prosperity and democracy.

In the same way that the Turkish military's long-standing public support for modernization and democratization would have been fatally compromised in the eyes of average Turks had the officers actively opposed the Copenhagen criteria, Egypt's leadership would confront a similarly stark choice if it rejected Washington's incentives. Public opinion has always mattered more in the Turkish context than in Egyptian politics, and the image of the United States in Egypt pales in comparison to the relative popularity of EU membership in Turkey; that said, Cairo is not impervious to U.S. policy or to public opinion. In response to the intersection of internal political pressure and Washington's rhetorical emphasis on democracy in the Middle East, beginning in 2003, President Mubarak sought to position himself as a reformer overseeing a reformist government. To reject Washington's incentive-based approach would further confirm that the chasm between the Egyptian government's principles and its practice remains wide and that the military-political leadership has little intention of reducing this gap—something that average Egyptians already suspect.

The empirical evidence indicates that the military establishments of Egypt, Algeria, and Turkey (until 2002–2004) have been adept at ensuring the integrity of their regimes. Yet countries with authoritarian political systems are not necessarily fated to manifest nondemocratic politics in perpetuity—forever is, after all, a long time. The

European Union's relationship with Turkey and the potential of incentive-based approaches to democracy promotion in Egypt and other nondemocratic systems suggest that the pathological stability of authoritarian politics can be unraveled. In the cases of Egypt and Algeria, the political will of external actors to pursue "positive conditionality" is critical to forging democratic transformation. The promise of incentive-based approaches to reform requires additional research, but it may be a more productive area of inquiry than past analyses that place emphasis on civil society, economic development, or punitive approaches to nondemocratic states.

Conclusion

Prior scholarly work on Egyptian, Algerian, and Turkish politics underestimates the stability of these regimes because analysts tended either to overlook the complex and dynamic relationship of relatively autonomous military establishments to these political systems or misconstrued the role of the officer corps. Although the claims of the modernization paradigm were disconfirmed more than two decades ago, there is a tendency among analysts to see "genuine democratization" in what are essentially tactical liberalizations and modifications of authoritarian political orders. Certainly, the emergence of multiparty presidential elections in Egypt or the relatively free and fair conduct of elections in Algeria are noteworthy developments. It is also crucial to understand, however, that such developments are reversible and are often undertaken primarily to benefit nondemocratic elites seeking to improve the legitimacy and efficiency of the prevailing system. Rather than elections, the relative relaxation of police powers, or the number of demonstrators in the streets, institutional changes that weaken the formal instruments of political control—along the lines of Turkey's reforms that began in 2002—are a more accurate indicator that a transition from authoritarianism is under way. Yet even then it would be premature to declare that a country is firmly on an irreversible democratic trajectory given the importance of informal institutions.

The Turkish transition highlights how external actors can nurture a political environment more conducive to peaceful, democratic change. It is unfashionable in the Middle East to acknowledge publicly the importance of external actors for fear this may be construed as an effort to impose democracy from abroad. However, the United States and other interested outside parties, such as the French in Algeria, can use a combination of incentives and political benchmarks to encourage a democratic transition. Without an external catalyst for change it is likely that familiar patterns of authoritarian politics will endure in military-dominated states like Egypt and Algeria.

One • A Logic of Regime Stability

1. The exception, of course, is Iran. The Iranian revolution replaced an authoritarian regime, which was based on the legitimacy of Pahlavi rule and Iranian nationalism, with a very different type of authoritarian order based on religious messianism.

2. Perhaps the best way to think about stability is through a metaphor: Stability is the range of oscillation around a center and/or the frequency of a wave. Though extremes may occur on either end of each wave, events predictably return to the center line.

3. See Eva Bellin, "The Robustness of Authoritarianism in the Middle East: Exceptionalism in Comparative Politics," *Comparative Politics* 36, no. 2 (January 2004): 139–158.

4. Samuel P. Huntington, *Political Order in Changing Societies* (New Haven: Yale University Press, 1968), 4.

5. Ergun Özbudun, *Contemporary Turkish Politics: The Challenges to Democratic Consolidation* (Boulder: Lynne Rienner Publishers, 2000).

6. David Collier and Ruth Berins Collier, *Shaping the Political Arena* (Princeton: Princeton University Press, 1991), chap. 1; Paul Pierson, "Increasing Returns, Path Dependence, and the Study of Politics," *American Political Science Review* 94, no. 2 (June 2000): 251–267; Peter A. Hall and Rosemary C. R. Taylor, "Political Science and the Three Institutionalisms," *Political Studies* 54 (1996): 941.

7. George Tsebelis argues persuasively that institutions result from the conscious choice of individuals who determine that previous institutions did not serve their interests. See Tsebelis, *Nested Games: Rational Choice in Comparative Politics* (Berkeley: University of California Press, 1990).

8. Kiren Aziz Chaudhry, *The Price of Wealth: Economies and Institutions in the Middle East* (Ithaca: Cornell University Press, 1997).

9. Douglass C. North, *Structure and Change in Economic History* (New York: Norton, 1981); Douglass C. North and Barry R. Weingast, "Constitutions and Commitment: The Evolution of Institutions Governing Public Choice in Seventeenth Century England," *Journal of Economic History* 59, no. 4 (December 1989): 803–832; Margaret Levi, *Of Rule and Revenue* (Berkeley: University of California Press, 1988).

10. Peter A. Hall and Rosemary C. R. Taylor, "Political Science and the Three Institutionalisms," *Political Studies* 54 (1996): 936–957.

11. Turkey did enact reforms in 1995 and 2001, but the thoroughgoing transformation of the political system did not begin until 2002.

12. Juan J. Linz and Alfred Stepan, *Problems of Democratic Transition and Consolidation* (Baltimore: Johns Hopkins University Press, 1996).

13. Denis J. Sullivan and Sana Abed-Kotob, *Islam in Contemporary Egypt: Civil Society vs. the State* (Boulder: Lynne Rienner Publishers, 1999), 24; Jenny B. White, *Islamist Mobilization in Turkey: A Study in Vernacular Politics* (Seattle: University of Washington Press, 2002), 205.

14. See www.confinesociales.org/directorio.

15. Ellis Goldberg, "Why Isn't There More Democracy in the Middle East?" *Contention* 5, no. 2 (winter 1996): 145.

16. Claude E. Welch Jr. "Military Disengagement from Politics: Paradigms, Processes, or Random Events," *Armed Forces and Society* 18, no. 3 (spring 1992): 323; see also Larry Diamond and Marc F. Plattner, eds., *Civil-Military Relations and Democracy* (Baltimore: Johns Hopkins University Press, 1996); David R. Mares, ed., *Civil-Military Relations: Building Democracy and Regional Security in Latin America, Southern Asia, and Central Europe* (Boulder: Westview Press, 1998); Rebecca Schiff, "Concordance Theory: The Cases of India and Pakistan," in *Civil-Military Relations: Building Democracy and Regional Security in Latin America*, ed. David R. Mares (Boulder: Westview Press, 1998), 27–44.

17. For a complete discussion of civil-military relations in several important Latin American countries, see J. Samuel Fitch, *The Armed Forces and Democracy in Latin America* (Baltimore: Johns Hopkins University Press, 1998).

18. Peter D. Feaver, "The Civil-Military Problematique: Huntington, Janowitz, and the Question of Civil Control," *Armed Forces and Society* 23, no. 2 (winter 1996): 154.

19. Clement Henry Moore, *Politics in North Africa: Algeria, Morocco, and Tunisia* (Boston: Little, Brown, 1970).

20. The definitive work on the Muslim Brotherhood remains Richard P. Mitchell's *The Society of Muslim Brothers* (New York: Oxford University Press, 1969). Also see Hadi Ragheb Awdah and Hasanayn Tawfik Ibrahim, *The Muslim Brotherhood and Politics in Egypt* (in Arabic) (Cairo: Mahroussa Center for Research, Training and Publishing, 1996); Sana Abed-Kotob, "The Accommodationists Speak: Goals and Strategies of the Muslim Brotherhood in Egypt," *International Journal of Middle East Studies* 27 (1995): 321–339; Raymond William Baker, "Afraid for Islam: Egypt's Muslim Centrists between Pharaohs and Fundamentalists," *Daedalus* (summer 1991): 41–68; Hasan Hanafi, "The Relevance of the Islamic Alternative in Egypt," *Arab Studies Quarterly* 4, no. 1–2 (spring 1982): 54–74.

Two • *The Egyptian, Algerian, and Turkish Military Enclaves*

1. Reinhard Bendix, *Nation-Building and Citizenship* (Berkeley: University of California Press, 1977).

2. See, for example, Manfred Halpern, *The Politics of Social Change in the Middle East and North Africa* (Princeton: Princeton University Press, 1963); Lucian W. Pye, "Armies in the Process of Political Modernization," in *The Role of the Military in Underdeveloped Countries*, ed.

John J. Johnson (Princeton: Princeton University Press, 1962), 69–89; and Edward Shils, "The Military in the Political Development of New States," in ibid., 7–67.

3. S. E. Finer, writing in 1962, was more cautious than his colleagues about the role military forces could play in these critical areas. Finer cautioned that the military "lacked . . . title to govern." For his part, Samuel Huntington seemed to share Finer's apprehensions but nevertheless recognized that the military was superbly placed to provide for order and economic development. See S. E. Finer, *The Man on Horseback: The Role of the Military in Politics* (London: Pall Mall Press, 1962), and Samuel P. Huntington, *Political Order in Changing Societies* (New Haven: Yale University Press, 1968).

4. Throughout the text the term *military enclave* will be used interchangeably with *military establishment, officers,* and *military.*

5. James C. Scott, *Seeing Like a State: How Certain Schemes to Improve the Human Condition Have Failed* (New Haven: Yale University Press, 1998), 87–102.

6. John Waterbury, *The Egypt of Nasser and Sadat: The Political Economy of Two Regimes* (Princeton: Princeton University Press, 1983), xv.

7. Ümit Cizre Sakallioğlu, "The Anatomy of the Turkish Military's Political Autonomy," *Comparative Politics* 29, no. 2 (January 1997): 151–166.

8. Quandt states: "The army's motives in intervening are apparent on one level. They were protecting their institutional prerogatives, throwing over an unpopular president to survive. The senior officers were protecting a comfortable way of life as well, since many had gotten rich from power." He cautions against underestimating the officers' nationalist sentiment, which was also a primary factor in their decision to nullify the elections of 1991 and oust Chadli. See William B. Quandt, *Between Ballots and Bullets: Algeria's Transition from Authoritarianism* (Washington, DC: Brookings Institution, 1998), 61.

9. See, for example, John Waterbury, "A Note on Egypt: 1973," American Universities Field Staff Report 18, no. 4; William Hale, *Turkish Politics and the Military* (New York: Routledge, 1994); Bradford L. Dillman, *State and Private Sector in Algeria: The Politics of Rent-seeking and Failed Development* (Boulder: Westview Press, 2000).

10. Interview, Ankara, May 1, 2000.

11. This was not always the case, however. In January 1977, faced with widespread demonstrations and violence in response to an IMF-sponsored plan that removed subsidies for basic goods, Egyptian president Anwar Sadat called on the military to quell the growing disturbances. Egypt's senior command refused to do so until Sadat reversed the policy.

12. Interview with U.S. government officials, Cairo, September 27, 1999; see Robert Springborg, *Mubarak's Egypt: Fragmentation of the Political Order* (Boulder: Westview Press, 1989), 104–118; and Robert Springborg, "The President and the Field Marshal: Civil-Military Relations in Egypt Today," *Middle East Report* (July-August 1987): 5–16.

13. Interview with a former employee of the Central Auditing Organization, Cairo, January 12, 2000.

14. Interview with Egyptian military officers, Cairo, September 24, 2004.

15. *Maghreb Confidentiel,* October 16, 1997, cited in Bradford L. Dillman, *State and Private Sector in Algeria: The Politics of Rent-seeking and Failed Development* (Boulder: Westview Press, 2000), 95.

16. Dillman, *State and Private Sector,* 3.

17. "IMF Concludes 2004 Article IV Consultation with Algeria," *Public Information Notice* 5/10 (Washington, DC: International Monetary Fund, January 28, 2005).

18. The officers who deposed the Menderes government in 1960 were motivated, in part, by downward pressure on their salaries. Although Turkish commanders have parlayed their positions into lucrative jobs in the private sector after retirement or leveraged commissions from the private sector, the rampant corruption and venal pursuit of wealth that has become a problem among officers in Egypt and Algeria is largely alien to members of Turkey's military elite.

19. Gerassimos Karabelias sums up the relationship between the Turkish military and the economy well: "Their [the Turkish Armed Forces'] economic activities have assisted not only in increasing the degree of the political and financial autonomy of the officer corps from the civilian government but also in developing closer, direct ties between the military establishment and leading industrialists both in Turkey (e.g., Koç, Eczacıbaşı, and Sabancı Holdings) as well as abroad (e.g., American, German, French, Israeli and Russian military and high-tech companies)." See Gerassimos Karabelias, "The Evolution of Civil-Military Relations in Post-War Turkey, 1980–95," *Middle Eastern Studies* 35, no. 4 (October 1999): 140–141.

20. Lale Sariibrahimoğlu, "At the Crossroads," *Jane's Defence Weekly* 42, no. 21 (May 25, 2005): 22–29.

21. Haras Jumhuriya, Jandarma, Western Study Group, Village Guards, Sécurité Militaire (SM), and Centre de Commandement de la Lutte Antisubversive to name just a few.

22. Murat Aydin, "6th EU Adaptation Package Forwarded to Prime Ministry," *Zaman*, May 23, 2003, www.zaman.com/default.php?kn=2334.

23. See General Ahmed Fahkr, "Speculation about the Egyptian Military and Conflict Management: Strategic Goals of the Egyptian Armed Forces," (in Arabic), *al-Gumhuriya*, January 20, 1985; interview with President Hosni Mubarak, *al-Ahram*, July 3, 1986 (Cairo: State Information Service); General Ahmed Fahkr, "Hot Topic of the Summer: The Egyptian Military Budget," (in Arabic), *al-Ahram*, July 25, 1986.

24. Lahouari Addi, "Algeria's Army, Algeria's Agony," *Foreign Affairs* 77, no. 4 (July–August 1998): 49.

25. Yahia H. Zoubir, "Algerian-Moroccan Relations and their Impact on Maghribi Integration," *Journal of North African Studies* 5, no. 3 (autumn 2000): 47.

26. The Civil Harmony Law went into effect after it passed in a referendum on September 16, 1999, and expired on January 13, 2000. In the intervening four months, Islamist activists not involved in terrorist activities in Algeria were granted a general amnesty while those who were involved in violence and turned themselves in to authorities were treated with leniency.

27. "The Return of Uneasy Tranquility," *Economist*, March 11, 2000.

28. Interview with a former senior Turkish official, Ankara, June 6, 2000. At first blush, the controversy surrounding the deployment of U.S. troops to Turkey to take part in Operation Iraqi Freedom in March 2003 weakens this claim. Yet expectations that the officers would support the United States in Iraq were based on erroneous assumptions about how the officers viewed Iraq, neglect of Turkish history, and a misapprehension of domestic Turkish politics. Not unlike the first Gulf war, Turkey's senior command was decidedly ambivalent about an invasion of Iraq. Risk averse, committed to Atatürk's maxim "peace at home, peace in the world," Turkish officers have been seized with the prospect of chaos on their southern border. They are particularly

concerned that an autonomous or potentially independent Iraqi Kurdistan would fuel nationalist agitation in Turkey's own Kurdish region neighboring Iraq. As a result, the status quo in Iraq
was not unduly disturbing to Turkish commanders. Moreover, the officers did not signal their
preferences prior to the March 8, 2003, vote on U.S. troop deployment because the officers stood
to gain regardless of the outcome. If the vote was positive, then the military would have benefited
from an enhanced relationship with the United States both militarily and financially. If the
officers did not intervene and parliament voted against U.S. troop deployment (as was the case),
two purposes would be served: (1) The officers could not be accused of interfering in the political
process—an issue that had stung the military just prior to the European Union's December 2002
meeting in Copenhagen during which the Turks failed to receive a date for accession negotiations, in part due to the role of the military; (2) a negative vote would, the officers calculated,
weaken the Islamist-based government of Prime Minister Recep Tayyip Erdoğan, who had
promised the United States a positive outcome. As the Iraq war unfolded, the United States grew
closer to Iraqi Kurdish factions, the Turkish economy suffered a temporary setback without the
prospect of massive U.S. aid, other U.S. allies were winning Washington's praise, and Erdoğan's
government faced criticism in Ankara as well as Washington.

29. M. Hakan Yavuz, "Cleansing Islam from the Public Sphere," *Journal of International
Affairs* 54, no. 1 (fall 2000): 36.

30. The EU Commission's "Regular Report on Turkey's Progress towards Accession," 1998–
2001, pointed to the problematic nature of civil-military relations in Turkey. Since changes to the
structure of the MGK, the EU has softened its criticism in this area, but it has noted the continuing influence of the officers. The commission's 2004 report, which ultimately recommended
that Turkey be given a date for membership negations, identified a number of ways the Turkish
military continued to influence the political arena.

31. Interview with a retired Egyptian military officer, Cairo, November 8, 1999.

32. There is no database on the use of Supreme State Security Court (not to be confused
with the State Security Court, which was abolished in 2003) and military tribunals to prosecute
individuals advocating for political reform. Yet there is no lack of evidence that this court has
been systematically used against the regime's political opponents. The most well-known of
these cases was the detention and trial of Saad Eddin Ibrahim and the staff of the Ibn Khaldun
Center for Development Studies over their advocacy for clean elections and greater respect for
human rights. The leader of the Egyptian Organization for Human Rights, Hafez Abu Sadeh,
went into exile in Paris for several years to avoid prosecution in the Supreme State Security
Court. In 2002 alone, 300 members of the Muslim Brotherhood were arrested and referred to
this court, although most were released after varying periods of detention. However, in July of
that year, a military tribunal handed down sentences ranging from three to five years for an
additional 22 members of the Brotherhood who had been arrested in 2001. For a detailed
discussion, see "Egypt: Country Report on Human Rights Practices—2002," www.state.gov/
g/drl/rls/hrrpt/2002/18274.htm.

33. Recalling the period immediately following Algerian independence, one former Algerian officer stated: "Colonel Boumediène placed himself voluntarily behind Ahmed Ben Bella
who was placed in the presidency, always guarding the means of real power [in Algeria], that is
the Army." See General Yahya Rahal, *History of Power—A Testimony* (in French) (Algiers:
Casbah Editions, 1997), 153–154.

34. Minister of Defense Khaled Nezzar indicated in the early 1990s that the Algerian military supported democracy as long as a "just mean" was established in the National Assembly (i.e. an arrangement in which no single party could wield significant power). Quoted in Robert Mortimer, "Islamists, Soldiers, and Democrats: The Second Algerian War," *Middle East Journal* 50, no. 1 (winter 1996): 21.

35. Hugh Roberts, "From Radical Mission to Equivocal Ambition: The Expansion and Manipulation of Algerian Islamism, 1979–1992," in Martin E. Marty and R. Scott Appleby, *Accounting for Fundamentalisms: The Dynamic Character of Movements* (Chicago: University of Chicago Press, 1994): 438.

36. The 1961 legislative elections—the first balloting after the 1960 coup—produced a victory for the newly formed Justice Party. Even though the party's personnel and leadership bore a distinct resemblance to the outlawed Demokrats, the military leadership permitted Justice to come to power. In 1983, the junta that had ruled Turkey for the previous three years publicly indicated its preference for the National Democracy Party under the leadership of Turgut Sünalp, a retired general. Nevertheless, when Turgut Özal's Motherland Party won a parliamentary majority, the officers honored the results. Four years later the officers did not interfere in a national referendum, which allowed Bülent Ecevit, Süleyman Demirel, Alparslan Türkeş, and Necmettin Erbakan to return to politics. The military had banned these politicians from the Turkish political arena for life in the aftermath of the 1980 coup.

37. Interview with a Turkish military officer, Washington, DC, March 5, 2002; interview with a Turkish military officer, Ankara, July 5, 2000.

38. See, for example, address delivered by President Hosni Mubarak on the Occasion of the 50th Anniversary of the 1952 Revolution, www.presidency.gov.eg/html/22-July2002_Speech .html; Gamal Kamal, "Mubarak Visits the Tomb of the Unknown Soldier, Reads the Sura on the Spirits of Sadat and Abd al-Nasser; The President to Members of the Supreme Military Council 'Comprehensive Power' Requires a Powerful Armed Forces; Field Marshal Tantawi 'We Will Not Forget Our Role . . . in Achieving the Victory'" (in Arabic), *al-Gumhurriya,* October 6, 1999; "Field Marshal Hussein Tantawi in a Conversation on 'Good Morning Egypt,'" (in Arabic), *al-Gumhurriya,* October 6, 1995; "Our Policy is Maintenance of Military Strength, Protection of National Sovereignty, Preservation of Peace" (interview with Defense Minister Yusef Sabri Abu Talib, in Arabic), *al-Ahram,* October 5, 1989; and address delivered by President Hosni Mubarak on the Occasion of the 34th Anniversary of the July Revolution, July 23, 1986 (Cairo: State Information Service).

39. In September 1963, *el-Djeich* declared, "It was in the fierce combat of the Algerian people against the oppression of the foreign regime in which the army of the national revolution was born. It is thus the Army of National Liberation." In an article titled "19 March 1962: Victory of the Revolution and of the People," the military's monthly magazine reminded Algerians: "A glorious result of the war of liberation that began on the 1st of November 1954 by the FLN and its lance, the ALN; the date of 19 March 1962 signifies the triumph of the army's battle for national independence, justice, and liberty," *el-Djeich,* March 1970. And on the anniversary of the revolution in 1975, the military proclaimed, "The ANP (Armée Nationale Populaire), heir to our glorious ALN is renewing the flame of the 1st of November 1954 for the battle of building the nation," *el-Djeich,* November 1975. These examples illustrate the type of nationalist rhetoric Algeria's military enclave employed in *el-Djeich* in the period between 1963 and 1985. In 1986, the

magazine was no longer published for public consumption, but this should not imply that public acceptance of the officers' nationalist narrative was no longer important or needed. Instead, *el-Djeich*'s editorials on significant issues of the day, which are invariably laced with nationalist discourse, have been routinely reprinted in Algeria's newspapers, particularly the daily *el-Watan*.

40. Abdelkader Yefsah, *The Process of Legitimation of Military Power and the Construction of the State in Algeria* (in French) (Paris: Éditions Anthropos, 1982), 106; John Ruedy, *Modern Algeria: The Origins and Development of a Nation* (Bloomington: Indiana University Press, 1992), 206.

41. Quoted in I. William Zartman, "The Algerian Army in Politics," in *Man, State, and Society in the Contemporary Maghrib*, ed. I. William Zartman (New York: Praeger, 1973), 217.

42. Şerif Mardin, "Religion and Secularism in Turkey," in *Atatürk: The Founder of a Modern State*, ed. Ali Kazancigil and Ergun Özbudun (Hamden, CT: Archon Books, 1981), 208.

43. Quoted in George S. Harris, "The Role of the Military in Turkish Politics, Part I," *Middle East Journal* 19, no. 1 (winter 1965): 56, n. 4, and in Cengiz Çandar, "Redefining Turkey's Political Center," *Journal of Democracy* 10, no. 4 (October 1999): 131.

44. General Kenan Evren in *12 September in Turkey: Before and After*, prepared by the General Secretariat of the National Security Council (Ankara: Ongun Kardesler Printing House, 1982), xi.

45. Interview with a Turkish military officer, Ankara, July 5, 2000; interview with a Turkish military officer, Washington, DC, May 15, 2001.

Three • *The* Pouvoir Militaire *and the Failure to Achieve a "Just Mean"*

1. Michael C. Hudson, for example, referred to Algeria's political system as "the most liberal" in the Arab world. Unfortunately for Hudson, this evaluation was published at the same moment Algeria's military establishment declared a state of siege and arrested the FIS leadership in response to the general strike of April–June 1991. See Michael C. Hudson, "After the Gulf War: Prospects for Democratization in the Arab World," *Middle East Journal* 45, no. 3 (summer 1991): 417. See also, Saad Eddin Ibrahim, "Crises, Elites, and Democratization in the Arab World," *Middle East Journal* 47, no. 2 (spring 1993): 292–306.

2. *Le Monde*, September 12, 1963, quoted in Abdelkader Yefsah, *The Processes of Legitimation of the* Pouvoir Militaire *and the Construction of the State in Algeria* (in French) (Paris: Éditions Anthropos, 1982), 117. A year before Boumédienne's statement, Ahmed Ben Bella made the following comments concerning the Algerian military: "It is necessary to work out its [the military's] reconversion, not because it constitutes a base for military dictatorship but because without the support of this mass of men we would be unable to construct the new Algeria. We have magnificent cadres, politically educated. The best of them should take their place in the party, for the future of the country is the party." See Maria Antoinetta Macciocchi, "An Interview with Ben Bella," in *Man, State, and Society in the Contemporary Maghrib*, ed. I. William Zartman (New York: Praeger, 1973), 124–127, reprinted from *L'Unità*, August 12, 1962.

3. William B. Quandt refers to the military establishment and related security services as "the real powers behind the president"; *Between Ballots and Bullets: Algeria's Transition from Authoritarianism* (Washington, DC: Brookings Institution, 1998), 23.

4. John Ruedy, *Modern Algeria: The Origins and Development of a Nation* (Bloomington: Indiana University Press, 1992), 209.

5. Mahfoud Bennoune, *The Making of Contemporary Algeria, 1830–1987: Colonial Upheaval and Post-Independence Development* (New York: Cambridge University Press, 1988), 111; Hugh Roberts, "From Radical Mission to Equivocal Ambition: The Expansion and Manipulation of Algerian Islamism, 1979–1992," in *Accounting for Fundamentalisms: The Dynamic Character of Movements,* ed. Martin E. Marty and R. Scott Appleby (Chicago: University of Chicago Press, 1994), 437; "Toward an Army of Tontons Macoutes" (interview with Abdelkader Yefsah, in French), *Le Nouvel Observateur,* January 19–25, 1995. It is important to note that by the mid-1970s, the Council of the Revolution comprised only nine members. In the decade after the 1965 coup, both Boumédienne's consolidation of power and the willingness of the officer corps to allow one of their own—particularly one with the president's charisma and stature—to manage the affairs of state resulted in an almost two-thirds reduction of the council.

6. Interview with Abderrezak Bouharra (in French), *el-Watan,* January 23, 2001.

7. Preamble, Constitution of the Democratic and Popular Republic of Algeria (in French), September 1963.

8. Ibid.

9. Jean-Claude Vatin, "Religious Resistance and State Power in Algeria," in *Islam and Power,* ed. Alexander S. Cudsi and Ali E. Hilal Dessouki (Baltimore: Johns Hopkins University Press, 1981), 119–157; Ernest Gellner, "The Unknown Apollo of Biskra: The Social Base of Algerian Puritanism," *Government and Opposition* 9, no. 3 (summer 1974): 277–310. See also Lahouari Addi, *Algeria and Democracy: Power and Political Crisis in Contemporary Algeria* (in French) (Paris: Éditions la Découverte, 1995), 27–33.

10. Preamble and Articles 4 and 5, Constitution of 1963.

11. Article 63 affirmed, "The Constitutional Council judges the constitutionality of laws and legislative ordinances after the execution by the president of the republic or the president of the national assembly."

12. Articles 70–73, Constitution of 1963.

13. For a complete discussion of the 1976 National Charter, see John Nellis, "The Algerian National Charter of 1976: Content, Public Reaction, and Significance," Occasional Paper no. 2 (Washington, DC: Center for Contemporary Arab Studies, 1980).

14. The charter was ratified overwhelmingly in June 1976. Of the 91.6 percent of the eligible voters who participated in the referendum, 98.5 percent approved of the charter. See Nellis, "The Algerian National Charter," 1.

15. Preamble, Constitution of the Democratic and Popular Republic of Algeria (in French), November 1976.

16. Ibid.

17. Articles 7, 125, 127, and 128, Constitution of 1976.

18. Articles 157–161, 187, Constitution of 1976.

19. Article 184, Constitution of 1976.

20. Chapter 1, Section 1, Enhanced National Charter of the Democratic and Popular Republic of Algeria (in Arabic), February 1986, in *Official Gazette of the Republic of Algeria,* 162.

21. Ibid.

22. Chapter 1, Section 2, Enhanced National Charter of the Algerian Democratic and Popular Republic (in Arabic), February 1986, in *Official Gazette of the Republic of Algeria,* 162.

23. Preamble, Constitution of the Democratic and Popular Republic of Algeria (in French), February 1989.

24. Article 40, Constitution of 1989.

25. Of the period between the 1965 coup d'état and the 1976 constitution, Ammar Koroghli has written, "Upon acceding to power . . . the army intended to institute a political system adapted to the exigencies of development, considered the priority of priorities. Moreover, the officers in power proceeded to 'constitutionalize' themselves according to classic processes: promulgation of a constitution followed by presidential and legislative elections"; *Political Institutions and Development in Algeria* (in French) (Paris: Éditions L'Harmattan, 1988). Abdel-kader Yefsah has described the officers' efforts to "give the impression of a civilian power"; *The Processes of Legitimation,* 107. Séverine Labat has characterized the Algerian political system as "dressed in the finery of democratization"; "Islamism and Islamists: The Emergence of New Types of Politico-Religious Militants," in *Islamism and Secularism in North Africa,* ed. John Ruedy (New York: St. Martin's, 1994), 103–121.

26. Abassi Madani pointed out this rigged quality of Algeria's political order. In early 1990, he asked *Horizons:* "Who preserved the resources of the Boumédienne period? And the same now? The laws that they promulgated are the rulings that were elaborated to profit their interests"; interview with Abassi Madani, *Horizons,* January 14, 1990.

27. Following the military's intervention in 1992, the officers made Mohamed Boudiaf the head of the High State Council, engineered the assumption of former minister of defense Liamine Zeroual to replace Boudiaf, and when Zeroual decided not to seek another presidential term, Algeria's senior commanders ensured the election of Abdelaziz Bouteflika.

28. The text of Law 89-11 (in French) is reprinted in *el-Moujahid,* August 10, 1989, and *Maghreb-Machrek* 127 (January–March 1990): 200–205.

29. Arun Kapil, "Liberalization and the Question of Democracy in Algeria, 1979–1992" (Ph.D. diss., University of Chicago, 1999), 399.

30. Hugh Roberts, "The Struggle for Constitutional Rule in Algeria," *Journal of Algerian Studies* 3 (1998): 19–30; Lahouari Addi, "Algeria's Army, Algeria's Agony," *Foreign Affairs* 77, no. 4 (July–August 1998): 44–53.

31. Anthony J. Pazzanita, "From Boumedienne to Benjedid: The Algerian Regime in Transition," *Journal of South Asian and Middle Eastern Studies* 15, no. 4 (summer 1992): 65.

32. The military has often used conclaves—for which there are no formal provisions—as a forum to discuss and develop a military consensus on important issues of the day. Kapil argues that, in fact, the military conclave is "the supreme decision-making body" in Algeria; "Liberalization," 616.

33. By 1976, the Council of the Revolution had been reduced from 26 to 9 members, and Boumédienne governed through the Council of Ministers, whose membership was distinct for its lack of military officers. Moreover, the president of the republic now "embod[ied] the unity of leadership of the Party and the State" and was furnished with enhanced powers in relation to the APN and the judiciary. The president was able to issue laws by decree and dissolve parliament. As the head of the Supreme Council of Magistrature, he could influence everything from pardons to the constitutionality of laws and regulations. See Articles 152 and 162, Constitution of 1976.

34. Roberts, "Struggle for Constitutional Rule," 24.

35. John Nellis indicates that regime legitimacy was an important factor in the development of the 1976 National Charter; see "The Algerian National Charter," 2.

36. Ruedy, *Modern Algeria*, 233.

37. Mohamed Harbi makes a similar point about Algeria's *"ouverture sous contrôle"*; see his "The Tragedy of Democracy without Democrats" (in French), *Le Monde*, April 13, 1994.

38. Yahia H. Zoubir, "Stalled Democratization of an Authoritarian Regime: The Case of Algeria," *Democratization* 2, no. 2 (summer 1995): 117. Zoubir also uses the term "democratic facade."

39. Quandt argues, for example, that Algeria's military remains so decisive because it is less divided than any other group in Algerian society; see *Between Ballots and Bullets*, 78.

40. Claire Spencer, "Algeria in Crisis," *Survival* 36, no. 2 (summer 1994): 158.

41. Roberts "Struggle for Constitutional Rule," 25, 98; I. William Zartman, "The Algerian Army in Politics," in *Man, State, and Society in the Contemporary Maghrib*, ed. I. William Zartman (New York: Praeger, 1973), 212.

42. Michael Willis, *The Islamist Challenge in Algeria: A Political History* (New York: NYU Press, 1998); Robert Mortimer, "Islamists, Soldiers, and Democrats: The Second Algerian War," *Middle East Journal* 50, no. 1 (winter 1996): 18–39; Hugh Roberts, "Doctrinaire Economic and Political Opportunism in the Strategy of Algerian Islamism," in *Islamism and Secularism in North Africa*, ed. John Ruedy (New York: St. Martin's, 1994), 123–147; Ahmed Rouadjia, "Discourse and Strategy of the Algerian Islamist Movement (1986–1992)," in *The Islamist Dilemma: The Political Role of Islamist Movements in the Contemporary Arab World*, ed. Laura Guazzone (London: Ithaca Press, 1995), 69–103.

43. Hugh Roberts has wondered why, in light of the party's cultivation of the great mass of disaffected, mostly young, men and its populist positions on a variety of other important issues, the FIS leadership seemingly supported Chadli's program of economic liberalization; "From Radical Mission to Equivocal Ambition," 459. Yet FIS support for Chadli's reforms was not a contradiction of the Front's populism but actually reflected the party's vast and varied constituency, as well as differences with the Majlis ash-Shura. Thus, the collective FIS leadership maintained a number of discernible positions on the Algerian economy, one of which was economic liberalism.

44. Chadli's reforms hardly resembled a radical alteration of Algeria's economy. Rather, the program left the state-owned sector largely intact. While providing more room in the economy for Algeria's small private sector, Chadli's goal was, in fact, to spur more nimble public industries. The unfortunate result of these policies was a liberalized economy, but one that lacked the institutions to underpin the effective functioning of a market. In such an environment, inefficiencies and distortions remained, rendering every step of the business process—planning, supply, investment, and even licensing—risky ventures. For a complete discussion, see Bradford L. Dillman, *State and Private Sector in Algeria: The Politics of Rent-seeking and Failed Development* (Boulder: Westview Press, 2000).

45. *Project of the Political Program of the Islamic Salvation Front* (in French), Algiers, March 7, 1989.

46. The Front called state planning and state-owned industry "pretext[s] for suffocating freedoms," which had led to the chronic unemployment of young men and the country's

dependency in all areas including everything from military equipment and consumer goods to agricultural items. Yet, the official FIS policy statement also targeted the deleterious consequences of Chadli's policies, notably the exploitation of the consumer and the rise of intermediaries, whom they saw as nothing more than parasites; See "Economic Axis," *Project of the Political Program of the Islamic Salvation Front,* 5.

47. "Economic Axis, Part IV—Finance," *Project of the Political Program of the Islamic Salvation Front,* 9.

48. Article 37, Constitution of 1976; Article 8, Constitution of 1989.

49. Interview with Abassi Madani, *Horizons,* January 14, 1990.

50. "Platform of Political Demands of the FIS," reprinted in Mustafa al-Ahnaf et al., *Algeria According to Its Islamists* (in French) (Paris: Éditions Karthala, 1991), 49–51.

51. Dirk Vandewalle, "Islam in Algeria: Religion, Culture, and Opposition in a Rentier State," in *Political Islam: Revolution, Radicalism, or Reforms?* ed. John Esposito (Boulder: Lynne Rienner Publishers, 1997), 35.

52. Pradeep K. Chhibber, "State Policy, Rent Seeking, and the Electoral Success of a Religious Party in Algeria," *Journal of Politics* 58, no. 1 (February 1996): 137.

53. Dillman, *State and Private Sector in Algeria,* 75.

54. Ibid, 3.

55. The FIS position on the issue of corruption was given a significant boost in March 1990 with former Prime Minister Abdelhamid Brahimi's accusation that $26 billion had been siphoned from the national treasury. The charge is questionable given that the amount of money Brahimi cited just happened to equal the precise amount of Algeria's national debt at the time.

56. "Political Axis," *Project of the Political Program of the Islamic Salvation Front,* Part D, 4.

57. *Platform of Political Demands of the FIS* (in French), reprinted in al-Ahnaf et al., *Algeria According to Its Islamists,* 49–51.

58. In 1987 the Sécurité Militaire was reorganized and named Délégation à la Prévention et à la Sécurité, but Algerians continued to refer to the organization by its original name or acronym, SM.

59. Interview with Abassi Madani (in French), *Jeune Afrique* 1543 (July 25–August 1, 1990): 3–6. On the question of relations with Morocco, Abassi, in an apparent overture to King Hassan II, invoked the memory of the monarch's father, Mohamed V, and his solidarity with Algeria during its revolutionary struggle with France. Building on this theme, the FIS spokesman and leader declared, "We have concluded that we are part of the same nation with the same destiny," coyly adding, "The King follows the FIS attentively and vows not to miss any televised debate concerning it."

60. "Abassi Madani: Between Municipalities and Legislatures" (interview with Fatiha Akeb and Mohamed Balhi, in French), *Algérie-Actualité* 1298 (August 30–September 5, 1990): 8–9.

61. Article 19, Constitution of 1963; Article 55, Constitution of 1976; Article 39, Constitution of 1989.

62. In fact, not only was open discussion of these issues informally discouraged, but its prohibition was to some extent formally codified. For example, under Law 90-07, which opened the print media to private ownership, journalists were enjoined not to disclose any information that could undermine national security—the interpretation of which was left to the appropriate authorities. The penalty for violating this provision was five to ten years in

prison. Moreover, the discussion of foreign policy was formally obstructed even in the National Popular Assembly. Article 121 of the 1989 constitution prohibited members from initiating discussion in this area. The president of the republic or the president of the National People's Assembly could, however, request deliberations on a foreign policy–related matter.

63. Yahia H. Zoubir, "Algerian-Moroccan Relations and their Impact on Maghribi Integration," *Journal of North African Studies* 5, no. 3 (autumn 2000): n. 18.

64. "The Army and the Political-Religious Current" (in French), *Algérie—Revue de Presse* 354-3 (April 1991): n.p. In January 1986, the Central Directorate of the Political Commission of the ANP ended mass circulation of *el-Djeich*. When the officer corps wanted to inform the Algerian public and politicians of its thinking on important issues of the day, the contents of the magazine's editorials were reprinted in Algerian newspapers. The excerpts cited here were published in the April 4, 1991, edition of *Horizons* and in *el-Moujahid* on April 7 of the same year.

65. Quoted in Yahia H. Zoubir, "The Painful Transition from Authoritarianism in Algeria," *Arab Studies Quarterly* 15, no. 3 (summer 1993): 98.

66. Jean-Claude Vatin has written: "The constitution of 1963, the *Charte d'Alger* in 1964 and the governments of 1963 and 1965 made clear that Islam would be preserved . . . Reinforcing a young state was the only way to secure independence. Moreover, there was no other structure to answer the needs of development, to help solve the crisis of adaptation while preserving national unity at the same time." See Jean-Claude Vatin, "Religious Resistance and State Power in Algeria," in *Islam and Power,* ed. Alexander S. Cudsi and Ali E. Hilal Dessouki (Baltimore: Johns Hopkins University Press, 1981), 140.

67. "Political Axis," *Project of the Political Program of the Islamic Salvation Front,* 3.

68. *Platform of Political Demands of the FIS* (in French), reprinted in al-Ahnaf et al., *Algeria According to Its Islamists,* 49–51.

69. Interview with Abassi Madani (in French), *Jeune Afrique* 1543 (July 25–August 1, 1990): 4.

70. Bradford Dillman, "Parliamentary Elections and the Prospects for Political Pluralism in North Africa," *Government and Opposition* 35, no. 2 (spring 2000): 227.

71. François Burgat reports, however, that the hydrocarbon industry was "hit by the full force of the strike and that the cost to the national economy had been quite high." See François Burgat and William Dowell, *The Islamic Movement in North Africa,* 2nd ed. (Austin: University of Texas Press, 1997), 294–295.

72. Roberts, "From Radical Mission," 466–468.

73. "The Army and the Political-Religious Current" (in French), *Algérie—Revue de Presse* 354-3 (April 1991): n.p.

74. Ibid.

75. Willis, *The Islamist Challenge,* 184 n. 60.

76. Vandewalle, "Islam in Algeria," 38.

77. *Project of the Political Program of the Islamic Salvation Front,* 2–3, 15. Ahmed Rouadjia makes a similar point concerning the Front's penchant for borrowing heavily the "nationalist phraseology" of the FLN. See his "Discourse and Strategy of the Algerian Islamist Movement," 69–103.

78. Abdelkader Yefsah has pointed out two factors that were critical to Algerian legitimacy: industrialization and nationalist authenticity. See *Processes of Legitimation,* 121.

79. "Sheikh Abassi Madani: No to the Application of *Sharia*, French Is as Useful as Arabic, the Arab Maghreb Union Is Multiple, but the *Umma* Is One" (interview with Abassi Madani, in French), *Arabies*, July 1990: 20–22.

80. By the late 1980s the senior officer corps featured a dwindling number of personalities with any kind of significant link to the internal *maquis*, or who were even prominent in the army of the frontiers, which detracted from the ANP's ability to hold itself out as the natural and logical preserve of Algerian nationalism.

81. Interview with Abassi Madani by Fatiha Akeb and Mohamed Balhi (in French), *Algérie-Actualité* 1298 (August 30-September 5, 1990): 8–9.

82. As part of its efforts to restore order during the October 1988 rioting, the military not only fired on demonstrators, killing anywhere from 150 to 500 Algerians, but also used a tactic associated with the French occupation: torture. According to François Burgat, the army's use of torture irrevocably tarnished the officers' nationalist credentials with the Algerian people. See Burgat and Dowell, *The Islamic Movement in North Africa*, chap. 11.

83. For a complete discussion, see Lahouari Addi, *Algeria and Democracy: Power and Political Crisis in Contemporary Algeria* (in French) (Paris: Éditions la Découverte, 1995): 55–74.

84. Ibid.

85. Thus, in addition to forsaking the role of such organizations as the Mouvement pour le Triomphe des Libertés Démocratiques, Union Démocratique du Manifeste Algérien, and the Association of Algerian *Ulema*, the military establishment synthesized its role in the war with that of the internal *maquisards*, who bore the brunt of the conflict with the French. Despite that the ALN sat out most of the conflict on the Tunisian and Moroccan frontiers, on the 31st anniversary of the Algerian revolutions, *el-Djeich* declared: "In light of the disproportion of power between the two forces (the ALN and the French army) in number of soldiers and in matériel of war, the National Liberation Army imposed on the enemy an appropriate form of combat: the guerilla who harasses the enemy positions, disperses its forces, and breaks down its morale . . . "; Mahieddine Filali, "The National Liberation Army, From Formation to Organization" (in French), *el-Djeich* 270 (November 1985): 16.

86. "The Army and the Political-Religious Current" (in French), *Algérie—Revue de Presse* 354-3 (April 1991): n.p.

87. Ibid.

88. "Objective Number One: Protect Their Privileges" (interview with Abdelkader Yefsah, in French), *Le Nouvel Observateur*, January 19–25, 1995, 23. See also Rémy Leveau, "Algeria between the Tank and the Minaret" (in French), *Telerama*, August 24, 1994; Quandt, *Between Bullets and Ballots*, 61; and Roberts, "From Radical Mission," 438.

89. Some may argue that the military's apparent unwillingness to intervene is testament to their democratic credentials. As Generals Chelloufi, Nezzar, and others have indicated, the military supported the transition to democracy. Even such a fierce critic of the military as Algerian sociologist Lahouari Addi suggested in a 1991 column in *Le Monde* that the military establishment recognized the need for democratic change. Yet, subsequent events suggest otherwise, and as William Quandt has noted, the military cannot be credited with democratic credentials; *Between Ballots and Bullets*, 44.

90. Daniel Brumberg, "Islamists and Power Sharing: A Comparative Assessment of Middle

East and Southeast Asian Cases," working paper, U.S. Institute of Peace, Washington, DC, summer 1998, 14. Chadli's opponents within the FLN were so dissatisfied with his economic reform program that this faction considered nominating another candidate for president.

91. Willis, *The Islamist Challenge,* 128–129.

92. This was the exact amount of Algeria's external debt at the time. See ibid., 129.

93. Roberts, "From Radical Mission," 462.

94. To understand the way the military establishment viewed Chadli, Hamrouche, and their apparent relationship with the FIS, see "The Hamrouche-Chadli-FIS Connivance" (in French), chap. 8 of *Memoirs of General Khaled Nezzar* (Algiers: Chihab Editions, 2000).

95. Reported in *The Guardian,* December 16, 1991.

96. Willis, *The Islamist Challenge,* 238–239.

97. Abed Charef, *Algeria: The Grand Skid* (in French) (La Tour d'Aigues: Éditions de l'Aube, 1994), 236; Nezzar, *Memoirs,* 235.

98. Nezzar, *Memoirs,* 236.

99. Willis, *The Islamist Challenge,* 238–239; Hugh Roberts, "The Algerian State and the Challenge of Democracy," *Government and Opposition* 27, no. 4 (autumn 1992): 441; interview with an Algerian government official, Washington, DC, January 2, 2001; interview with Yahia H. Zoubir, Orlando, FL, November 18, 2001.

100. Nezzar, *Memoirs,* 237. This theme is also emphasized in Mohammed Muqadam, "Algeria: Coup Plotters Isolated after Retiring," (in Arabic), *al-Hayat,* August 24, 2001; Yahia Rahal, *A History of Power: A General's Testimony* (in French), (Algiers: Casbah Editions, 1997); Hamid Barrada, "The Striking Changes of Khaled Nezzar" (in French), *Jeune Afrique* 1858–1859 (August 14–27, 1996): 26–29; Omar Belhoucet, "Khaled Nezzar's Testimony" (in French), *El Watan,* May 15, 1996; and Khaled Nezzar, "Duty and Truth" (in French), *el-Watan* May 15, 1996.

101. Nezzar, *Memoirs,* 240.

102. The army did not act without considerable support. Under the umbrella of what was called the Comité National pour la Sauvegarde de l'Algérie, Algerian "civil society" pressed for the military's intervention. The Comité National pour la Sauvegarde de l'Algérie was comprised of the Union Générale des Travailleurs Algériens; the Ligue Algérienne des Droits de l'Homme; a range of women's organizations; and private sector associations. With the outside support of political parties such as the Rassemblement pour la Culture et la Démocratie and Parti de l'Avant-Garde Socialiste, it sought the cancellation of the elections so, its constituent organizations believed, the democratic process could be preserved.

103. "The Magazine *el-Djeich* and the Army on the Constitution" (in French), excerpts from *el-Djeich* reprinted in *el-Moudjahid,* March 15, 1990.

104. Though the Constitutional Council was formally an advisory body established under Section III (Audit/Control and Consultative Institutions), Algeria's judiciary, despite what the country's constitutions had declared, was not an independent branch of government. Lahouari Addi indicates that the judiciary, in its application of the law, fell well below international standards. See "From the Shadow of Terror the Army Seizes Power" (in French), *Le Monde Diplomatique* (February 1998): 1, 16–17; "Algeria's Army, Algeria's Agony," *Foreign Affairs* (July/August 1998): 44–53.

105. According to Presidential Decree 89-196 of October 1989, the Haut Conseil de Sécurité did have prerogatives related to domestic security issues, but only in an advisory capacity.

Article 4 of the decree states, "the HCS offers advice to the president of the republic on all aspects of security related to the national and international domains"; reprinted in *el-Moujahid*, January 13, 1992.

106. Presidential Decree 89-196 establishes an eight-person council, but at the time, Sid-Ahmed Ghozali held both the prime ministerial and economic portfolios and Chadli, of course, had been forced to resign.

107. *Proclamation of the High Security Council* (in French), reprinted in *el-Watan*, February 15, 1992. These constitutional articles, upon which the military justified its actions, addressed the following issues: The relationship between government and the presidency (75); the functions of the head of the government and the National Popular Assembly (79); the independence of the judiciary (129); the role of the judiciary in protecting society, liberty and the fundamental rights; and the functions of the Constitutional Council (153).

108. These included the following: "With respect to the dispositions of the present constitution, the political parties are not to be founded on a religious, linguistic, racial, gender, corporatist, or regional basis; political parties are prohibited from recourse to partisan propaganda bearing/carrying the mentioned elements in the above line; obedience to foreign interests or parties is proscribed; political parties are not to resort to violence or to coercion." See the Constitution of the Democratic and Popular Republic of Algeria, November 28, 1996, www.algeria-watch.de/farticle/docu/constit.htm.

109. Human Rights Watch, *Algeria's Human Rights Crisis* 10, no. 2 (August 1998): 15.

110. Article 120, Constitution of 1996; Mona Yacoubian, "Algeria's Struggle for Democracy," Occasional Paper no. 3, Council on Foreign Relations, New York, 1997.

111. Algerian government officials like to point out that the 1999 presidential elections featured seven candidates. Yet, six of those candidates dropped out of the race just prior to the balloting due to concerns that the military establishment had predetermined the outcome in favor of its candidate, Abdelaziz Bouteflika.

112. Addi, "Algeria's Army," 50.

113. For the complete text of the Charter for Peace and National Reconciliation, see www.el-mouradia.dz/arabe/infos/actualite/actualite.htm or www.el-mouradia.dz/francais/infos/actualite/algerieact.htm.

114. Although then-chief of staff General Mohamed Lamari affirmed that the officers were "ready to accept any candidate, even an Islamist," this position was disingenuous. Even so, Bouteflika obtained a mandate that eluded him after the 1999 polling when his six challengers dropped out of the race the day before the election claiming, among other accusations, that the military had rigged the polls in Bouteflika's favor. With 58 percent of eligible voters participating, 85 percent supported the incumbent president. European and other observers declared the actual polling free and fair, but the magnitude of Bouteflika's victory (his primary challenger garnered just 8 percent of the vote) and a number of questionable practices by the Constitutional Council, Interior Ministry, and the state-affiliated media during the campaign indicated manipulation of the process in favor of the incumbent. For example, in early March 2004, the Constitutional Council rejected the candidacy of Ahmed Taleb Ibrahimi, a former government minister with close ties to the Islamic Salvation Front. Ibrahimi was widely considered a strong challenger who could have forced Bouteflika into a second round of voting. The Bouteflika-controlled council ruled that Ibrahimi, who garnered more than a million votes in 1999 even

though he withdrew from the race the day before the election, had failed to secure the requisite 75,000 signatures. Also, in violation of regulations concerning the use of state resources for political purposes, for several weeks before the campaign Algeria's state television broadcast a series of paeans to Bouteflika immediately after the evening news, which itself featured extensive positive coverage of the president. Finally, the Interior Ministry made it impossible for campaign representatives to verify the accuracy of the voter list. It released the official registry for public scrutiny but only after voter registration had closed, prompting allegations that electoral authorities had manipulated the list in Bouteflika's favor.

Four • *Institutionalizing a Military-Founded System*

1. See, for example, Mark N. Cooper, *The Transformation of Egypt* (London: Croom Helm, 1982), and "The Demilitarization of the Egyptian Cabinet," *International Journal of Middle East Studies* 14 (1982): 203–225; Raymond A. Hinnebusch Jr., *Egyptian Politics Under Sadat: The Post-Populist Development of an Authoritarian-Modernizing State* (Boulder: Lynne Rienner Publishers, 1988); Raymond A. Hinnebusch, "The Formation of the Contemporary Egyptian State from Nasser and Sadat to Mubarak," in *The Political Economy of Contemporary Egypt,* ed. Ibrahim Oweiss (Washington, DC: Center for Contemporary Arab Studies, 1990), 188–209; Ibrahim A. Karawan, "Egypt," in *The Political Role of the Military: An International Handbook,* ed. Constantine P. Danopoulos and Cynthia Watson (Westport, CT: Greenwood Press, 1996), 107–121; Ali Dessouki and Gehad Audah, "Military and Development: The Dynamics of Role Change—the Case of Egypt," paper presented to the 14th World Congress of the International Political Science Association, Washington, DC, August 28–September 1, 1988; R. Hrair Dekmejian, *Egypt under Nasir: A Study in Political Dynamics* (Albany: State University of New York Press, 1971). This chapter does not take issue with the broad facts surrounding the events of the late 1960s and early 1970s as they relate to Egypt's military establishment. The officers did give up their role in the day-to-day governing of the country and as a result there was a concomitant reduction of officers in successive Egyptian cabinets. Analyses such as those cited above conspicuously give short shrift to factors that undermine the analytical connection between a reduction in raw numbers of officers involved in Egyptian politics and administration and compromised influence.

2. In contrast to Abdel-Malek or Perlmutter, I do not consider Egypt—or Algeria or Turkey—to be "military regimes" in which officers thoroughly penetrate the state apparatus at a variety of levels. Malek was writing during the first 15 years after the Free Officers' coup/revolution when this was, indeed, the case. Perlmutter, perhaps because he was convinced that Nasser and his collaborators had failed miserably in developing durable political institutions, did not recognize that the military could retain its significant influence in a setting that was something other than the "personalist and praetorian rule" he asserted. The Free Officers and their successors have been rather successful in developing an institutional setting in which the military continues to dominate but, with the exception of the president, does not govern. Thus, instead of an Egyptian military regime, it is more apt to refer to Egypt's military-dominated system. See Anouar Abdel-Malek, *Egypt: Military Society* (New York: Vintage Books, 1968), and Amos Perlmutter, *Egypt: The Praetorian State* (New Brunswick, NJ: Transaction Books, 1974).

3. P. J. Vatikiotis, "Some Political Consequences of the 1952 Revolution in Egypt," in *Political*

and Social Change in Modern Egypt, ed. P.M. Holt (New York: Oxford University Press, 1968), 369–370. This is by no means to suggest that Egypt's military establishment was united in its support for the Free Officers movement. Indeed, once it became clear that Nasser and his colleagues did not intend to hand the reins of government back to civilians, opposition to the Free Officers developed within the ranks of the officer corps. Most notably, General Mohamed Neguib, who had led the Free Officers at the time of the coup, opposed his erstwhile allies along with a number of other commanders who rallied around Neguib. After the Free Officers outmaneuvered Neguib in April 1954, his supporters were purged.

4. Joel Gordon, *Nasser's Blessed Movement: Egypt's Free Officers and the July Revolution* (Cairo: American University in Cairo Press, 1996): 13.

5. Gamal Abdel Nasser quoted in Gehad Audah, "The State of Political Control: The Case of Nasser 1960–1967," *Arab Journal of the Social Sciences* 2, no. 1 (April 1987): 98.

6. For a complete discussion, see Abdel-Malek, *Egypt: Military Society*; P. J. Vatikiotis, *The Egyptian Army in Politics: Pattern for New Nations?* (Bloomington, Indiana University Press, 1961); Derek Hopwood, *Egypt: Politics and Society, 1945–1984,* 2nd ed. (Boston: Unwin and Hyman, 1985); P. J. Vatikiotis, *The History of Modern Egypt,* 4th ed. (Baltimore: Johns Hopkins University Press, 1991); James Jankowski, *Nasser's Egypt, Arab Nationalism, and the United Arab Republic* (Boulder: Lynne Rienner Publishers, 2002).

7. Vatikiotis, "Some Political Consequences," 368.

8. Salah Issa, *Constitution in the Dustbin: A Tale of the 1954 Constitution* (in Arabic), (Cairo: Cairo Center for the Study of Human Rights, 2001).

9. Preamble, Constitution of the Republic of Egypt (Cairo: State Information Service, 1956).

10. Draft of the Charter, United Arab Republic Information Department, Cairo, May 21, 1962, 26–27.

11. Ibid, 9–10.

12. Article 89, Constitution of United Arab Republic 1964 (in Arabic), *al-Dasatir al-Misriya, 1805–1971* (Cairo: al-Ahram Foundation, 1977).

13. After the defeat, a number of senior officers including the commander of the air force, Lieutenant General Sidqi Mahmud, the minister of war, Colonel Shams Badran, and several others were placed on trial and forced to account for the poor performance of the armed forces. In the end these officers received lenient sentences.

14. "March 30 Programme," in E. S. Farag (trans.), *Nassar Speaks: Basic Documents* (London: Morsett Press, 1972), 165–166.

15. Preamble and Articles 64–65, Constitution of the United Arab Republic 1971 (in Arabic), *al-Dasatir al-Misriya 1805–1971* (Cairo: al-Ahram Foundation, 1977).

16. Article 71, Constitution of 1971.

17. Constitution of the Arab Republic of Egypt, 1980 (Cairo: State Information Service, May 1980). See also Nathan J. Brown, *Constitutions in a Non-constitutional World: Arab Basic Laws and the Prospects for Accountable Government* (Albany: State University of New York, 2002), chap. 6.

18. Article 194, Constitution of 1980.

19. Some accounts of contemporary Egyptian history suggest that Nasser created the ASU as a counterweight to the increasingly autonomous military establishment under the command of his close confidant Field Marshal Amer. This narrative indicates further that Nasser sought to

discredit the military establishment when he placed the field marshal at the helm of the Committee to Eradicate Feudalism in the hope that the officers would distinguish themselves for their brutality, thus alienating society. Yet this analysis leaves open an important question: Given the rhetoric of both Nasser and his fellow officers concerning the malevolent role of Egypt's capitalists and land-owning "feudalists," why would the military's destruction of this class—brutal or otherwise—tarnish the officer corps' image? It seems plausible that both Nasser and Amer were not as ideologically pure as official rhetoric might suggest and the field marshal's appointment to lead the committee was to prevent devastating an important segment of society. Despite agricultural reform and sequestration of private property and businesses, particularly during the first decade after the coup, the landowning and capitalist classes were not systematically destroyed. Indeed, as early as 1964, the Egyptian government began to reverse aspects of its earlier policies in these areas.

20. Kirk J. Beattie, "Egypt: Thirty-five years of Praetorian Politics," in *Military Disengagement from Politics,* ed. Constantine P. Danopoulos (London: Routledge, 1988), 218; John Waterbury, *The Egypt of Nasser and Sadat: The Political Economy of Two Regimes* (Princeton: Princeton University Press, 1983), 383; Shahrough Akhavi, "Egypt: Diffused Elite in a Bureaucratic Society," in *Political Elites in Arab North Africa,* ed. I. William Zartman (New York: Longman, 1982), 230.

21. These organizations were required to conduct their activities within the parameters of "democratic socialism, social peace and national unity." For a complete discussion, see Marat Terterov, "Lessons from Political Liberalization," *Civil Society* 5, no. 54 (June 1996): 19.

22. For a complete discussion of Law 40/1977 and its implications for political participation, see Hassanein Tawfiq Ibrahim and Hadi Ragheb Audah, *The Muslim Brotherhood and Politics in Egypt: A Study in the Electoral Alliances and Parliamentary Practices of the Muslim Brotherhood in the Framework of Limited Political Pluralism, 1984–1990* (in Arabic) (Cairo: Mahroussah Book, 1995), 40–44; Eberhad Kienle, *A Grand Delusion: Democracy and Economic Reform in Egypt* (London: I. B. Tauris, 2001), 28–30.

23. Fauzi Najjar "Elections and Democracy in Egypt," *American-Arab Affairs* 29 (summer 1989): 103–104.

24. "Egypt: Elections Concerns," *News from Middle East Watch,* November 15, 1990, 1; Carrie Rosefsky Wickham, "Beyond Democratization: Political Change in the Arab World," *PS—Political Science and Politics* 27, no. 3 (1994): 508; Najjar, "Elections and Democracy," 97–98.

25. "Citizen's Rights and Democracy" (in Arabic), National Democratic Party Position Paper, September 2004, 16–18.

26. Gamal Essam El-Din, "A Controversial Law," *al-Ahram Weekly,* July 7–13, 2005.

27. Kienle, *A Grand Delusion,* 98–102.

28. For the complete text of the Emergency Law, see Abd al-Moneim Husni, *A Compendium of Egyptian Law and Statutes* (in Arabic), vol. 6 (Giza: Merkaz Husni l-il-Dirasaat al-Qaanuniyah, 1987): 292–306. Many of Egypt's most restrictive laws, including the Military Police Act; the Protection of the Internal Front and Social Peace or the "Law of Shame"; the NGOs Law of 1964 and its later incarnations; and the Law to Protect Democracy in the Syndicates, are based on, superseded by, or reinforced with the Emergency Law.

29. The state of emergency was lifted for a 10-month period in 1980–1981, but was reinstated in the period just before Anwar Sadat's assassination.

30. Appeals made to Egypt's Court of Cassation fall into two categories—review and cassation. Those appeals sustained based on review may result in invalidation of the verdict and acquittal or retrial. Appeals held on the cassation may only result in a retrial before a new three-judge panel of the Supreme State Security Court. If, however, a defendant is found guilty a second time and makes a second appeal to the Court of Cassation, that court is permitted to rule on the facts of the case. For a complete discussion see "The State of Egypt vs. Free Expression: The Ibn Khaldun Trial," Human Rights Watch, New York, January 2002.

31. www.ndp.org.eg/modifications/THE_AMENDMENT_TO_ARTICLE_76%20.htm.

32. See, for example, Waterbury, *The Egypt of Nasser and Sadat;* Ahmed Abdalla, "The Armed Forces and Democratic Development in Egypt," in *The Army and Democracy in Egypt* (in Arabic), ed. Ahmed Abdalla (Cairo, Sinai Publishers, 1990); Raymond A. Hinnebusch Jr., *Egyptian Politics under Sadat: The Post-Populist Development of an Authoritarian-Modernizing State* (Boulder: Lynne Rienner Publishers, 1988); Maisa Gamel, *The Political Elite in Egypt* (Beirut: Center for the Study of Arab Unity, 1998).

33. Interviews with retired military officers, Cairo, November 8 and December 7, 1999; January 18, 22, 24, 2000.

34. According to this interlocutor when speaking of the Egyptian presidency, "We are all military"; interview with a retired military officer, Cairo, December 7, 1999.

35. Part 5, Chapter 1, Articles 76, 78, 82–84, Constitution of 1980.

36. Interview with retired Egyptian military officers, Cairo, October 8, 1999; January 18, 2000.

37. Interview with a retired Egyptian military officer, Cairo, January 18, 2000. In the immediate aftermath of Sadat's death, Dr. Sufi Abu Talib, the speaker of the People's Assembly, did assume the duties of the president for the remainder of October 6 until Mubarak was nominated president on October 7, but even as Abu Talib did so, Mubarak was preparing to assume the office.

38. Interviews with retired military officers, Cairo, November 22, 1999; January 22, 2000.

39. Interview with an Egyptian military officer, Washington, DC, April 26, 2005.

40. In addition to the president, one informant explains, the staff of the presidency is composed almost exclusively of currently serving or retired military officers who have a significant role in the administration of the state. Accordingly, these officers are routinely deployed throughout the ministries and agencies to impress upon the vast bureaucracy the priorities of the leadership.

41. Both Ahmed Abdalla and Mona Makram Ebeid have made similar points with regard to the hegemony of the Egyptian executive in general. See, for example, Abdalla's monograph on Egypt's 1995 elections, *Parliamentary Elections in Egypt: What Egypt . . . What Parliament . . . and Which Egypt?* (Amsterdam: Amsterdam Middle East Papers, 1995); Mona Makram Ebeid, "Egypt's 1995 Elections: One Step Forward, Two Steps Back?" *Middle East Policy* 4, no. 3 (March 1996): 119–136.

42. Interview with a retired military officer, Cairo, January 22, 2000.

43. Gordon, *Nasser's Blessed Movement,* 48–49.

44. Raymond A. Hinnebusch Jr., "The Formation of the Contemporary Egyptian State from Nasser and Sadat to Mubarak," in *The Political Economy of Contemporary Egypt,* ed. Ibrahim Oweiss (Washington, DC: Center for Contemporary Arab Studies, 1990), 199.

45. See Michael Farhang, "Terrorism and Military Trials in Egypt: Presidential Decree No. 375 and the Consequences for Judicial Authority," *Harvard International Law Journal* 35 (winter 1994): 225–237.

46. Though the High Constitutional Court refused to rule on the substance of Law 153/ 1999, the justices did indicate that several of the proposed statute's provisions were unconstitutional, forcing the government to modify the text. See "Stifling Civil Society in Egypt: Proposed New Law on Associations is a Step Back for Political Pluralism," *Lawyers Committee for Human Rights,* May 31, 2002, www.lchr.org/defender/middle_east/egypt/laws/e_laws_main.htm. For a discussion on the independence of Egypt's judicial branch, see Kienle, *A Grand Delusion.*

47. Gehad Audah, "The 'Normalization' of the Islamic Movement in Egypt from the 1970s to the Early 1990s," in *Accounting for Fundamentalisms: The Dynamic Character of Movements,* vol. 4, ed. Martin E. Marty and R. Scott Appleby (Chicago: University of Chicago Press, 1994): 388.

48. Ibrahim A. Karawan, "Egypt," in *The Political Role of the Military: An International Handbook,* ed. Constantine P. Danopoulos and Cynthia Watson (Westport CT: Greenwood Press, 1996), 112.

49. Interview with retired Egyptian officers, Cairo, January 22, 24, 2000; Abdalla, "Armed Forces and Democratic Development," 1464.

50. Ibrahim and Audah, *The Muslim Brotherhood and Politics in Egypt,* 68.

51. For a complete discussion of the Muslim Brotherhood's grievances during Sadat's tenure, see, for example, Mohamed Abd al-Quddus, "The Corrective Revolution that the People Want!!" (in Arabic), *ad-Dawa* (May 1978): 52–53; "The American Elections . . . A Smack to Those Who Pride Themselves with False Election Results in the Arab-Islamic World" (in Arabic) *al-Itisam,* December 1980, 3; Abd al-Moneim Said Aly and Manfred W. Wenner, "Modern Islamic Reform Movements: The Muslim Brotherhood in Contemporary Egypt," *Middle East Journal* 36, no. 3 (summer 1982): 336–361; Saad Eddin Ibrahim, "An Islamic Alternative in Egypt: The Muslim Brotherhood and Sadat," *Arab Studies Quarterly* 4, no. 1–2 (spring 1982): 75–93; Raymond W. Baker, "Afraid for Islam: Egypt's Muslim Centrists Between Pharaohs and Fundamentalists," *Daedalus* 10, no. 3 (summer 1991): 41–68.

52. On the Brotherhood's repudiation of violence, see Sullivan and Abed-Kotob, *Islam in Contemporary Egypt,* 59–65; Richard P. Mitchell explains that the Ikhwan's violence between the 1930s and early 1950s was a response to both Egypt's situation—nominal independence—and the organization's frustration with the state of the country's politics in which either the palace or the *Wafd* dominated with heavy British interference. To Brotherhood activists, the collusion of Egypt's politicians with the forces of imperial penetration was an affront to Egyptian nationalism and thus rendered them legitimate targets. Still, Mitchell reveals that there was considerable tension within the Muslim Brotherhood on the question of violence—the existence of *al-gihaz al-sirri* (secret apparatus) notwithstanding—as Hasan al-Banna advocated "persuasion and advice" rather than the "force of the hand." See Mitchell, *The Society of the Muslim Brothers,* 319–320.

53. Audah, "'Normalization' of the Islamic Movement," 375; Jon B. Alterman, "Egypt: Stable, but for How Long?" *Washington Quarterly* 23, no. 4 (autumn 2000): 111.

54. Gilles Kepel, "Islamists versus the State in Egypt and Algeria," *Daedalus* 124, no. 3 (summer 1995): 109–127.

55. Sullivan and Abed-Kotob, *Islam in Contemporary Egypt*, 21–22.

56. For a complete discussion of the Brotherhood's economic agenda in the period just before and after the Free Officers' coup, see Mitchell, *The Society of the Muslim Brothers*, 272–282.

57. This coalition began to crystallize even while ten members of the Brotherhood sat in the People's Assembly under the umbrella of the Hizb al-Wafd, as the Labor party was in many respects a more philosophically compatible partner for the Ikhwan. Al-Amal was founded in 1978 to play the role of Sadat's leftist opposition and although the party, under the leadership of Ibrahim Shukri, fulfilled this function for a time, al-Amal became a forceful critic of Sadat and the general direction of Egypt's domestic and foreign policies. Both Shukri and his outspoken lieutenant, Adel Hussein, had previously been firmly disposed toward Marxism and leftist critiques of Egyptian politics, but in the late 1970s and early 1980s they both underwent a conversion that placed them and elements within the party on the same political and cultural terrain as the Ikhwan. As a result, an important feature of the alliance was the transformation of Labor's newspaper, *ash-Sha'ab*, into a tribune of the Brotherhood. This is not to suggest that the publication solely reflected Brotherhood thinking, as leftist columnists and politicians continued to contribute. Yet, although in the course of establishing the alliance both the Ikhwan and al-Amal did make a number of compromises, the Brotherhood's penetration of both the party and its newspaper—particularly in the continuing absence of the Brotherhood's magazine *ad-Dawa*—at times rendered the two organizations indistinguishable. Indeed, a comparison of the founding principles of al-Amal, the organization's electoral program of 1984, and the platform of what came to be known as al-Tahaluf al-Islami (the Islamic Alliance) demonstrates the significant influence of the Ikhwan on the Labor Party. Ibrahim and Audah, *The Muslim Brotherhood and Politics in Egypt*, 310; Program of the Socialist Labor Party (in Arabic), Cairo, 1978; Electoral Program of the Labor Party List (in Arabic), *ash-Sha'ab*, March 17, 1987.

58. Electoral Program, Section VI/2E: Planning and Public Sector; Section VI: Economic Development, *ash-Sha'ab* March 17, 1987.

59. Ibid.

60. Bjorn Olav Utvik, "Filling the Vacant Throne of Nasser: The Economic Discourse of Egypt's Islamist Opposition," *Middle East Insight* (January–February 1995): 27–28.

61. Electoral Program, Section V: Treatment of Problem Pertaining to the Standard of Living.

62. Mohamed Hamid Abul-Nasr, "Open Letter to Mubarak" (in Arabic), *al-Sha'ab*, February 17, 1987.

63. Electoral Program, Section III: Spreading Morals and Closing the Gates of Corruption.

64. Ibid.

65. Robert Springborg, *Mubarak's Egypt: Fragmentation of the Political Order* (Boulder: Westview Press, 1989), 104–118; interview with U.S. government officials, Cairo, September 27, 1999; interview with retired Egyptian military officers, Cairo, November 8, 22, 1999; January 18, 2000.

66. Interview with a former employee of Egypt's Ministry of Finance, Cairo, January 12, 2000. This retired official explained that a special unit within the Central Auditing Organization does review the military's budget and finances, but that its findings are released neither to other sections of that agency nor to the public.

67. Interview with a retired Egyptian military officer, Cairo, November 8, 1999; Robert Springborg, "The President and the Field Marshal: Civil-Military Relations in Egypt Today," *Middle East Report* 147 (July-August 1987): 10; For discussions of the military's activities related to national service see, for example, Ahmad Hamroush, "The Military in National Service" (in Arabic), *Ruz al-Yusuf,* May 14, 1999; Ahmad Hamroush, "Question of the Hour: What Is the Army Doing in the Face of Terror?" (in Arabic), *Ruz al-Yusuf,* January 3, 1994; and Springborg, *Mubarak's Egypt.* The Gihaaz Mashru'at al-Khidimat al-Wataniya (National Service Projects Organization), which the military established in 1978, was the agency vested with much of the responsibility to oversee the armed forces' economic initiatives, particularly in areas related to agriculture and infrastructure. Officially the NSPO is a semimilitary organization, which means that its principals are generally appointed from within the officer corps and that the organization's financing and activities are largely outside the purview of state auditors.

68. "Field Marshal Abu Ghazala in the Conversation of the Week" (in Arabic), *Al-Musawwar,* May 13, 1988. Egypt's fiscal year 2000 request for U.S. military assistance makes the same argument, indicating that a continuation of U.S. aid is the fastest and most efficient means to achieving Egyptian "economic security" and "military self-sufficiency." See Egypt's FY 2000 Request for Military Assistance: United States–Egyptian Military Cooperation: A Partnership for Peace, Stability, and Progress.

69. Interview with a retired Egyptian military officer, Cairo, November 9, 1999.

70. Interview with Egyptian military officials, Cairo, September 23, 2004.

71. Mohamed Abul-Nasr, "Valuable Freedom" (in Arabic), *Liwa al-Islam,* July 1990, 4–5.

72. Brotherhood spokesmen freely related that they sought to use the institutions of the Egyptian political system in an effort to ultimately alter those institutions. In February 1989, Maamoun Hudeibi stated, "I've said many times, we entered elections under the slogan 'Islam is the solution.' How can it be that we participate in the existing system when we are trying to change it in the preferred manner—by changing institutions with institutions?" Quoted in Sullivan and Abed-Kotob, *Islam in Contemporary Egypt,* 330.

73. Interview with Muslim Brotherhood Supreme Guide Umar al-Talmasani, *al-Majalla* June 9–15, trans. by Foreign Broadcast Information Service, June 13, 1984, D2–3.

74. Electoral Program, Section I: Reform of the Governing System by True Democracy, Part 3: Peaceful General Elections.

75. Kienle, *A Grand Delusion,* 53–54.

76. Electoral Program, Section II: Applying Islamic Law.

77. The position of vice president has been left vacant throughout the Mubarak period.

78. Electoral Program, Section I: Reform of the Governing System by True Democracy, Part 1: Reconsideration of the Constitution.

79. Issam al-Arian, a prominent member of the Muslim Brotherhood has stated, for example, "The Brothers consider constitutional rule to be the closest to Islamic rule . . . We are the first to call for and apply democracy." Cited in Sullivan and Abed-Kotob, *Islam in Contemporary Egypt,* 48.

80. *Texts and Analysis of the Statements of President Hosni Mubarak, President of the Republic to the People's Assembly* (in Arabic) (Cairo: People's Assembly, 1999), 26.

81. Address delivered by President Mohamed Hosni Mubarak before the Joint Meeting of the People's Assembly and the Shura Council, November 12, 1986 (Cairo: Egyptian State Information Service).

82. Interview with a retired Egyptian military officer, Cairo, January 18, 2000.

83. It should be noted that the High Constitutional Court did enjoy financial autonomy.

84. Electoral Program, Section I: Reform of the Governing System by True Democracy, Part 4: Independence of the Judiciary.

85. Electoral Program, Section I: Reform of the Governing System by True Democracy, Part 2: Abolition of Laws and Practices Inconsistent with Democracy; Section II: Applying Islamic Law.

86. Sullivan and Abed-Kotob quote the deputy secretary-general of the Engineers' syndicate, Abu al-'Ala Madi who asserted in *ad-Dawa* (printed in Pakistan) that Egypt's restrictive laws are, in part, to blame for violence perpetrated against the state; *Islam in Contemporary Egypt*, 62.

87. Vatikiotis, *The History of Modern Egypt*, 388–389; Hopwood, *Egypt: Politics and Society*, 41–42.

88. Quoted in Saad Eddin Ibrahim, "An Islamic Alternative in Egypt: The Muslim Brotherhood and Sadat," *Arab Studies Quarterly* 4 no. 1–2 (spring 1982): 87.

89. Nasr, "Open Letter to President Mubarak." In *Philosophy of the Revolution*, Nasser, in his meditations on Egypt's role in the first Arab-Israeli war, wrote: " . . . when the Palestine crisis began, I was utterly convinced that the fighting in Palestine was not taking place on foreign soil, nor was our participation going beyond the requirements of simple friendship. It was a duty made obligatory by the necessity of self-defense."

90. Mustafa Mashour, "This Conference . . . Between Whom? With Whom? To Whose Benefit?" (in Arabic), *ash-Sha'ab*, October 22, 1991.

91. Initially, prominent members of Egypt's senior command, such as General Mohamed Abdel Ghani el-Gamasy, were either skeptical of the benefits of the relationship with the United States or, like Lieutenant General Saad el-Shazly, downright hostile. The memoirs of both Shazly and Gamasy betray a considerable wariness of the United States and its intentions. Shazly writes critically of U.S. support for Israel's demands in the period immediately following the October 1973 war, whereas Gamasy voices unease with U.S. military transfers to Egypt that began in the late 1970s—particularly in comparison to the U.S.-manufactured weapons in Israel's arsenal. See Lieutenant General Saad el-Shazly, *The Crossing of the Suez* (San Francisco: American Mideast Research, 1980); Mohamed Abdel Ghani el-Gamasy, *The October War: Memoirs of Field Marshal el-Gamasy of Egypt* (Cairo: American University in Cairo Press, 1993). Gamasy and Shazly's successors—officers like Mubarak, Yusuf Sabri Abu Talib, Ahmed Abdel Halim, and the quintessentially pro-American Mohamed Abdel Halim Abu Ghazala—recognized the attendant benefits of the orientation toward the United States, particularly in the area of military modernization. There is, however, an undeniable logic to the U.S.-Egyptian relationship that is based on Cairo's ties to Jerusalem. As Ismail Sabri Abdallah, former minister of planning and a deputy vice-president under Sadat, put it, "For us to have good relations with the United States, we had to spend a night in Tel Aviv." This may be a somewhat crude characterization of Egyptian diplomacy, yet Abdallah's remark reveals a grain of truth to the Islamist counter-narrative: Israel, and more specifically, Egypt's relations with Israel, is critical to the maintenance of Egypt's strategic ties to America. As a result, the dynamics of the trilateral relationship constrain Egyptian foreign and security policy.

92. Electoral Program: Section VII National Security and Foreign Relations.

93. Ibid.

94. Yves Heller and Alexander Buccianti, "International Repercussions: The Impotence of Opposition in Egypt" (in French), *Le Monde,* February 19, 1991.

95. Ibid.; "The Islamic Group in the Gulf War" (in Arabic), *Ruz al-Yusuf,* February 18, 1991.

96. The Ikhwan were not alone in their efforts to open various aspects of Egypt's foreign and security policy to public discussion, nor was the organization always the most vocal in some areas. Still, the Brotherhood's rhetoric entered them into the field of defense and security policy—strictly a closed military zone. Concerning the decision to dispatch forces to the Persian Gulf, for example, Ahmed Abdalla has written: "The only institution to discuss the decision to send Egyptian troops to the Gulf before the decision was made was the general command—no parties, not even the ruling party, nor the cabinet, and certainly not parliament." Ahmed Abdalla, "Mubarak's Gamble," *Middle East Report* 168 (January–February 1991): 19.

97. Unlike their Algerian counterparts, the Brotherhood sought to avoid a head-on collision with Egypt's military establishment, preferring instead to burnish their own nationalist credentials through demonstrations (which were quickly suppressed) in cooperation with other opposition groups, press conferences, and petition drives urging the withdrawal of Egyptian forces from the Persian Gulf. 'Abd al-Hayy Mohamed, "Faculty and Student Unions, the Professional Associations Reject the Military Alliance" (in Arabic), *ash-Sha'ab,* September 18, 1990; Magdi Ahmad Husayn, "We Reject an American Framework Giving it a Blank Check for [the United States] to Control Policy, Oil, and Security in the Gulf" (in Arabic), *ash-Sha'ab,* September 18, 1990; 'Abd al-Hayy Mohamed, "All Political Parties and Forces Express their Support for the Iraqi People" (in Arabic), *ash-Sha'ab,* January 29, 1991.

98. Spingborg, "The President and the Field Marshal . . . ," 6; Abdalla, "The Armed Forces . . . ," 1458. Though the Islamists remained wary of Abu Ghazala for his widely (and correctly) perceived pro-American worldview, the Brotherhood viewed him, in general, with favor. In late October 1986, for example, Mohamed Abd al-Qudus, a prominent member of the Ikhwan, published an article in *ash-Sha'ab* entitled, "Sons of the Country: A Salute to the Field Marshal," in which Abu Ghazala was praised for his role in the October war, his piety, and his message that the armed forces belonged to all the people of Egypt.

99. "Field Marshal Abu Ghazala in the Discussion of the Week" (in Arabic), *al-Musawwar,* May 13, 1988; "Our Policy Is to Defend the Power of the Army, Protection of the Nation, and Preservation of Peace" (in Arabic), *al-Ahram,* October 5, 1989; "The Strong Armed Forces' Duty Is Peace, Countries of the World Pursue Military Cooperation with Egypt" (in Arabic), *al-Akhbar,* January 10, 1993.

100. General Ahmad Fakhr, "Hot Discussion of the Summer: The Egyptian Military Budget" (in Arabic), *al-Ahram,* July 25, 1986.

101. "Mubarak Addresses Egyptian Troops in Saudi Arabia," Middle East News Agency, October 22, 1990, trans. Foreign Broadcast Information Service, October 23, 1990. The minister of defense, General Yusuf Sabri Abu Talib, and Chief of Staff Safa ad-Din Abu Shanaf echoed the sentiments of their deputy in Saudi Arabia in their many statements to the press during the Gulf War.

102. "Mubarak Comments on Crisis during Religious Speech," Cairo Domestic Service, February 11, 1991, trans. Foreign Broadcast Information Service, February 14, 1991.

103. Joel Campagna, "From Accommodation to Confrontation: The Muslim Brotherhood in the Mubarak Years," *Journal of International Affairs* 50, no. 1 (summer 1996): 290–291.

104. Ibid, 295.

105. Saad Eddin Ibrahim, "Reform and Frustration in Egypt," *Journal of Democracy* 7, no. 4 (October 1996): 132.

106. Kienle, *A Grand Delusion*, 38; Cassandra, "The Impending Crisis in Egypt," *Middle East Journal* 49, no. 1 (winter 1995): 15.

107. Carrie Rosefsky Wickham, "Beyond Democratization: Political Change in the Arab World," *PS—Political Science and Politics* 27, no. 3 (1994): 508; also see Carrie Rosefsky Wickham, *Mobilizing Islam: Religion, Activism, and Political Change in Egypt* (New York: Columbia University Press, 2002), chap. 8.

108. Audah, "The 'Normalization' of the Islamic Movement," 404; interview with a retired Egyptian military officer, Cairo, January 18, 2000; interview with a former U.S. government official, Washington, DC, September 20, 2000.

109. Geneive Abdo, *No God but God: Egypt and the Triumph of Islam* (New York: Oxford University Press, 2000), 96–97.

110. Interview with a retired Egyptian military officer, Cairo, December 22, 1999.

111. Recalling this period, one retired Egyptian military officer stated, "There is no room for the fundamentalists (*usuliyyun*) in Egyptian politics, this movement must die out." Interview, Cairo, January 18, 2000.

112. Interview with a Western government official, Cairo, January 6, 2000. As Mona Makram Ebeid explains, it was not just Egyptian leaders who were concerned about another Algeria, but also Egyptian liberals and secularists who feared the Islamists more than the prevailing authoritarian order. See Mona Makram Ebeid, "Democratization in Egypt: The 'Algeria Complex,'" *Middle East Policy* 3, no. 3 (1994): 119–124.

113. Interview with a retired Egyptian military officer, Cairo, February 26, 2000.

114. Asef Bayat, "Revolution without Movement, Movement without Revolution: Comparing Islamic Activism in Iran and Egypt," *Comparative Study of Society and History* 40, no. 1 (1998): 168; Ahmed Abdalla, "Egypt's Islamists and the State: From Complicity to Confrontation," *Middle East Report* 183 (July–August 1993): 29.

115. Kienle, *A Grand Delusion*, 87.

116. Ibid., 295–296.

117. In May 2005, Issam al-Arian, a senior member of the Muslim Brotherhood, was arrested for "participating in a banned organization and planning unauthorized protests." At the time of al-Arian's arrest, 325 other members of the Brotherhood were also taken into custody. Al-Arian was arrested again in May 2006 for protesting in favor of judicial independence.

Five • Turkish Paradox

1. Kazım Karabekir and Ali Fuat Cebesoy were two of Mustafa Kemal's closest nationalist conspirators in the period following the collapse of the Ottoman forces at the end of World War I, yet political rivalries within and among the nationalist officers led to Kemal's falling out with Karabekir and Ali Fuat. Though these two officers played a role in the military campaign to push the Greeks, French, British, and Italians from Anatolia, they had no political role once this objective was accomplished and the Turkish Republic was proclaimed.

2. Senior-ranking Ottoman military commanders were divided in their support for

Kemal's nationalist project. There were some officers (mainly older and retired officers) who remained loyal to the sultan and others who sought to avoid a commitment to either side in the nationalist struggle until it was clear who would prevail. There were also officers who resigned their commissions in an effort to evade a potentially devastating fratricidal conflict.

3. There was significant opposition within the Grand National Assembly to this proposal from the *hocas* (men of religion) and even some of Kemal's closest military collaborators. For example, Marshal Fevzi Çakmak reportedly expressed reservations about the elimination of the sultanate. Nevertheless, the resolution passed unanimously.

4. For a complete inventory of what is now regarded as the Kemalist reforms, see Binnaz Toprak, "The Religious Right," in *Turkey in Transition: New Perspectives,* ed. Irvin C. Schick and Ertuğrul Ahmet Tonak (Oxford University Press, 1987), 223.

5. Şerif Mardin, "Religion and Secularism in Turkey," in *The Modern Middle East,* ed. Albert Hourani, Philip Khoury, and Mary C. Wilson (Berkeley: University of California Press, 1993), 363–365.

6. James Brown, "The Military and Society: The Turkish Case," *Middle Eastern Studies* 25, no. 3 (July 1989): 387.

7. Quoted in Bernard Lewis, *The Emergence of Modern Turkey,* 2nd ed. (New York: Oxford University Press, 1968), 256.

8. Ibid.

9. Articles 68–70, Constitution of the Turkish Republic (1924), unofficial translation, U.S. Embassy, Ankara, December 26, 1944.

10. See Andrew Mango, *Atatürk: The Biography of the Founder of Modern Turkey* (Woodstock, NY: Overlook Press, 1999), chap. 19.

11. Article 51, Constitution of 1924.

12. Article 2 as amended in 1928, Constitution of 1924.

13. Articles 56 and 57, Constitution of the Turkish Republic (1961), *Official Gazette of the Turkish Republic* 10859, July 20, 1961.

14. Article 147, Constitution of 1961.

15. The 1971 coup did not result in a new constitution.

16. The National Security Council of the 1980–1983 period is different from the constitutionally mandated advisory body of the same name that was established in the 1961 constitution.

17. Preamble, Constitution of the Turkish Republic (1982), *Official Gazette of the Turkish Republic* 17874, November 20, 1982.

18. Ilkay Sunar and Binnaz Toprak, "Islam and Politics: The Case of Turkey," *Government and Opposition* 18, no. 4 (1983): 426; Şerif Mardin, "Ideology and Religion in the Turkish Revolution," *International Journal of Middle East Studies* 2 (1971): 208.

19. Feroz Ahmad, "Politics and Islam in Modern Turkey," *Middle Eastern Studies* 27, no. 1 (January 1991): 7.

20. Article 69, Constitution of 1982.

21. Articles 5, 78, and 90 are designed to limit opposition politics and expressly prohibit, "communist parties, parties oriented toward ethnic separatism, religious distinctions and racial differences." Articles 66, 91, and 92 elaborate on articles in the constitution that prohibit parties from establishing auxiliary branches and "extra-party organizations such as clubs, associations, labor unions, co-operatives, foundations, occupational and professional associations." More-

over, these types of organizations, which are to remain nonpolitical, are prohibited from offering financial support to political parties. According to Article 96, new parties are not permitted to take the names or symbols of parties previously banned, and Article 97 requires that not only must all parties adhere to the decisions of the MGK, but they must also refrain from criticizing or opposing these decisions. Constitution of 1982; see also Law 2820: Political Parties Law (in Turkish) *Official Gazette of the Turkish Republic* 18027, April 24, 1983; Ilter Turan, "Political Parties and the Party System in Post-1983 Turkey," in *State, Democracy and the Military: Turkey in the 1980s,* ed. Metin Heper and Ahmet Evin (Berlin: deGruyter, 1988), 69.

22. Umit Cizre Sakallioğlu, "Parameters and Strategies of Islam-State Interaction in Republican Turkey," *International Journal of Middle East Studies* 28, no. 2 (May 1996): 251 n. 60. The TGNA repealed Article 163 in 1991. Yet as important as this step may be, the Political Parties Law of 1983 and the 1991 Law for the Struggle against Terrorism retain provisions similar to those of Article 163.

23. Article 312, Penal Code of the Turkish Republic, quoted in Nilufer Narli, "The Rise of the Islamist Movement in Turkey," *MERIA Journal* 3, no. 3 (September 1999): n. 12.

24. Supporters of the banned Demokrat Partisi, roughly half the Turkish electorate, were prohibited from participating in the Constituent Assembly.

25. James Brown, "The Military and Society: The Turkish Case," *Middle Eastern Studies* 25, no. 3 (July 1989): 388.

26. Article 104, Constitution of 1982.

27. Article 105, Constitution of 1982.

28. During the first three decades of the republic, the power of the military establishment was not based on formal legal institutions but rather on the influential positions many officers occupied—most prominently, the president of the republic. Although Article 40 of the 1924 constitution placed the armed forces under the auspices of the Grand National Assembly, these powers were delegated to the president of the republic who, during the first 27 years of the republic's existence, were Mustafa Kemal and Ismet Inönü, the two leading members of the Turkish military enclave. Others such as the chief of staff, Marshal Çakmak, exercised significant influence within the Council of Ministers, though he was not formally a member of that body. And, as noted, officers occupied many seats within the TGNA, though they were prohibited from command positions during their tenure in the legislature.

29. Article 111, Constitution of 1961. The National Security Council comprised the president of the republic, the prime minister, minister of defense, the minister of foreign affairs, the minister of interior, the chief of the General Staff, the four service chiefs, and the secretary-general of the MGK (an officer).

30. Feroz Ahmed, *The Making of Modern Turkey* (New York: Routledge, 1993), 130.

31. Ibid.

32. Turkish Armed Forces, "Defense White Paper 2000," www.msb.gov.tr/Birimler/GnPPD/GnPPDBeyazKitap.htm#WHITE%20PAPER.

33. Mehmet Ali Birand, *Shirts of Steel: An Anatomy of the Turkish Armed Forces* (London: I. B. Tauris, 1991), 22. In the 1980s, Birand—one of Turkey's leading journalists—gained unprecedented access to the Turkish military academy and staff colleges. *Shirts of Steel* is the only available account (in both Turkish and English) of the education and socialization of Turkey's future military officers.

34. "Ecevit Denies Claims of Interfering in Military Assignments," July 5, 1998 www .turkpulse.com/armed.htm.

35. Party Program of the Justice and Development Party (in Turkish), n.d.

36. Yavuz, "Cleansing Islam," 40.

37. For some analysts, including Metin Heper, Aylin Güney, Fuat Keyman, Jacob Landau, and Dankwart Rostow, there is one key fact crucial to determining the democratic credentials of Turkey's military establishment—each time the Turkish military has intervened, it has returned the reins of government to civilian representatives. From this, these scholars have drawn the conclusion that the Turkish officer corps has internalized the principles of democracy. Heper and Güney, in their effort to demonstrate the democratic credentials of Turkey's senior officers, examined the memoirs and statements of former chiefs of staff Generals Kenan Evren and Doğan Gureş in an article entitled "The Military and Democracy in the Third Turkish Republic." While there is no denying the fact that both officers sound like committed democrats, their actions betray something quite different. Evren, who was the leader of the 1980 intervention, which, given the political violence that shook Turkey in the late 1970s, was not an irresponsible act of military power, nevertheless presided over a thorough depoliticization of Turkish society. Gureş, who was chief of staff in the early and mid-1990s, was noted for his unwillingness to countenance civilian criticism of the military and zealously guarded the military establishment's autonomy in developing Turkey's national security policy.

38. According to a textbook used at the Military Academy, "All the commanders, officers, and NCOs of the Turkish Armed Forces must be trained to be aware of the difference between intervention in and actual participation in politics, and between being outside and above politics in the course of fulfillment of their duties and responsibilities, in line with loyalty to Ataturkist principles." See Birand, Shirts of Steel, 86.

39. Public opinion polls reveal that the military is the most trusted state organization, far outstripping the police and various components of the bureaucracy, as well as Turkey's civilian political elite. See, for example, polling done by Fikret Adaman, Ali Çarkoğlu, and Burhan Şenatalar for the Turkish Economic and Social Foundation at www.tesev.org.tr/eng/events/ corrp27feb2001.php; Ustun Erguder, Yilmaz Esmer and Ersin Kalaycioğlu, An Assessment of Turkish Society (in Turkish) (Istanbul: Turk Sanayicileri ve Isadamlari Dernegi, 1991), 22; Hürriyet poll, June 16–22, 1997.

40. Ergun Özbudun, Contemporary Turkish Politics: Challenges to Democratic Consolidation (Boulder: Lynne Rienner Publishers, 2000), 151.

41. Interview with a Turkish military officer, Washington, DC, August 9, 2001.

42. For a complete discussion, see Ali Çarkoğlu and Binnaz Toprak, Religion, Society, and Politics in Turkey (in Turkish), (Istanbul: Turkish Economic and Social Studies Foundation, 2000).

43. General Çevik Bir, one of Turkey's most outspoken officers during the mid-1990s, declared to an audience in Washington, DC, shortly after the municipality of Sincan celebrated "Jerusalem Night" in early 1997 that "We [the Turkish Armed forces] are the insurance for the secular system and democracy"; "Bir: Court Martial is Desirable" (in Turkish), Milliyet, February 24, 1997. Beyond these types of press statements, the military has consistently—through its National Security Policy documents—designated "religious fundamentalism" as an "imminent threat" to the state. See Lale Sariibrahimoğlu, "Military Prepares a New National Security Policy

Document," *Turkish Daily News,* August 8, 2001; also see Turkish Armed Forces, "Defense White Paper 2000." In an April 2005 speech to the Turkish War Academies Command, General Özkök listed "religious fundamentalism and Kurdish separatism" as two primary threats to Turkish unity. In the context of Turkish politics, this was a clear warning from the senior command that the civilian, Islamist-led government should not step beyond certain bounds.

44. For a complete discussion of the "Turkish-Islamic Synthesis," see Gokhan Çetinsaya, "Rethinking Nationalism and Islam: Some Preliminary Notes on the Roots of 'Turkish-Islamic Synthesis' in Modern Turkish Political Thought," *The Muslim World* 89, no. 3–4 (July–October 1999): 350–376.

45. Ümit Cizre Sakallıoğlu, "Parameters and Strategies of Islam-State Interaction in Republican Turkey," *International Journal of Middle East Studies* 28, no. 2 (May 1996): 231.

46. This vision was based on the philosophy of Necmettin Erbakan's *Milli Goru̇ş* (National Outlook) movement dating back to the 1960s. In general, the guiding principles of this movement called for a return to religious values, emphasized Turkish culture, and hearkened back to the height of Ottoman power. Against this backdrop, Refah promised Turks freedom, happiness, security, democracy, and moral as well as material progress. Critics of the party indicated that the program was everything from incoherent and naïve to irresponsible and even dangerous. Yet Refah's adversaries failed to understand that even though the Islamist's platform and policies may have been everything the party's foes believed it to be, this did not compromise the effectiveness of the program as an emotionally and materially satisfying counter-narrative.

47. For a complete discussion of Turkey's experiment with ISI, see John Waterbury, *Exposed to Innumerbale Delusions: Public Enterprise and State Power in Egypt, India, Mexico, and Turkey* (New York: Cambridge University Press, 1993).

48. Henri Barkey offers a compelling case when he suggests that the 1980 coup saved the economic reform package. These policies, which Turgut Özal developed, had actually been slated for implementation in January 1980 but partisan political battles delayed and ultimately threatened their realization. See Henri J. Barkey, *The State and the Industrialization Crisis in Turkey* (Boulder: Westview Press, 1990), 180.

49. Haldun Gülalp, "Political Islam in Turkey: The Rise and Fall of the Refah Party," *The Muslim World* 89, no. 1 (January 1999): 27.

50. M. Hakan Yavuz, "Political Islam and the Welfare (Refah) Party in Turkey," *Comparative Politics* 30, no. 1 (October 1997): 72.

51. "RP Explains Its 'Just Order'," trans. Foreign Broadcast Information Service, December 5, 1995, 1–2; see also Necmettin Erbakan, *Just Economic Order* (in Turkish), (Ankara: Semih Ofset Matbaacılık, 1991).

52. See Ernst B. Haas, *Nationalism, Liberalism, and Progress: The Rise and Decline of Nationalism,* vol. 1 (Ithaca: Cornell University Press, 1997).

53. Sami Zubaida, "Turkish Islam and National Identity," *Middle East Report* 199 (spring 1996): 12.

54. As Jenny B. White argues, by the 1990s, Refah had taken the place the Turkish Left had historically occupied. See *Islamist Mobilization in Turkey: A Study in Vernacular Politics* (Seattle: University of Washington Press, 2002).

55. "Erbakan Favors Islamic Union over European Union," *Turkish Daily News,* February 16, 1995.

56. "RP Explains Its 'Just Order'," 4.

57. "Erbakan Reads Government Program at Assembly," Ankara TRT Television Network, July 3, 1996, trans. Foreign Broadcast Information Service, July 5, 1996.

58. Birand, *Shirts of Steel*, 147–153. The compensation for both officers and civilian employees of the Turkish military establishment is not commensurate with that of their counterparts in the private sector.

59. Serdar Şen, *Armed Forces and Modernism* (in Turkish) (Istanbul, 1996), 159–162.

60. Semih Vaner, "The Army," in *Turkey in Transition: New Perspectives*, ed. Irving C. Schick and Ertuğrul Ahmet Tonak (Oxford: Oxford University Press, 1987), 253.

61. Karabelias, "Evolution of Civil-Military Relations," 140–141.

62. Interview with a Western official, Ankara, June 12, 2000.

63. Ömer Taspinar, "Kemalist Identity in Transition: A Case Study of Kurdish Nationalism and Political Islam in Turkey" (Ph.D. diss., Johns Hopkins School of Advanced International Studies, 2001), 217.

64. "Turkish Nationalism, Islamic Movement, and Muslim Identity—Case Study: Necmettin Erbakan and the Turkish Welfare Party," UASR Regional Report 2 (Springfield, VA: UASR Publishing Group, 2000), 9–10.

65. Gülalp, 28; Murat Çemrik, "The Unnoticed Face of the Milli Görüş Movement (MGM): Nationalism," unpublished manuscript (n.d.).

66. For a complete text of the speech, see *New Istanbul, New Turkey, New World* (in Turkish), October 10, 1993, 71–77.

67. The trip to Libya was nothing less than a debacle. Though the Refah leader had come to Tripoli as a first step in his effort to forge closer relations with the Arab and Muslim world, al-Qadhafi embarrassed Erbakan. At the departure ceremony for the Turkish prime minister and his delegation, the Libyan leader lectured his guests about Turkey's treatment of its Kurdish minority. Turkey's establishment newspapers faithfully reported the episode with thinly veiled glee, adding to their copy pictures of a red-faced Erbakan standing uncomfortably with al-Qadhafi on the tarmac at Libya's international airport.

68. Article 85 of the Internal Service Act (1961) states that the "Armed Forces shall defend the country against internal as well as external threats, if necessary by force."

69. Interview with a former senior Turkish government official, Ankara, June 6, 2000.

70. See, for example, Hale, *Turkish Politics and the Military;* Metin Heper and Aylin Güney, "The Military and Democracy in the Third Turkish Republic," *Armed Forces and Society* 22, no. 4 (summer 1996): 619–642; Aylin Güney, "The Military, Politics and Post-Cold War Dilemmas in Turkey," in *Political Armies: The Military and Nation Building in the Age of Democracy*, ed. Kees Koonings and Dirk Kruijt (London: Zed Book, 2002), 162–175.

71. Henri J. Barkey and Graham E. Fuller, *Turkey's Kurdish Question* (Lanham, MD: Rowman and Littlefield, 1998), 139–140.

72. Commenting on Erbakan's ideas concerning Muslim solidarity as a means of resolving the conflict in the southeast specifically and more generally addressing the potential problems associated with increased Kurdish ethnic identity, one Turkish officer stated: "We have heard these kinds of proposals before, we know all about neo-Ottomanism as it is called. It will not work." Interview with a Turkish military officer, Ankara, July 5, 2000.

73. In practice, the senior command routinely outlines an array of pressing security problems facing the country from the Balkans, Adriatic, Mediterranean, and Middle East in public statements as well as official documents including what is called the Defense White Paper and the National Security Concept. See for example, Turkish Armed Forces, "Defense White Paper 2000."

74. Not only did Erbakan have to forfeit a campaign promise, but the military seemingly deliberately sought to put the prime minister in situations that would undermine his prestige with the Refah faithful. For example, Erbakan was forced to countenance what must have seemed like a parade of senior Israeli military officers visiting Ankara. In addition, the Turkish Chief of Staff, Ismail Hakki Karadayı, compelled the prime minister to meet with civilian Israeli officials such as Foreign Minister David Levy.

75. Yavuz, "Cleansing Islam," 36.

76. Necmettin Erbakan, cited in Hebar Abdullah, "Turks Wary of EU Membership, Islamist Welcomes Intervention," *I-View,* September 15, 2000.

77. "I Have Not Changed" (interview with Necmettin Erbakan by Sedat Ergin, in Turkish), *Hürriyet,* February 22, 1996.

78. Muzaffer Bal, "Erbakan: The Military Forces Will Welcome the RP Government," (in Turkish), *Milliyet,* December 15, 1995.

79. For a discussion of Milli Görüs, see Birol A. Yeşilada, "The Refah Party Phenomenon in Turkey," in *Comparative Political Parties and Party Elites: Essays in Honor of Samuel J. Eldersveld,* ed. Birol A. Yeşilada (Ann Arbor: University of Michigan Press, 1999), 123–150.

80. Bal, "Erbakan."

81. Interview, Ankara, July 5, 2000. One middle-ranking officer indicated that although he yearns for democracy and civilian control, he would not hesitate to intervene if he and his colleagues deemed it necessary to preserve Kemalism. Interview with a Turkish military officer, Washington, DC, March 5, 2002.

82. Hayri Birler, "Military Prosecutor Warns against RP Victory," *Turkish Daily News,* November 28, 1994.

83. Sezai Sengun, "The Army Warns Erbakan about Reactionaryism" (in Turkish), *Hürriyet,* July 24, 1996. Interestingly, the military's response represented a dynamic that was not new. In 1987, for example, the military effectively short-circuited Turgut Özal's public discussion of civil society and the need for less state (i.e. military) supervision with the timely release of a report outlining the threat of fundamentalism.

84. Interview with a Turkish military officer, Washington, DC, May 10, 2001.

85. Erbakan and other Refah leaders often moderated their critique of Turkish nationalism when engaging audiences in the Anatolian heartland with few Kurds.

86. Dieter Bednarz and Paul M. Schumacher, "The Country Will Explode" (interview with Necmettin Erbakan of the Refah Partisi), *Der Spiegel,* June 16, 1996, 136–140, trans. Foreign Broadcast Information Service.

87. Bal, "Erbakan."

88. For a complete discussion of vernacular politics, see White, *Islamist Mobilization in Turkey.*

89. Article 24, Constitution of 1982.

90. At its Fifth Party Conference, Refah embraced "the American version" of secularism.

See Aslı Aydıntaşbaş, "The Malaise of Turkish Democracy," *Middle East Report* 209 (winter 1998): 34.

91. "RP Ready for a Referendum on Constitutional Reforms," *Turkish Daily News*, June 15, 1995.

92. Birand quotes one officer telling him, "I measure a politician not by his education but by the priority he gives to country and nation. Politicians are not concerned 'for the state' as much as we are. They talk about Atatürk's principles and all that only because they're wary of us or afraid of some reaction . . . ," Birand, *Shirts of Steel*, 75–76.

93. Jenny B. White, "Pragmatists or Ideologues? Turkey's Welfare Party in Power," *Current History* 96, no. 606 (January 1997): 30.

94. Sengun, "The Army Warns Erbakan about Reactionaryism."

95. The fact that Nakşibendi brotherhoods had been a critical component of support for Refah since the party's founding in 1983 only heightened the officers' calculation of threat. As Birol Yeşilada has written: "In their strategy for political domination, known as *takiyye* (dissimulation), the *Nakşibendis* always emphasized the need to conquer the state from within by aligning themselves with powerful sources of capital and political actors (ultimately including the armed forces) . . . Furthermore, according to *takkiye* rule, any action of a fellow member that aimed at conquering the state but that might violate Islamic code is acceptable because a state of war (*Dar ul-Harb*) exists between the believers and the enemies of Islam"; Yeşilada, "The Refah Party Phenomenon," 139.

96. On the importance of the bureaucracy during the Ottoman period, see Ahmet Ö. Evin, "Bureaucracy," *Private View* 1, no. 2 (spring-summer 1996): 47–51; Mardin, "Religion and Secularism in Turkey," 347–374; and Şerif Mardin, "Center-Periphery Relations: A Key to Turkish Politics?" *Daedalus* 102, no. 1 (Winter 1973): 169–190.

97. Şerif Mardin, "Religion and Politics in Modern Turkey," in *Islam in the Political Process*, ed. James Piscatori (London: Cambridge University Press, 1983), 147.

98. The officers' concern with the bureaucracy is part of a pattern that emerged in the 1950s as the Demokrat Partisi sought to replace those bureaucrats affiliated with the Republican People's Party with its own activists. Notwithstanding the 1960 coup d'état, which banned DP supporters, packing the bureaucracy with party activists became a common practice over the following three decades as representatives from across Turkey's political spectrum (including Islamists) were placed throughout the state's administrative structures. In subsequent coups, but particularly that of 1980, the military expressed its dismay over what it believed to be the deleterious effects of the politicization of the bureaucracy. See, Ersin Kalaycıoğlu, "The Logic of Contemporary Turkish Politics," *MERIA Journal* 1, no. 3 (September 1997): 10; Yeşilada, "The Refah Party Phenomenon," 130; Sencer Ayata, "Patronage, Party, and State: The Politicization of Islam in Turkey," *Middle East Journal* 50, no. 1 (winter 1996): 45; Sunar and Toprak, "Islam and Politics," 430–432; General Secretariat of the National Security Council, *12 September in Turkey: Before and After* (Ankara: Ongun Kardeşler Printing House, 1982).

99. "Transformation of the Welfare Party," *Turkish Daily News*, October 14, 1996.

100. Ayla Ganioğlu, "Erbakan RP Seen as Harmful to Coalition," *Turkish Daily News*, July 15, 1996.

101. Ismail Küçükkaya, "Interesting Appointments," (in Turkish), *Sabah*, August 11, 1996.

102. White, "Pragmatists or Ideologues?" 29.

103. Interview with a Western official, Ankara, June 16, 2000.

104. "Erbakan on New Initiatives for Defense Industry," Ankara TRT Television, August 2, 1996, trans. Foreign Broadcast Information Service, August 8, 1996.

105. Interview with a Western government official, Ankara, April 7, 2000.

106. Interview with a retired Turkish military officer, Istanbul, April 28, 2000.

107. Interview with a Turkish military officer, Ankara, July 5, 2000.

108. Tolga Şardan, "The MGK's Report on Reactionaryism" (in Turkish), *Milliyet*, February 27, 1997.

109. Niyazi Günay, "Implementing the 'February 28' Recommendations: A Scorecard," Washington Institute Research Note no. 10, May 2001.

110. Oya Armutçu and Sezai Sengun, "RP Engaged in Reactionary Activities" (in Turkish), *Hürriyet*, June 11, 1997.

111. At the time of the Constitutional Court's decision, the TGNA was in the process of approving a number of amendments to Turkey's legal structure. Turkish politicians and political commentators suggested that justices wait in rendering their opinion so that Fazilet would have the advantage of being judged against regulations that ostensibly made it more difficult to close a political party. In the end, it mattered little as Fazilet was found guilty of being a "center of anti-secular activity," which was proscribed in both the old set of regulations as well as the new ones.

112. Between the November 2002 election and changes to the constitution and the penal code, Erdoğan was essentially in political limbo. Although he was unquestionably the leader of the party with the largest number of seats in the Grand National Assembly, the president of the republic was unable to ask him to form a government because Erdoğan remained barred from holding a seat in the parliament and thus a senior government position. Instead, Erdoğan's deputy, Abdullah Gül, served as prime minister in a short-lived government. With the necessary constitutional amendment and legal reforms carried out, Erdoğan ran for a parliamentary seat in a by-election held in March 2003 and ultimately became the prime minister of Turkey's 59th government.

113. "Three Visas from the Military" (in Turkish), *Milliyet*, May 9, 2000; "NSC Can Enlarge" (in Turkish), *Milliyet*, July 25, 2000; interview with a Turkish military officer, July 5, 2000 (Ankara).

114. In August 2004, Ambassador Mehmet Yiğit Alpogan, Turkey's former representative in Greece, became the first civilian secretary general of the National Security Council.

115. "Regular Report on Turkey's Progress towards Accession," Commission of the European Communities, Brussels, October 6, 2004, 22.

116. "MGK Advisor Reacts to the Seventh EU Package," *ZAMAN*, July 29, 2003; "Turkish General Slams EU-Linked reform Curbing Military's Power," *EU Business*, August 8, 2003, www.eubusiness.com/afp/030825170303.quksi3vb.

117. "Refah Party Deputy Leader Gül Interviewed on Party Policy," *Milliyet*, February 28, 1995, trans. Foreign Broadcast Information Service, March 6, 1995.

118. "Is It a Waning Influence?" *Economist*, June 12, 2003.

119. For more on the Turkish military's internal service codes, see Saban Iba, *National Security State: Global and Turkish Documents on National Security Ideology and Institutions* (In Turkish), (Istanbul: Civiyazilari, 1998).

Six • Toward a Democratic Transition?

1. Stephen P. Cohen, *The Pakistan Army* (New York: Oxford University Press, 1998), 105.

2. "Pakistan: Transition to Democracy?" International Crisis Group Report no. 40, October 3, 2002, 21.

3. James T. Quinlivan, "Coup Proofing: Its Practice and Consequences in the Middle East," *International Security* 24, no. 2 (fall 1999): 131–165.

4. See J. Samuel Fitch, *The Armed Forces and Democracy in Latin America* (Baltimore: Johns Hopkins University Press, 1998).

5. See Nikola B. Schahgaldian, *The Iranian Military under the Islamic Republic* (Santa Monica: Rand Corporation, 1987); William F. Hickman, *Ravaged and Reborn: The Iranian Army, 1982* (Washington, DC: Brookings Institution, 1982). This is the same kind of dynamic that befell the Iraqi military during the U.S. invasion of Iraq in March 2003.

6. Adam Przeworski, Michael Alvarez, Jose Antonio Cheibub, Fernando Limongi, "What Makes Democracies Endure?" *Journal of Democracy* 7, no. 1 (January 1996): 39–55.

7. For a complete discussion of the relationship between business and the state, particularly in Tunisia, see Eva Bellin, *Stalled Democracy: Capital, Labor, and the Paradox of State-Sponsored Development* (Ithaca: Cornell University Press, 2002).

8. Amendment 13, FY2005 Foreign Operations Appropriations Act (H.R. 4818), 108th U.S. Congress.

9. Reflecting on the Adalet ve Kalkinma Party's first eight months in office, Turkish Foreign Minister Abdullah Gül told an American audience in July 2003: "Among the first agenda items on the new Turkish parliament were two major political reform packages. These were related to the process initiated by the previous government to upgrade the Turkish legislation on fundamental rights and freedoms in conformity with the European Union standards. That was not all. Last month we passed another political reform package further harmonizing our legislation with those of Europe."

10. See Steven A. Cook, "The Right Way to Promote Arab Reform," *Foreign Affairs* 84, no. 2 (March/April 2005): 91–102.

11. Thomas Carothers, "Recent U.S. Experience in Democracy Promotion," *IDS Bulletin* 26, no. 2 (1995): 62–69; Gordon Crawford, *Foreign Aid and Political Reform* (London: Palgrave, 2001); Olav Stokke, "Aid and Political Conditionality: Core Issues and the State of the Art," in *Aid and Political Conditionality,* ed. Olav Stokke (London: Frank Cass, 1995), 1–87.

12. Annual Report 2003–2004 and "Citizens Rights and Democracy" (in Arabic), *National Democratic Party,* September 2004.